# YOKO ONO

# YOKO ONO

## AN ARTFUL LIFE

### DONALD BRACKETT

**sh.**
SUTHERLAND
HOUSE
TORONTO, 2022

*This one is for the late Kevin Courrier,*
*who first recommended that I tell Yoko's story.*

*For my good friend Gerry Watson, who first forced me*
*to listen to her groundbreaking music.*

*And for my ever-supportive partner,*
*Dr. Mimi Gellman, because of who she is.*

*"I'm walking on thin ice, paying the price
for throwing the dice in the air . . ."*

Yoko Ono

("Walking on Thin Ice")

Sutherland House
416 Moore Ave., Suite 205
Toronto, ON M4G 1C9

First edition, April 2022

If you are interested in inviting one of our authors to a live event or
media appearance, please contact sranasinghe@sutherlandhousebooks.com
and visit our website at sutherlandhousebooks.com for more
information about our authors and their schedules.

Manufactured in Canada
Cover designed by Lena Yang
Book composed by Karl Hunt

Library and Archives Canada Cataloguing in Publication
Title: Yoko Ono : an artful life / Donald Brackett.
Names: Brackett, Donald, 1951- author.
Identifiers: Canadiana 20220162387 | ISBN 9781989555583 (hardcover)
Subjects: LCSH: Ono, Yōko. | LCSH: Artists—United States—Biography. |
LCGFT: Biographies.
Classification: LCC NX512.O56 B73 2022 |
DDC 700.92—dc23

ISBN 978-1989555583

# Contents

*Prologue: Who and What*                                          ix

PART ONE  BEFORE THE BEGINNING:
          BUILDING A DREAM                                         1

   CHAPTER ONE    A Map of Two Territories                         3

   CHAPTER TWO    No East or West in Dreams                       21

   CHAPTER THREE  Hold Back the Dawn                              35

   CHAPTER FOUR   Across the Great Divide                         45


PART TWO  WORLDS IN COLLISION:
          ENDURING THE LIVING MOVIE                               57

   CHAPTER FIVE    Baby's in Black                                59

   CHAPTER SIX     Nowhere Plans for Nobody                       73

   CHAPTER SEVEN   Help Me If You Can                             91

   CHAPTER EIGHT   I'm Looking Through You                       107

CHAPTER NINE    Cross Purposes      121

CHAPTER TEN    The Expanding Field      138

CHAPTER ELEVEN    Honeymoon with History      158

CHAPTER TWELVE    A New Lease on Life      177

PART THREE   AFTER THE END:
                 LEARNING TO SWIM ALONE      193

CHAPTER THIRTEEN    Passing the Time      195

CHAPTER FOURTEEN    Burning Bridges      212

EPILOGUE    What Did It All Mean?      228

Index      250

# PROLOGUE

# Who and What

W HO IS YOKO ONO? What is Yoko Ono? It is important to ask both questions because throughout her long life she has been both a living person and an aesthetic phenomenon—admired, vilified, and profoundly misunderstood in each role.

The merest outline of her life is fascinating. Born to a Tokyo family of merchant aristocrats, she was raised in an unusual combination of pampered luxury and benign neglect, traditional Japanese values and permissive American influences. During the Second World War, her native city was firebombed beyond recognition and her homeland devastated and humiliated by history's first application of nuclear warfare. She later graduated from Japan's best schools and dropped out of Sarah Lawrence College to live with the first of her three husbands in bohemian New York. That marriage in ruins, she returned to Tokyo, spent time in an asylum, married a dangerous American jazz musician and had her first child. When that marriage also deteriorated, she landed in London in the arms of arguably the most famous rock star alive, John Lennon, at the time he was parting ways with the Beatles. She and Lennon abandoned England for a new life in New York; less than a decade later, he was shot dead on the sidewalk outside of their apartment. Ever since, she has been keeper of the Lennon flame, a hugely successful businesswoman, one of New York's most beloved and iconic citizens, and a globally recognized activist.

At the same time, her artistic achievements are diverse and impressive. Trained in traditional voice, music, and visual arts, she carved a role for herself in the America's avant-garde, combining Western conceptual and performance art practices with unique Eastern influences at happenings in the Greenwich Village loft scene alongside such luminaries as John Cage, Marcel Duchamp, and Peggy Guggenheim. Swept up in the feverish politics of the 1960s, she infused her work with the causes of feminism and peace, and expanded her repertoire with experimental films. Her bed-ins and bag events with Lennon, a natural outgrowth of her earlier performance pieces, changed the nature of artistic activism in the 1970s, while their oft-maligned musical collaborations heralded a new era of collaboration between popular music and the avant-garde. At the dawn of the punk and grunge eras, Yoko's solo work found new popularity among a younger generation of musicians, and during the remix-happy Aughts, she became a darling of DJs and enjoyed a long series of number one dance-chart hits. In 2009, she received the Golden Lion award for lifetime achievement at the Venice Biennale. Six years later was the subject of a major retrospective at The Museum of Modern Art.

Through it all, she has been a lightning rod for controversy and hatred: accused of stealing Lennon from his first wife and breaking up the Beatles; of being dismissive of Lennon's legacy, hoarding it for herself, and cashing in on it. She has been reviled as a drug addict, bad parent, and careless wife, and dismissed as a shock artist and talentless attention-seeker with puerile ideas and bad taste. Yoko Ono, said the legendary critic Lester

Bangs, "couldn't carry a tune in a briefcase." Perhaps no other artist in our times has been subject to as much racism and misogyny. It has never been easy.

But that still doesn't tell us everything about Yoko Ono. Not even close.

She can be seen as many combinations of things, some of them contradictory. A living person and an aesthetic phenomenon. A small, fragile-looking person and a huge force of energy. A human being with a personal history and a profoundly puzzling myth. An enormous celebrity, one of the first to be famous for being famous, and a serious artist who worked in obscurity through much of her career. A dedicated outsider who became the ultimate insider. An intensely private person who has lived and worked in a startlingly public and revealing manner. An elusive persona and a lightning rod for some of our most extreme emotions. An independent-minded feminist best known for her relationship with a sometimes misogynistic man. Most recently, she has been wrapped in several layers of personal and cultural heroism which she both embodies and denies.

She can be viewed as a series of collisions, some of them intentional, others not, some of them violent, others fruitful. Born in tradition-laden Japan, she collided with the idea of America, and the more experimental versions of the American dream. She collided with modern art and music. She collided with John Lennon and the biggest rock group in history. She collided with our fears of the other, the limits of our tastes, with sudden widowhood, the world of business, the digital age, and so much else that has happened in our times.

This book is an attempt to capture some of the 'all' of Yoko Ono, the person and the myth, and the radically talented artist behind both. It attempts to see her as a human being in her own right, and also to read her as an object of her own creation, perhaps her own greatest piece of art—she has always insisted that "we" are the art. The avant-garde tradition from which she springs is all about merging art and everyday life, and enthusiastically erasing the traditional barriers between art, artist, artwork, and audience. There was a lot of romantic, utopian idealism and social experimentation in her scene, and it is clear in retrospect that the movement's reach often exceeded its grasp, but it is only by looking at the whole of her world that we can hope to understand and appreciate her importance to our culture.

That she has lived as if her life is art is nowhere more apparent than in her harrowing 1969 film *Rape (Chase)*, which leaves its audience feeling both seduced and shamed by its overwhelming scrutiny of an unknown woman followed down the street by a rogue cameraman who stalks her even into the security of her own home. This was one of the first films to use the newly invented, hand-held Eclair camera, and it is eerily prescient about today's suffocating social media environment.

It is also what the Ono-Lennons themselves were experiencing in the brutal public chase that marked their careers and life together, at least until the chase ended on that New York sidewalk. Yoko and John were real people in a captivating melodrama that ended in pain, sorrow, loss, and separation. Her visionary film about the evaporation of privacy captured the alienation and public scourging she endured in her living movie. Maybe that's life imitating art. Maybe it's the other way around. For Yoko, it's all one and the same. Much of what she experienced was intended for us to consume personally, and much of it was, including unintended tragedy.

During the times he was providing me with helpful insights into the subject and themes of this book, my friend, the experimental filmmaker Mike Myers, insisted that he knew the one and only possible title for a book on Yoko Ono, her music, and her partnership with John Lennon:

"You have to call it 'Yoko Ono: An Artful Life.'" After all, he reasoned, she lived her life as though it were art, and she became a brand name in doing it. "That brand might mean different things to different people but it is still an instantly recognizable brand."

What is the nature of the brand? It's a difficult question, but for me Yoko is a time-ghost, which is the literal meaning of the word *zeitgeist*. She has always embodied a defining mood or spirit of her times. Not *the* mood or spirit of her times, exactly, because she often appeared to be out of place and out of time, or clearly ahead of her time in her conceptual art practice, experimental music and film, political and social activism, and maybe especially her radical feminism. A lot of these zones of encounter were still under construction as she worked, leaving her to embody a future that had yet to arrive, but it always did, as she always seemed to know it would. It's no wonder they called her a witch.

How did she do it? How was she so consistently able to see history eventually arriving in some place she had long occupied? That's where we come in. While we're all watching her, Yoko is sometimes deliberately, sometimes accidentally holding a mirror up to us, giving us fascinating insight into ourselves as individuals and as a collection of individuals we like to call a culture. As a result, she is constantly evolving into a manifestation of whatever we imagine her to be, or what we ourselves are becoming. We share in her brand, even if it often takes us time to realize it, even if it's not always pretty. And that's exactly how she wanted it.

Yoko Ono is definitely someone worth knowing better. One of the many retrospectives of her work launched since the turn of the century is being held at the Vancouver Art Gallery from October 2021 to May 2022. Titled *Growing Freedom: The Instructions of Yoko Ono*, the show gathers important pieces from across the spectrum of her long artistic career. It suggests a view of art that can be cultivated like a garden, with individual works resembling flowers in a landscape of free thought, free expression, and, perhaps most importantly, the freedom to be who you really are. I overheard a visitor who had asked our questions—who and what is Yoko Ono?—come away from the exhibit surprised and impressed. "I thought she was a big part of music history, but now I realize she's a big part of art history, and just history, period."

# PART ONE

# BEFORE
# THE BEGINNING:
# BUILDING A DREAM

*"A dream you dream alone is only a dream.*
*A dream you dream together is reality."*

Yoko Ono, *Grapefruit*, 1964

# CHAPTER ONE

# A Map of Two Territories

VEN A LOFTY AERIAL VIEW of Yoko Ono's genealogy is impressive. One particular forebear, her great-grandfather Atsushi Saisho, traces the family ancestry back to the ninth-century religious figure Saisho, who was the founder of a radical Buddhist sect and involved in both political intrigues and ecclesiastical soap operas. He was considered almost a saint by some followers, and a devil by others (not unlike Yoko's own later acclaim), and had bestowed upon him the title of Daishi—great teacher. He was the first priest in Japan to be so gloriously identified.

Saisho and his sibling branch initiated a powerful and influential dynasty, one so impactful, in fact, that it contributed in a major way to the overthrow of the ancient tradition of feudal military dictatorship, or *shoguns*, and restored to full sovereignty the sanctified role of emperor. Great-Grandfather Saisho was instrumental in social and political movements associated with the Imperial Household Council, a prestigious courtier clique that held sway under the highly progressive Mejii restoration that bridged the nineteenth and twentieth centuries. Mejii was to be the first emperor to accept any Occidental people arriving from off the Japanese mainland.

As a court adviser through the imperial council, Saisho was also involved in shifting the royal court from Kyoto, where it had languished for over a thousand years, to a new location in the new capital city, Tokyo. The only error Saisho apparently made in his successful career near the summits of imperial power was producing a female rather than a male heir. Despite this interruption in the traditional course of inheritance and prestige in Japan, Saisho supported his daughter Tsuruko's equally unconventional choice to study English and music at a college in Tokyo. It's hard not to take note of this early evidence of feminist courage in Ono's long family background.

Tsuruko displayed a few other unique personality traits, among them an embrace of the minority and generally suspect religion of Christianity, a faith that would flow onward to Yoko's own father. She wed one Eijiro Ono, who was descended from a long line of samurai-scholar warriors. Eijiro would excel at a college in the new capital city and exhibit similarly worldly traits, such as pursuing a postgraduate degree in America at the University of Michigan, where he was awarded a doctorate in economics. He was thus the first in Yoko's lineage to migrate to the West, as well as the first to legitimize the vocation of making money—lots of it.

Setting up yet another pattern in the family's structure, that of shuttling back and forth between the West and his homeland, Eijiro Ono rose to prominence as an executive in the Bank of Japan. He first became a branch manager, later joined the board of directors, and eventually rose to be president of the Japan Industrial Bank prior to his retirement and passing in 1927.

Ono's third son, Yeisuke, Yoko's father, also proved himself academically, and demonstrated an early interest in music, especially Western church music, which he learned under the tutelage of his mother. His musical skills were sufficient to gain him entry into polite society. He would often perform in Karuizawa resorts peopled by foreign diplomats, new-money mavens, and youthful aristocrats.

It was this passion for music, especially Western idioms such as jazz, that he passed on to his daughter. Indeed, he seems to have transmitted to her almost by osmosis his fascination with experimental twentieth-century music by the likes of Schoenberg, Ruggles, and Cowell. While he did not embrace all the extravagant experiments he might have witnessed at Karuizawa recitals, along with some startling discussions of Dadaist and Surrealist visual art, he was astute enough to hold his own among them, especially since he was seemingly capable of enthralling them all with his own facility for equally racy jazz idioms.

It was at these events that he was first observed, then admired, and then loved by a shy, quiet, pretty twenty-year-old named Isoko Yasuda. They embarked on a kind of unspoken courtship, each dazzled by the other's combination of demure good looks and talent. The almost thirty-year-old Yeisuke figured it was time for him to take life seriously and get married, but there were obstacles, starting with Isoko's Buddhist parents, who were taken aback by Yeisuke's exotic Christianity. Another roadblock was Yeisuke's almost embarrassing interest in being a musical performer. Show business was not considered a lofty pursuit in respectable Japanese circles.

The senior Yasudas were so unenthusiastic about the match that they withheld news of their daughter's relationship from her fragile maternal grandmother, whose health was an issue. She was recently widowed. Her conservative husband, Zenjiro, had been killed in a grim encounter with violent left-wing extremists on a Tokyo street corner. As the founder of the Yasuda Bank, he was an easy target, the scion of one of Japan's biggest and richest international business consortiums. He had intended to elevate his son-in-law, Isoko's father, Iomi Teitairo, as his successor, while also pulling strings to have him named the Japanese equivalent of an earl.

Yoko's mother had been the youngest of eight children in a family that quite literally lived in a shining house on the hill, within strolling distance of the royal palace. She and her siblings were sheltered and insulated in a manner consistent with their high social position. Isoko seldom saw what we might call normal children and, in fact, Yeisuke may have been the first commoner with whom she became familiar, let alone intimate, much to her parents' dismay. He was from a relatively affluent and upper-echelon clan, but far removed from the rarefied air breathed by Yasudas, who were Japanese analogues of the Getty or Rockefeller dynasties in the West. They had been identified for ages with the *zaibatsu*, the immensely powerful clique of financial and industrial conglomerates at the core of Japanese business.

It is not difficult to see what Isoko saw in Yeisuke. By all accounts, he was handsome, charming, great fun at a party, a good golfer, an adept player of the classical game of Go, all in addition to being an accomplished pianist. Almost everyone he met found him warm and inviting, but his prospective in-laws could not get over his musical ambitions. To their eyes and ears, Yeisuke's music was barely a legitimate profession, let alone one with a future.

Under pressure from his own parents, who approved of the match, and his prospective in-laws, Yeisuke agreed to put aside his delusions of a life of art and music and take his place in the Yokohama Bank business his father had established. He resisted the wishes of his in-laws that he convert to Buddhism. The couple wed in December 1931.

Demonstrating his dedication to his new role, Yeisuke agreed to transfer to an American branch of his father's bank. He moved two weeks before his daughter, Yoko, was born back in Tokyo, at 8:30 a.m. during a blizzard on February 18, 1933. She was a Pisces, in the Year of the Bird.

Yoko's early life was an ironic combination of stressful deprivation in the midst of wealth, opulence, and social privilege. Her father was literally absent for the first three years of her existence. Her mother, Isoko, was responsible for the upkeep of their Yasuda mansion, as well as maintenance of the family's lifestyle and social standing. She operated as a queen bee in a hive of attendants. Yoko, in thrall to her mother's grace and beauty, would shadow her around their home and join her at the afternoon tea parties held in their opulent garden in the company of other society ladies. At such gatherings, Isoko displayed her cute doll of a daughter to her friends, and allowed her to serve them tea and crumpets, but in private Yoko was on the receiving end of a constant stream of criticisms for her supposed lack of beauty and charm.

Mother and daughter eventually joined Yeisuke in San Francisco, beginning Yoko's exposure to the hybrid life: she was bilingual from infancy, learning English in America, while still maintaining a privileged position in Japanese society. Moving to San Francisco did little to bring her closer to her father, however, who would only meet with her by appointment.

Yeisuke was making progress in his financial career in the US but events in the homeland interrupted his family's new life. Throughout Yoko's early years, Japan was awash in aggressive expansionist attitudes. Shortly before her birth, it established its puppet state in Manchuria, and by 1937 it was at war with China. The rest of the world was meanwhile lurching toward the Second World War. With these dark clouds on the horizon, Isoko took Yoko and her younger brother, the American-born Keisuke, back to Tokyo.

Yoko was enrolled at kindergarten level in the renowned Peers School, the Gakushuin, a noble Tokyo institution that was, as the name suggests, available only to relatives of the Imperial Family or members of the parliament's House of Peers. It was an obvious destination for Yoko, given that her maternal grandfather, the banker Yasuda Zenjiro, had been a noble since about 1915. Her schooling was interrupted almost immediately, however. In 1940 Isoko feared that if the United States and Japan declared war on each other, she might be interned in Japan and never see Yeisuke again. She made the bold decision to return to America, not anticipating that internment would loom large for her in the US, as well.

Isoko and her children set sail from San Francisco and caught up to Yeisuke in his new posting, New York, in the spring of 1941. They hoped to settle into a new life in a new city, but tensions between Japan and the US only increased. Months before Japan's attack on Pearl Harbor, the peripatetic clan packed up and returned to the East. Yeisuke was positioned at his bank's Hanoi branch. Yoko, by this point in her childhood intimately familiar with ocean liners, was enrolled at a Christian primary school in Tokyo operated by the Mitsui family and catering to Japanese children who had returned from abroad.

Her father endured some unsavory postings in the early years of the war, including one in Vichy-controlled France. In 1942, after Japan's invasion of Indochina, he was the representative of the "Southeast Asia Co-Prosperity Sphere," his country's euphemism for its occupation of Indochina. Years later, his wife was said to refer to Yeisuke as a "Class B war criminal," which may or may not have been accurate. Nothing in US archives substantiates the claim, apart from General Douglas MacArthur's edict that *all* must share the blame for the war. If Isoko did say anything along those lines, she was likely speaking in a vernacular sense, as in "he did what needed to be done, he followed orders from head office," even if head office was something infernal.

The Takasumi school provided Yoko a safe refuge from the global conflagration as well as a highly progressive education. She continued to study English and the arts. Simultaneously, she was privately tutored in the Bible (her father's background), Buddhism (her mother's background), and the piano (Yoko's foreground).

Already there were tensions in Yoko's relationship with her mother, who was never free with her affections. "While her father was a remote figure in her infancy, her dutiful mother showed but rarely any overt emotion or physical fondness towards her ideally seen but not heard daughter," wrote Alan Clayson in a journalistic profile of Yoko. Much of the mother-daughter contact was filtered through the attentions of some thirty servants who ensured that Yoko was scrupulously clean, using alcohol and cotton wool to achieve otherworldly spotlessness. "Ostensibly," continues Clayson, "Isoko cared less about [Yoko's] happiness than the good opinion of her peers via displays of material wealth and attending social functions."

As what Yoko called "a nice girl from a nice family," her mother had learned *ikebana* (flower arrangement) and various other formalized aspects of Japanese culture. She also knew Japanese singing styles and could read Japanese musical scores. These skills she passed along to her daughter. One particular style of music was *nagauta*, derived from the Kabuki theater. These songs are chanted epics or ballads accompanied by *shamisen*, a three-stringed banjo-type instrument, and sometimes drums. Yoko learned to read Japanese musical scores, with their minimal indications of pitch and sound duration. Both the intense performance style of Kabuki and the tones of *nagauta* would leave their marks on her.

The curator/writer Edward Gomez elaborates on her musical education: "As a youngster, Ono attended kabuki performances with her mother and also heard the melancholy strains of popular *enka* songs on the radio. Her parents sent her to Jiyu Gakuen, another prestigious Tokyo school, where she began piano lessons at the age of four. Known for its music-centered curriculum, the school gave early career starts to several notable Japanese composers. In a typical assignment, pupils were told to listen for and notate everyday sounds and noises."

Ono would continue her piano lessons into adolescence but admitted, "I was too shy to play in front of my father, I would go and play in the next room, just to let him know I was working." Her father was more judgmental than encouraging. He routinely examined his daughter's fingers for signs of her professional potential, eventually concluding that she would never become a concert pianist.

Yoko was quoted by journalist Jerry Hopkins as feeling bereft and alone as a result of an enforced regime where she was expected to withhold any feelings of dissatisfaction toward her parents, even ones that might be wholly suitable given the disciplines enforced upon her amid all the ostentatious display. "Inside me, I could feel a certain rejection of my mother's show of her possessions, but I got over it as I got older."

The war was largely distant until March 9, 1944, when almost a quarter of Tokyo was incinerated in the notorious firebomb raids. Affluent and privileged, the Ono family was well protected in its private family bunker in the Azabu district, some distance from the horrible destruction downtown. But they were close enough that Isoko, fearful for their safety, embarked on another perilous move. She took her children to a farming village on the outskirts of the fashionable Karuisawa mountain resort, where her husband used to play lounge piano. Despite their near regal status, the family suffered deprivation in the village. Yoko and her brother helped to sustain the family by trading some of their luxury goods, lovely but now useless, for food and supplies essential to their survival.

Yoko, at some points, would look back on this rural interlude almost wistfully. She recalled seeking shelter in the domain of the imagination with her brother, Keisuke: "Lying on our backs, looking up at the sky through an opening in the roof, we exchanged menus in the air and used our powers of visualization to survive." When her brother was hungry and unhappy, Yoko would ask him, "What kind of dinner would you like?"

"Ice cream."

"Good, let's imagine our ice cream dinner."

They did, "and he started to look happy," said Yoko later. "I realized even then that just through imagining, we can be happy. So we had our conceptual dinner and this is maybe my first piece of art."

On other days, she was less whimsical about the forced evacuation: "My mother had some crazy idea that this would be a nice time to get in touch with nature. She bought, sight unseen, a farmhouse that turned out to be only half-finished. The farmers wouldn't give us any food, and my mother took the next train back to Tokyo." That was when Yoko began begging and bartering for food and staples.

Still, it wasn't all despair. "I had a very romantic picture of myself as a hero. I lived in a half-dream world."

The neighborhood children teased her for being "*bata kusai*" (smelling like butter), a taunt relating to both her urban nature and her wealthy, Americanized sensibility. In a sense, she was already an outsider, a foreigner, even in her own country. It was lonely, although "I didn't think of it as 'I'm a lonely child,'" she would later tell *Mojo* magazine with a certain resignation in her tone, "because that was the only life I knew."

She was twelve as the war approached its climax, an age when most girls are dealing with puberty and preparations for adulthood. Yoko was instead absorbing the most mind-altering violence ever perpetrated on an

11

enemy culture: the nuclear attack on her homeland by the other nation in which she'd grown up.

Isoko moved her children again, this time to a more secure location elsewhere in Tokyo. In April 1946, Yoko rejoined the Peers School, which had survived further firebombings owing to its fortunate location near the Imperial Palace. It was also far from the two major Japanese cities, Hiroshima and Nagasaki, obliterated by a mysterious type of bomb no one fully understood yet, but there was no escaping the devastation of total war. It was evident outside her school's windows. In his profile of Yoko, Murray Sayles describes her vantage point in harrowing detail: "A city all but returned, as the American General Curtis E. Lemay (sic) had promised, to the Stone Age. Sterile wastelands of twisted iron and blackened stone. People lived in holes clawed in the ground, roofed with stray sheets of iron. On every corner, famished woman tried to sell trinkets for food. In a terminal degradation of Japanese martial values, American servicewomen smiled for snaps in rickshaws pulled by Japanese men still wearing the tattered remnants of military uniforms. Japan under the occupation was a paradox: democracy imposed by a conqueror."

Tokyo residents, the Onos included, were preoccupied by the search for secure housing and food, and also haunted by doubts about human culture and the meaning of civilization. These penetrated even the thick walls of the Peers School itself. One unexpected side effect of the discrediting of Japan's male romantically aestheticized warrior mindset was a new postwar mentality that questioned values and traditions that had stood for centuries. Out of this emerged a new feminism. Women were allowed to cast political votes by the new westernized US-composed constitution of 1946, and new female members of parliament eventually succeeded in abolishing licensed brothels, long a stalwart of a male-dominated society.

Yoko remained in Tokyo during the radical transitions to follow: the abolition of the Peerage in 1947 and the resultant opening up of the school to anyone from anywhere. One example of this new and jarring egalitarianism was the enrollment of Yoko's classmate Crown Prince Naruhito alongside the son of a plumber from Melbourne, Australia, an outcome that might have contributed to Yoko's own fluid notions of social status.

Japanese arts and culture were also in turmoil, perhaps an inevitable outcome of the broader collapse in values, both economic and aesthetic. General MacArthur's occupation headquarters heavily censored all of what the Japanese media reported on, including any new, fresh, or daring cultural pursuits. Postwar democracy was fragile and fraught with pressures from within and without. Incredibly, though, Japan suddenly became a willing ally of its conqueror, enticed by the abrupt opening of gigantic American markets for Japanese products, the revival of its production system, newly formed alliances with Western banks and industrial concerns, and the accidental creation of a huge force field that soon would become recognized by the name of 'Japan Inc'. This, and the looming war with Korea, all contributed to Japan's embrace of the US, its rapid return to economic prosperity, and its modernist cultural revolution.

One thing that didn't much change was Yoko Ono's relations with her parents. She felt a distinct emotional frigidity in her mother. This odd maternal figure who did not want a child's tears to damage her mink coat even managed to make an obstacle of her own beauty. Yoko recalled Isoko saying that "she should feel lucky that her mother was so beautiful." Her looks mattered little to her daughter, who only wanted and needed human connection. "I often wished my mother had died so that at least I could get some people's sympathy," she said. "I got no support from my family at all."

Yoko felt daily that both her mother and father had wanted a son and not a daughter. "I was a sensitive child. You smell it, you understand that actually your father doesn't want you to be good. And then you think that you're not good, because you're not talented," she said in an interview with the Japan Society.

This paternal dynamic, torturous and immutable, had a range of effects on Yoko. In her most impressionable years, she was often left to live in her own imagination, which, together with being waited on by scores of servants, provided a weird sense of freedom. As Clayson expressed it, Yoko began to turn "into an astoundingly self-motivated, purposeful girl." Her mother, believing that she "somehow owned her child's life," characterized her daughter as willful, and "seldom paused to consider not only how different Yoko's values might be to hers, but whether Yoko had even formed any of her own. A symptom of a certain 'apartness' would come to the fore."

There was a sense of incompleteness, and an awareness of loss and absence in this apartness, but the independence it allowed her was real. She would always be able to retreat into the safe harbors of dreams, art, stories, poetry, and, later, music. She would carry into adulthood a wistful sense of herself as a heroic character. Yoko perceived the world as a zone of half measures, and life itself as an unfinished project, one to be consciously crafted as the needs of the moment dictated.

At the same time, she was being set up for a lifelong expectation of suppression, of having to fight your way to center stage, of having to scream loudly where others might whisper softly. It made her strong and strident, with a good amount of rage trapped in her small body. She also became a connoisseur of pain, building her own private repository of aches, miseries, and grudges. As John Lennon would later tell *Rolling Stone* magazine, "Her pain is such that she expresses herself in a way that hurts you—you really cannot take it."

When it came to thinking about her future, Yoko received mixed direction from her parents. At fourteen, she had announced to her father her desire to become a composer. He discouraged her, believing, according to his daughter, that "music composition was too hard for women." Her mother, meanwhile, warned her against marriage and parenthood, saying it had destroyed her own hopes for a painting career.

She graduated from the Peers School primary level in 1951 at the age of eighteen, and promptly enrolled to study philosophy at its sister institution, the Peers Gakushuin University. Created in 1847 and originally located in Kyoto, Gakushuin was highly exclusive, originally attended only by the Imperial Family or members of the House of Peers. It was a natural landing place for a member of the Yasuda clan. Despite its privileged, tradition-bound image, the university offered an eclectic and Westernized course of study. The founder of the school, Emperor Ninko, was an Oxford graduate himself. Yoko was thus further exposed to the hybrid lifestyle, a collision of Eastern and Western ideas and faiths, reinforcing what she had experienced at home with a Buddhist mother and a Christian father who moved effortlessly between Japan and the US.

She was the first female student admitted to the philosophy faculty, the first of her many firsts, although she dropped out after only two semesters. She set her sights on a writing career but her teachers were unimpressed by her unconventional style and strange form of delivery. "People said my stories were like poems and my essays were like fiction," she says. "In Japan, in those days, there was no genre called avant-garde. My schoolteachers denounced my work as bad because they judged it from existing standards." By the time there *was* an avant-garde in Japan, her work would still be criticized as something beyond even the new aesthetic standards.

Yoko resented the rigors of her structured education at Gakushuin, feeling like "a domesticated animal being fed information." But she did learn. Even later, when she was creating her mature work as a multimedia artist, she still regarded her early classical training as her foundation; its formalism gave her something to rebel against. She would follow the many experimental artists and musicians whose rigorous classical educations were starting points for rule-breaking and anti-formalist techniques.

In fact, Gakushuin was a perfect playground for a future experimenter: elite, permissive, blending East and West, and on the cutting edge of all things adventurous. Far from chafing against Westernization as an aberration, students at the school often shared a growing sense of the euphoric freedom associated with profound social change. Euphoria would become a hallmark of the Ono oeuvre, an ongoing sense of being on the verge of dramatic evolutionary developments, real or imaginary.

Yoko was reportedly precocious in all of her activities and pursuits, not just in her music or literature interests. Her cousin remarked that before the age of twenty, Yoko had already been involved in a series of romantic affairs, including one with an older man at Tokyo College, another with a professor at Gakushuin University, and another with the younger son of the emperor of Japan, Prince Toshi. The liberal attitudes of the university seemed quite suited to Ono's emotional temperament.

Her time at the university was short. The Ono family had relocated once again after the war, settling in the Manhattan suburb of Scarsdale, New York. In September 1952, Yoko joined them in their comfortable but hardly palatial ranch-style bungalow at 74 Carthage Road. She enrolled at Sarah Lawrence, a private liberal arts college a few miles out of town.

A privileged, progressive institution with a bright all-female student body, Sarah Lawrence College represented a certain kind of cutting edge in postsecondary education in the 1950s. There were no required courses, no majors, and no grades, and its environment encouraged a lofty kind of lifestyle and thinking, what Louise Blecher Rose described as a feeling that the college was only accidentally located in America, or even on earth. This would not have been a culture shock for Yoko. Rather, she already embodied her own kind of culture shock as a result of the social change and often contradictory influences she'd experienced by the age of twenty. The emerging feminist and freethinking ethos of the college would have appealed to her as someone who did not demand a consistent definition of personal identity or culture, and who was as comfortable with truth as with fiction.

Yoko studied poetry with Alastair Reid and English literature with Katherine Mansell, each of whom was as highly regarded in their field as they were at the college, and composition with the Viennese-trained Andre Singer. Her engagement with the college's visual arts department was especially fertile, leading her directly into the arms of the American avant-garde. She was encouraged to experiment in a drastically interdisciplinary manner, which suited her temperament perfectly. She pursued painting, photography, cinema, sculpture, installation, performance art, and eventually video, often at the same time.

The music department, too, encouraged Yoko to push the limits of traditional forms, and she did, sometimes further than the faculty advised. "My heroes were the twelve-tone composers—[Alban] Berg, [Anton] Webern, those people—and I was just fascinated by what they could do," she recalled. "I wrote some twelve-tone songs, but then my music went off into an area that my teacher felt was really a bit off the track . . . and he said, 'Well look, there are some people who are doing things like what you do, and they're called avant-garde.'"

One of her musical endeavors at the college echoed a childhood assignment she'd been given in Japan. She attempted to use Western musical notation to capture "the storm of birds singing." These were the sounds to which she awoke each morning. She found notation inadequate, and instead devised her first instruction-based composition, "Secret Piece" (1953). It reads: "Decide on one note you want to play. Play it with the following accompaniment: the woods from 5:00 a.m. to 8:00 a.m. in summer." Hand drawn beneath this brief text, staves (the horizontal lines in musical notion) appear without a time signature or measures. Two lonely half held notes on the bass hint at some sort of prolonged hum. Above the treble clef, Ono wrote: "With the accompaniment of birds singing."

One of her music instructors at the college, Meyer Kupferman, remembers Yoko as "particularly adept, the best in the class," and recalls "evidence of a strong intensity . . . she was tightly put together and intent on doing well. The other students were more relaxed. She wasn't relaxed, *ever.* At the same time, she was a shadow figure on campus. When you focused on her, she was fine, but then she sort of disappeared, like a phantom."

Other instructors struggled to remember anything at all about Yoko. Her freshman faculty adviser, Katherine Mansell, said: "I can picture her very clearly but I can't remember anything about her."

Her fellow students offered contradictory images of the immigrant art student, some calling her "sullen," others finding her "sweet." Richard Rabkin, who studied briefly with her at Harvard where she'd picked up extra credits required for her entry into Sarah Lawrence, found her "completely opaque," and said she "couldn't be too friendly with men. It required a degree of skill in appearing harmless to make friends with her. You had to be totally safe."

Rabkin did eventually gain the confidence of "this Japanese girl-woman," and marveled at her willingness to share her private life. He recalls that Ono's first attempts to write fiction were not very successful until she began drawing from her own experiences. Suddenly her work was harrowing. "I'm not sure what I expected, but I was not ready for the sadness she revealed. All her memories were painful. All of them." Rabkin was one of the first to encounter an Ono survival mechanism: the personal confrontation with painful limits, shaped into the content of her art and music.

Another classmate, Betty Rollin, describes four distinct social sets or scenes at Sarah Lawrence: northern Christian debutantes, young artist-bohemians, rich urban Jewish princesses, and an unclassifiable assortment of the eccentric and rich. Yoko "sort of fell into the artsy group and epitomized the unclassifiable," says Rollin. Other students in her orbit were Hope Cooke, who would marry the King of Sikkim, and Barbara Walters, the future television journalist, whose father operated one of the biggest nightclubs in New York.

Rollin found Yoko "ethereal and intelligent," and somewhat poetic, to the point of seeming to speak in haiku verse in conversations. Her lasting memory was of Yoko sitting alone under a tree reading a book: "Not aloof really, but removed, distant from the rest of us, somehow beyond our reach."

Another keen-eyed observer described Yoko, clad in exotic beatnik black, as a "ghostly" presence on campus.

On the whole, it does not appear that Yoko had a forceful impact on those around her. She stood out quietly at the college, aloof from others, inaccessible, and content to be alone with her own thoughts and dreams. At the same time, there were strong hints of her ambition and self-belief, a personal faith that she could become exactly what she imagined herself to be. Also, a willingness not simply to push the envelope, but to rip it to shreds. She displayed the flexibility, diversity, and eclecticism that a future curator would trace to her family background: "Ono's aristocratic heritage may account for her natural ease in moving among all the arts—music, poetry, performance and painting. Central to elite Japanese culture is the literati, or *bunjin*, ideal in which the practice of the three perfections, of painting, poetry, and calligraphy and the elegant pursuits of music and the board game *Go* are universally acknowledged as superior ways to refine the soul—life's loftiest goal. For Japanese literati, amateur delights were traditionally cultivated over professional gain, and spiritual content valued over technical proficiency. To move among and between art forms, seeking the higher self, that was the ideal."

Although there was little in the way of academic structure at Sarah Lawrence, Yoko still found enough to chafe against. She rebelled against the mandates of class attendance and assignments, preferring to read off-course books. She was learning, just not what her teachers were trying to impress upon her. One of her most daring aesthetic or "gesture" projects was a meditative performance art exhibition called *Lighting Piece*. It consisted of Yoko in a seated position, usually next to a piano, which would not be played, striking wooden matches and watching them as they slowly burned out in her fingers. The performance elicited shocked silence from her student audience.

Yoko spent much of her junior year in 1955 sequestered in the library, listening to recordings of international serialist, or twelve-tone composers, Alban Berg, Anton Webern, and Arnold Schoenberg. She would often be in the company of the quiet young Japanese composer Toshi Ichiyanagi, who was modeling himself on those masters' styles and atonal sensibilities. They shared a love of daring provocation in the arts, an ability to shift in and out of different creative disciplines, exploring the far edges of artistic expression, and soon, so much more.

# CHAPTER TWO

# No East or West in Dreams

URING HER YEARS AT Sarah Lawrence, Yoko Ono was increasingly at odds with her parents, and fearful that her towering family legacy would somehow swallow her whole. She viewed her mother and father, says curator Alexandra Munroe, "as artists who had failed to fulfill their talent in order to serve the cause of the suffocating Yasuda and Ono legacies. . . . [E]ither by resolve or impulse or both, [Yoko] determined to break away, to sunder her family's connection. The avant-garde, a world of ideas and possibilities, offered an escape at least to a conceptual freedom."

Yoko admitted as much herself: that "the pressure of becoming a Yasuda/Ono was so tremendous—intellectual, social, academic and bourgeois pressure. Unless I rebelled against it, I wouldn't have survived."

Her relationship with the young composer Toshi Ichiyanagi promised liberation from the claustrophobic web of home. She had officially been introduced to Toshi by Tanaka Kozo, son of a chief justice of the supreme court of Japan, who was studying at Columbia University in New York. Kozo felt Yoko's interest in music would provide a bond with Toshi, whose musical style others would describe as "walking an avant-garde tightrope without any net." Soon to be one of the most acclaimed of the postwar Japanese composers, he was one of a number of young Tokyo musicians seeking to rise Phoenix-like from the ashes of the world war.

Like so many other restless seekers, East and West, Ichiyanagi saw great possibilities in the form of a universal culture. In part, this project involved a reassessment of what was specifically Japanese and what was universally shared by all races and cultures. The idea was to hold both in some sort of uneasy but progressive balance. As he explained to a reporter from the *New York Times*, Ichiyanagi was looking for "a certain awareness that comes from looking at Japanese tradition from a contemporary viewpoint as well as a search for the logic and sensitivity of the East that has existed in the past and is now lost." Like Ono, he had a voracious appetite for the best of both worlds.

Although almost the same age as Yoko, Ichiyanagi was already accomplished, having been awarded the coveted Coolridge Scholarship at Juilliard, among other accolades. He was also a star pupil and later a copyist for the experimental composer Stefan Wolpe.

Yoko's romance with Ichiyanagi, like many of her past and future passions, seemed mostly a creation of her powerful will. Ichiyanagi was bowled over by her persuasive charms. In no time, she dropped out of Sarah Lawrence and moved into his West Eighty-Ninth Street brownstone. Later they would move together to 426 Amsterdam Avenue, another working-class address—all that Ichiyanagi's Juilliard scholarship would afford.

Their relationship was frowned upon by Yoko's parents, however much their resistance echoed what they themselves had met when disclosing their relationship to their parents years earlier, and for precisely the same reasons: the young man's relatively proletarian upbringing and unpromising artistic aspirations. Yoko's parents preferred a more conventional match for their increasingly wayward daughter, but there was no chance they were going to convince her to think practically, slow down, or change her mind. She was only twenty-two when she met Ichiyanagi, not yet fully formed, but it was already abundantly clear that patience and practicality were not her style.

Seeing the inevitability of their headstrong daughter's intentions, Yoko's parents eventually acquiesced to her wishes and reluctantly blessed the union of the déjà-vu couple, so much a mirror image of themselves. Although conspicuously absent from the formal wedding ceremony in the late spring of 1956, they did foot the bill for the lavish reception in a large Manhattan ballroom, and even persuaded the Japanese consul general to make some pertinent remarks in an after-dinner address.

The couple would only be married for a brief and intense six years, from the spring of 1956 until the fall of 1962, yet these were fertile years for both Ichiyanagi and Ono. It was especially valuable from Ono's perspective, as the newly emancipated Yasuda heiress was finally free to enter New York's burgeoning avant-garde scene alongside a bona fide experimental music maestro. So even though their relationship was stormy and competitive, eventually dissolving in rancor, separation, and divorce, she would always consider it worth the trouble, at least in the long run.

They lived a bohemian lifestyle in New York, struggling to make ends meet. In his liner notes to a compilation of Ono recordings, Robert Palmer, the longtime *New York Times* culture critic who followed the full arc of her career, captured the headiness of the times and the material circumstances in which Yoko was trying to make a new artistic home: "It was 1960. The Loft. A small, young Japanese woman stood at the bottom of an endless flight of stairs. It was a cold-water flat, there was no electricity, the ceiling wasn't very high, it was just a very long room.

The price was $50.50 per month. The loft was at 112 Chambers Street, in a rapidly changing area far downtown in Manhattan. It was just what Yoko Ono was looking for: ample space in which to build her art and life."

Yoko's early exhibitions did not garner either the press attention or the art collectors' investments that had been part of their mutual plan. Also not part of the plan were the demeaning odd jobs: the gifted Toshi forced to play piano in a bustling cocktail bar, and Yoko pretending to be a waitress in Greenwich Village cafés. Some of the cafés also exhibited her artwork, including *Painting to See the Sky* and *Painting to See the Room*, both of which had viewing holes drilled into unprimed canvas.

A few of the couple's efforts to support themselves were so out of character that in retrospect they almost seem like performance works in themselves: teaching calligraphy, lecturing on folk music, providing administrative duties for the Japan Society, which considered Yoko a cultural representative whom they proudly dispatched to city schools. She was philosophical about the latter role in conversation with the rock journalist Paul Trynka: "I would go there and demonstrate calligraphy and show what the tea ceremony was like. That paid pretty well. I did just about anything people do in those circumstances."

Their humble circumstances notwithstanding, the young couple and their growing circle of like-minded friends invented out of thin air what later came to be known and applauded as "loft culture," an alternative art, music, and cultural space that ran parallel to Manhattan's more staid, traditional concerts, dealers, and museum systems. These simpatico artists and musicians, experimentally inclined, agreed that the era of selling precious art objects to upper-class snobs or of methodically notating written music for orchestras to play with rigid and compulsively classical exactitude was largely over. They shared Yoko's strong sensation that something extraordinary was going to happen any minute.

And they were right. With their bare hands and wide-open minds, they fabricated a revolution in 1960s style and sensibility. Alongside their search for new sounds and images, they sought new ways to show and hear their work. Ono decided to eschew museums and concert halls and instead staged exhibits, installations, and concerts in the same art studio where she made her actual work. She invited her flock of radical friends to join her in this adventure and hosted some of the first loft concerts in New York. "The experimental loft music scene that would help make artists like Laurie Anderson and Philip Glass into stars and Soho real estate some of the most expensive in New York was still some twenty years in the future," writes Palmer.

Yoko remembers: "Everybody advised me not to do this, they said nobody's going to come all the way downtown to look at or listen to this." But she persisted, presenting her kind of visual art and music—the likes of Jasper Johns, Robert Rauschenberg, John Cage, David Tudor, Terry Riley, Steve Reich, Richard Maxfield, La Monte Young, and Tony Conrad, among others—in *her* way. It was an organic, often mesmerizing mix of East and West, emotionally Beat in tone, spiritual in motivation, and trance inducing.

"The day of the first concert it snowed very heavily," remembered Yoko. "Twenty-five people came." Among them were the not-quite-yet famous composer John Cage and his brilliant pianist, David Tudor, both friends of Toshi. These were people from the future. Legend has it that collector Peggy Guggenheim and her date, the painter Marcel Duchamp, also dropped by. "The concert may not have been a smashing success," writes Palmer, "but for Yoko Ono it was an auspicious beginning." Cage, he adds, "listened intently" to Yoko's performance, "head cocked in that sage way of his, sitting on an orange crate."

Beate Gordon, Yoko's Japan Society supporter, recalls her experiment with the minimalist composer La Monte Young: "We sat on orange crates.

There was a large piece of paper tacked to the wall. Yoko went to her refrigerator, took out a bowl of Jell-O and threw it at the paper. Then she took a couple of eggs and threw them. Then she took some Japanese sumi ink and started finger painting. Finally, she took out a match and lit the paper. I remember looking at the rickety loft and thinking—I'm going to die."

In an eerie presaging of Jimi Hendrix, Young would ignite his violin onstage, a flamboyant theatrical gesture to accompany his otherwise sedate and meditative drone music. Among his most notable compositions around this time was "Piano Piece for David Tudor #1, October 1960," which read: "Bring a bale of hay and a bucket of water onto the stage for the piano to eat and drink. The performer may then feed the piano or leave it to eat by itself. If the former, the piece is over once the piano has been fed, if the latter, it is over after the piano eats or decides not to."

Although they only occurred for a period of about seven months, these events, concerts, and exhibitions organized with La Monte Young and others in Yoko's Chambers Street loft have long been regarded as a historic watershed in American experimental arts. In addition to promoting her own work, the activities afforded a remarkable opportunity for some of the most adventurous of the new vanguard of artists to stretch their imaginations and flex their aesthetic muscles in tandem. It was almost a gymnasium of the mind.

The loft events also led to one of the most important associations of Ono's career. Early in the summer of 1961, she received a call from one of the artists who had performed at Chambers Street. He told her of "this guy who opened a midtown gallery on Madison Avenue and was planning to do exactly what I had been doing. . . ." All the Chamber Street Series artists were now lining up in front of his gallery, the artist said. "The guy got the idea when he came to one of the evenings at your loft. His name is George Maciunas. You were probably introduced. Do you remember him?"

Yoko didn't—hundreds of people had visited her loft—but the news made her miserable. "You're finished, Yoko," said the friend. "He's got all your artists."

Just as she was reconciling herself to the end of her loft series, she received a call from Maciunas. He invited her to do a show at his gallery. "Nobody ever thought of giving me a show yet in those days," she says. "So the guy who supposedly 'finished me off' is now giving me a show? Things work in mysterious ways." She was happy.

It was dusk when I visited the AG gallery for the first time. The staircase in the hall was already half dark. I went upstairs, and the door was wide open. I entered into an already dark room. I heard some people just whispering to each other and laughing in another room. The light was coming from that room. As I walked over, I saw a very handsome man, obviously European, with a beautiful woman sitting together at a table in candlelight. They both looked at me. I remember thinking what a romantic picture the two of them made! There was an IBM typewriter on the table gleaming in the dark. One of the artists had once commented, "That IBM typewriter! That alone must be something. Just means he's rich!" But turns out, everything was not as it seemed.

The very young and pretty woman George was sitting with was actually his mother. They used the candle because the electricity was cut off. And that great-looking IBM typewriter? It was a loaner. George also had phones everywhere. There was a story for that, too. He told me his phone service was listed under a new name every month. Whenever his phone was cut off, he just registered a new phone under a new name. . . . I, like the rest of the artists, just thought, "Wow!"

Yoko and Maciunas arranged a show of her work. She turned the fact that the gallery had no electricity to advantage, allowing the sunlight pouring through the windows to play on her canvases, "making beautiful, natural changes to them throughout the day."

Yoko chose to display her "instruction paintings." When people came to see the show, she would tour them around, explaining the meaning of each piece. Some of these items were entirely language oriented, others were manifestations of ideas that could more conventionally be approached as physical paintings, although the similarity ended there. Her instructions stipulated that a painting, or any artwork, really, can be divided into two separate zones: that of the instruction or stated idea, and that of the realization or personification of the idea. They can be both physical and mental, or neither.

The canvases at Maciunas's AG Gallery thus involved the viewer as an active participant in the completion of the work, in some cases requiring the visitor to step on the canvas as it lay on the floor, as with *Painting to be Stepped On*, or burned with a live candle, as with *Smoke Painting*. Such works of art were virtually alive: the process of their production was active and ongoing, not unlike the organic processes of which we ourselves are the living result.

"Yoko Ono has made a 'smoke painting,'" wrote Gene Swenson in *ARTnews* magazine. "It consists of a grimy unstrung canvas with a hole in it. Into the hole she has stuck a burning candle, withdrawing it when the canvas began to smolder and smoke on its own. The painting's limited life was shortened by one minute for this report, its living presence snuffed out by a damp cloth as soon as the idea became clear."

It was an exceptionally hot summer and few people took the time to enjoy these pieces in the robust and generous spirit in which they were conceived, made, and offered (although the great Japanese American sculptor Isamu Noguchi did make an appearance and stepped on *Painting to be Stepped on* in what Yoko remembered as "his elegant Zohri slippers." As understood by the participants, it was a rare spirit in the seriously constricted art world of the time: a spirit of pure and purposeless laughter which both celebrates being alive while also derailing our rational attempts to justify being alive.

Regardless of the low attendance, Yoko was playing an advanced role in the very early gestation period of both conceptual and minimal art, long before those terms even existed. Maciunas was obsessed with trying to put a name to their efforts:

> George said we had to have a name for this movement that was happening. "You think of the name," he told me. I said, "I don't think this is a movement. I think it's wrong to make it into a movement." To me, "movement" had a dirty sound—like we were going to become some kind of an establishment . . .
>
> The next day, George said, "Yoko, look." He showed me the word "Fluxus" in a huge dictionary. It had many meanings, but he pointed to "flushing." "Like toilet flushing!" he said, laughing, thinking it was a good name for the movement. "This is the name," he said. I just shrugged my shoulders in my mind.

Fluxus would become an international movement of collegial, likeminded artists, writers, and composers that flourished into the 1970s, famous for its experiments in new mediums and its creation of new art forms. Like the Dada movement, which had responded to the Great War with its rejection of logic, reason, and bourgeois values, Fluxus found its feet after the Second World War, taking Dadaists like Marcel Duchamp as inspiration, and locating meaning in artistic processes rather than artistic product. They were anti-commercial, anti-capitalist, artistic genre busters. Although they were too diverse and anarchic to agree on a manifesto, Dutch critic Harry Ruhé called them "the most radical and experimental art movement of the Sixties."

The impact of Fluxus in the larger culture is difficult to pin down, and is something on which art critics and art historians can't always agree, in part due to the ephemeral, anti-commercial, and sometimes even immaterial nature of its works, as well as its underground ethos. Seeing itself as a rearguard action, an anti-art movement opposed to the establishment system of museums and galleries, the marketing of art as fetishistic products for wealthy buyers, and especially the cult of personality around the artist, it had nothing in the way of institutional momentum.

Proponents such as Richard Dorment in *The Penguin Book of Art Writing*, suggest, quite rightly, that art need not last in order to be good, and that ephemeral events and objects might leave no visible residue yet still qualify as great and influential. But there's no getting around the problem of sustaining and calling attention to a movement when there's nothing to hang on the wall or sell at auction. Dorment acknowledges that apart from Maciunus, a natural-born promoter, and the composer John Cage, whom the movement looked to for inspiration, the only Fluxus artist anyone has heard of is Yoko Ono, and that would happen almost by accident.

Dorment believes it's a miracle that traces of Fluxus survive at all, and that it continues to exert an influence today. After all, a core belief of Fluxus is that Fluxus is already inside everyone, a part of who we are, a part of how we live, and that technically nobody and everybody can be a Fluxus artist. It's not a credo that guarantees your work entry into the collection of the Museum of Modern Art, yet, as Dorment observed, Fluxus lives on:

> In advertising, rock and roll, video and visual art, Fluxus is enjoying a comeback. This is because its aestheticizing attitude towards life, its idealistic belief that young artists can change society by turning people's attention toward the quality of everyday living, is compelling still. The several hundred artists who made up Fluxus wanted to transform society through social change. If that sounds pretentious, in reality Fluxus was light and witty, more Monty Python than Bertolt Brecht. It drew heavily on non-western visual traditions, refusing to distinguish between high and popular art, designating as "art" formal gestures, ritualized actions and a conscious aesthetic appreciation of the mundane . . . It was fun to know someone associated with *Fluxus*, since communications with them, often by post, were apt to contain bits of collage, poetry or instructions to perform a series of absurd ritualistic acts.

At the time Yoko was collaborating with Maciunus, Fluxus was barely an idea but people in the art world were watching. "Fluxus was the furthermost experimental group of its time," she said. "Anyone doing experimental work was aware of us and took ideas from us and then made them commercial. Their stuff was selling, but ours was too far-out to sell."

There was nevertheless a definite satisfaction in being at the leading edge of something. "We used to walk around [New York]," she remembers. "We felt good, like we owned the city. Both of us were totally bigheaded people. So, yes, we were the owners of something. Maybe not the city, but something . . . maybe not so tangible. . . . As they say, those were the days."

The year 1961 brought her more opportunities. In late November, she and Toshi staged two conceptual "operas" for an audience of 250 people in the recital room adjacent to the main auditorium of Carnegie Hall. One of the performances was the metaphysical musing *A Piece for Strawberries and Violin*. Its exotic lyrics consisted of a primal kind of wordless vocalization. The couple also presented an event called Grapefruit featuring a darkened stage with performers carrying heavy objects and trying to navigate an obstacle course through the near darkness. "The Carnegie Recital Hall concert of 1961 must have been particularly memorable," writes the *New York Times* music critic Robert Palmer. "There were electronic sounds, complete darkness, performers with contact microphones taped to their bodies hauling heavy objects across the pitch-black stage."

At one point in the *Grapefruit* event, remembered Yoko "two men were tied together with lots of empty cans and bottles around them, and they had to move from one end of the stage to the other very quietly and slowly without making any sounds. What I was trying to attain was a sound that almost doesn't come out. Before I speak, I stutter in my mind, and then my cultured mind tries to correct that stuttering into a clean sentence, and I wanted to deal with those sounds of people's fear and stuttering."

Another of Yoko's major appearances that same year was at the Village Gate nightclub, best known as a home for groundbreaking jazz musicians. Ono was one of three Japanese composers on the bill, along with Toshi and Mayazumi Toshiro. What she presented was anything but jazz. Her compositions included atonal music, laughter, nursery rhymes, and a commanding Kabuki stage presence. Much of Ono's avant ethos has surprising roots in this classical Japanese dance-drama, with its heavily stylized performances, as well as Noh, with its mixture of music, dance, and drama, and, later on, Butoh, the dance of darkness, with its intensely visceral emotional eruptions.

She was undoubtedly coming into her own as an artist, but no one, or very few, were prepared for her arrival. "As a Japanese-American artist emerging at a time when neither Asians nor women had much place in modernism's history, Ono had little framework for sustained critical support," writes the astute Alexandra Munroe. Few recognized her importance, and fewer still paid attention to such Asian forms such as haiku poetry, Noh drama, and Kabuki theater, and few "fathomed the complexity of Ono's cultural lineage that shaped her seemingly cryptic ideas of art."

"Ono's art," writes Munroe, "is directed at transformation, a faith in the mind's power to realize good through the act of visualization. Hers is a social art that relies on participants. If consciousness in Zen Buddhism equals *creativity in every moment*, then it is possible to see Ono's art as an ongoing practice of what she calls *fabricating consciousness*."

The indifference, rejection, and almost total lack of support she received for her work was naturally frustrating and dispiriting for an ambitious young artist. A point of her art, her mission, even, had been to press against her environment until it let her be, let her exist. She was searching for her place in a tumultuous, dislocative world, forever fearful that no one would take her work seriously, as though she did not exist at all. It did not help that her personal life was unraveling at the same time.

To some extent, Yoko's marriage to Toshi Ichiyanagi was an act of rebellion, an attempt to outrun the family ghosts she always believed were chasing her. The relationship proved unsustainable. The deeper Yoko delved into Manhattan's underground art scene, producing her groundbreaking and overlooked works, the greater the strains in her marriage. She was increasingly becoming a solo act. Toshi returned to Japan, permanently, it turned out, to continue his ascent to a stellar career as a modernist serial composer.

She had engaged in a series of liaisons, including one with her erstwhile collaborator, the composer La Monte Young. None of this was unusual in the loft scene, a merry-go-round of both love affairs and artistic experiments. Yoko had learned early on that a creative life as an artist was not conducive to traditional domestic habits, and she would always live this way, regardless of the consequences.

One of those consequences was an abortion, which occurred while she was still living with Toshi, and which he appeared to accept as a matter of course. Later on, Yoko would confide to *Esquire* magazine: "In New York I was always having abortions, because I was too neurotic to take precautions, I would go out and have an affair, and oh, I'm in a mess. My first husband was very kind to me."

The state of her marriage naturally worried her parents. In 1962, Yoko was given a welcome opportunity to exhibit and perform in a mini-tour of events in Tokyo organized by John Cage. She was preparing for the tour when two ominous-looking gentlemen from the Bank of Japan showed up at her loft. They were not there to watch her throw eggs at the wall but to "escort" her to the airport and "assist" her in traveling back to Tokyo. On her arrival, it became clear that her parents had hatched a plan to help her patch up her marriage with Toshi, who was occupying a flat owned by her family. Yoko was promptly installed in the flat.

Notwithstanding the abrupt manner of her reentry to Japan after almost a decade's absence, the journey would be momentous for Yoko. It would not heal her marriage, but she could see that she had changed, and so had Japan. Its experimental art scene was now in some ways far ahead of what was happening in the US. Unlike the indifferent, sometimes hostile reactions she was receiving from American audiences, Tokyo would welcome her almost like returning royalty, with open arms, eyes, and ears.

# CHAPTER THREE

# Hold Back the Dawn

Y EARS LATER, YOKO ONO would be asked about the risk
she took in abandoning the New York avant-garde scene in
1962, at the age of twenty-nine, just when it was coming into
its own and her career had perhaps its best chance of lifting off. If she
could do it again, would she have stayed in New York? Her response to
art critic Robert Enright was blunt: "No. There were many things that
I did that were inspired directly from the environment there in Japan.
Had I stayed in New York, I would have become one of those grand-
dames of the avant-garde, repeating what I was doing over and over
again."

Her answer suggests that a more fruitful approach to her decision
would be to look not at what she was missing in New York but at what was
going on in Tokyo. She was arriving home at an explosive moment for the
Japanese avant-garde. Artists were clamoring to lift art out of its familiar
institutions; mix genres; experiment with language, sound art, street
performance, and many other creative expressions rooted in the realities
of everyday life rather than working within the familiar conventions of

high art. Anti-art collectives were staging events, concerts, and exhibitions that were euphoric in their abandonment of orthodox modernism and its reliance on Western media and studio practices like oil painting.

"The East was emerging, like *Fluxus* did, in the cold aftermath of World War Two, where the hugely horrific consequences of modern rationalism were laid bare, and the Japanese avant-garde reveled in anarchistic forms of art and performance to subvert, parody, and critique the political establishment," writes the critic Dore Ashton. "It also took clear aim at aggressive Americanization, mass consumerism, nuclear threat, and found solace in existentialism, absurdism, and the Buddhist void."

Ono must have been a little taken aback to discover how artistically advanced Japan had become in her absence. Few would have expected a formerly conservative, tradition-bound culture such as Japan's to shrug off the past with such abandon and race headlong into a more hopeful, experimental future. But it was happening everywhere: in music, visual arts, and, especially, literature. Contemporary writers give perhaps the best insight into the emergence of this radicalized postwar Japanese culture. Authors such as Dazai Osamu in *Setting Sun* and *No Longer Human*, and Kobo Abe in *Woman of the Dunes* and *The Ruined Map*, as well as the remarkable Kenzaburo Oe in his harrowing *A Personal Matter* and especially, in *Teach Us to Outgrow Our Madness*, captured the social times which Ono survived and now reencountered. The nuclear aftermath, noted another Oe work, was front and center:

> The massive wreckage of life, limb, and livelihood caused by the atomic bombings of Hiroshima and Nagasaki, was, for single bomb attacks, unprecedented in human history. In trying to comprehend this extensive damage in the aftermath of the Pacific War, the Japanese faced many uncertainties and ambiguities.

It fell to artists to create "highly significant vehicles for thinking about the contemporary world over which hangs the awesome threat of vastly expanded nuclear arsenals." Individual creators would stir "our imaginative powers to consider the fundamental conditions of human existence; they are relevant to our present and to our movement toward all tomorrows. Because civilization is headed toward extinction or towards salvation from that fate, we inescapably face an 'unknown future.' The fundamental condition of life, then, is that we are assailed by overwhelming fear and yet, at the same time, beckoned by the necessity to rebuild hope, however difficult, in the face of that fear."

It turns out that a horrific recent past, an unknown future, and the imperative to rebuild hope can indeed combine for a remarkable flowering of experimental thinking. Key to it were the profound East–West connections of the postwar artists. Forbidden by official sanction in wartime from experiencing or sharing the arts of the enemy, Japanese artists now consciously sought out and plunged themselves into the West's most questionable and dangerous cultural export product: the avant-garde.

A marvelous group exhibition, *Asian Traditions/Modern Expressions: Asian American Artists and Abstraction, 1945–1970*, organized by the Zimmerli Art Museum at Rutgers, demonstrates the vigorous cross-fertilization that was occurring between the two cultures immediately following the war, with both sides attempting to erase all stylistic and intellectual boundaries. The art historian Jeffrey Wechsler, editor of the exhibition catalogue, notes that the shared dimension of the curatorial project has been subsumed beneath a considerable amount of "nationalistic and exclusivist fervor" among writers on postwar abstract expressionism, as well as the dominant presence of a few famous (mostly New York–based) artists, including Jackson Pollock and Mark Rothko. But, in reality, what emerged in this period was "a communal experiment in East/West artistic interaction."

The best and most accessible example of the experiment, as well as a superb example of the blossoming idea of *Gesamtkunstwerk*, or "total work of art," comes from the postwar filmmaker Hiroshi Teshigahara. He and his circle of artists and musicians, which included the vastly influential artist and critic Shuzo Takiguchi, and Japan's foremost modern composer, Toru Takemitsu, were determined to leap over all divisions between the arts in their search for new ways to express a universal creative force.

"When Teshigahara and his friends returned to Tokyo to scenes of unimaginable suffering," writes Dore Ashton, "they were obviously in no mood to accept . . . passive wisdom. . . . They were filled with consternation, and in some cases, loathing for their own past, and they strove to fill in the gaping lacunae in their own educations as swiftly as possible. They were keenly aware that as artists and writers not aligned with government bureaucracy, they bore the burden of dissent and independent thought."

Teshigahara and friends formed the Jikken Kobo, or Experimental Workshop, and sought a means of bridging old/new and East/West while also dissolving existing art forms into a single, simultaneously throbbing and selfless whole. It was this kind of all-inclusive thinking that would provide the context for all of Ono's future forays into the use of parallel art forms for mutual purpose.

Best known as the director of the gripping film based on Kobo Abe's *Woman in the Dunes*, Teshigahara had built a career of straying from familiar paths. Boundaries, for him, were obstacles to creation: deliberately and instinctively choosing paths that led beyond borders, as Dore Ashton observed: "Boundary markers do not concern him, whether between centuries or geographic regions. For him, they are meant to be crossed."

With artists such as the Jikken Kobo providing the intellectual fuel, the radical culture of postwar Japan was well on its way to redrawing its own aesthetic map, affording young art and philosophy students a new blueprint for their work. They could think freely about art, and literally manufacture new forms. These liberties, they believed, provided the foundations on which a new, utopian society could be constructed. That Japan and the West were both in the early stages of a long economic boom made liberal idealism and extreme social change seem, if not revolutionary, at the least eminently possible.

It was a highly charged world, and it gave a sense of urgency to everything the artists were doing, from cutting ties with the past to embracing the logic of a possibly impossible future. Catastrophe often encourages people to start from some hopeful ground zero and construct something out of nothing. Individual Japanese artists, writers, and musicians may have had "diverse experiences of the war and differing family backgrounds," said Oe, "but almost without exception, they were determined to renounce not only their brief personal pasts but also the entire Japanese ethos as they had learned to perceive it. As artists in their early twenties, they were determined to invent a new Japan." Teshigahara, the descendant of a glorious *ikebana* master, Sofu, came from as privileged a background as Yoko Ono, but they were equally determined as less fortunate artists to embrace what the great Australian critic Robert Hughes once called "the shock of the new."

Taro Okamoto, a prewar pioneer of the Japanese avant-garde, encouraged the new generation to "destroy everything with a monstrous energy like Picasso's, in order to reconstruct the Japanese art world." Ono was more than willing to do so, combining the influence of advanced Western practices with an indigenous oriental impulse. For the rest of her long career, she would be an active ambassador between the East and West avant-gardes.

In Tokyo in 1962 she participated in a wide range of experimental activities, among them Group Ongaku, Hi-red Center, and the blossoming career of her friend the innovative video artist Nam June Paik. Ono further cemented her progressive credentials and also forged a crucial link between the Eastern groups and *Fluxus,* helping to generate a fertile cross-cultural communication that would come to be called "post-atomic art," finding new and fresh meaning in the inherently irrational experience of contemporary urban life. It relied on extreme contrasts, humor, discordance, and the possibilities inherent in non-sense, social conscience, and the serious joke. Whether it contributed to lessening the assault of those irrational forces on human society is still open to debate.

Yoko Ono's 1962 concerts consisted of a dramatic cacophony of recorded and live speeches in different languages, staged in concurrence with her *Instructions for Paintings,* or what she called "paintings to be constructed in your head." These were further attempts at undermining the traditional art object of idealized representational illusions and establishing the idea of an art without any object at all, one whose content was "pure concept." As the art historian Reiko Tomii writes of Ono's bold enterprise: "Not only was paint replaced by language, the structural syntax of the medium was also laid bare. Moreover, the role of the viewer was reconfigured as an active agent who completed the artwork either physically by his/her making it, or simply as a mental process." Suddenly, the art *was* us, writ large.

Her collaborations with the young artists at the Sogetsu Art Center had the profound fervor generally associated with evangelical movements, and certainly, for them, the avant-garde and its freedoms were somewhat religious in scope and scale, or at least were highly spiritualized. They would often be accused of being obsessive in their ironic seriousness. Extravagant performances with mysterious content ensued, including Toru Takemitsu's experiment in concrete sound, *Water Music,* in 1960, and Yoko Ono's re-creation of her 1955 Sarah Lawrence College student work *Lighting Piece*. Unlike the stunned incomprehension of some visitors to her Manhattan loft performances, the Tokyo crowd met *Lighting Piece* with rousing recognition and acclaim. It made complete and utter sense to an Eastern vanguard tutored in postwar romanticism by Suzuki and Cage. They treated Yoko's bold statement as a kind of brilliant visual evocation of rock and roll.

She also premiered *Cut Piece*, a gestural stage act in which she carried a large-than-life pair of scissors into a sparse spotlight and invited the audience to cut away her clothes until she was practically naked and covering her breasts with her tiny hands. "They couldn't quite pinpoint it but something was disturbing them," she would say later. "There was a feminist sensibility that surfaced in 'Cut Piece' and I think it was hard for them to watch. I was making a statement but it was very difficult. We live in a world of illusion created by the mass media. The reality has always been hidden. I was trying to show what women go through. I didn't have any notion of feminism."

Now considered a classic of feminist art, *Cut Piece* was possibly Yoko's most daring public performance piece ever. Her chief raw material for the act was "some anger and turbulence in my heart," she later told *Record Collector* magazine. The intensity of feeling generated by the piece would stay with her: "That was a frightening experience, and a bit embarrassing. It was something that I insisted on—in the Zen tradition of doing the thing which is the most embarrassing for you to do, and seeing what you come up with and how you deal with it."

As she told another writer: "For art's sake, I would do just about anything."

There is an apparent absurdity in much of Yoko's work from this period. She demands that we accept artists who use "humorous nonsense for serious intent," dispensing with logic and its dictates, and inviting us into a unique dimension she calls a "mind-world." A good example of this strategy is her 1962 instruction painting *Sun Piece*, which asks the viewer to "watch the sun until it becomes square." This mind-world of Yoko's is preferable to the everyday world we inhabit and the clutter it leaves in our minds. As she told *Newsweek*, "The mind is omnipresent, events in life never happen alone, and history is forever increasing its volume. At this point, what art can offer (if it can at all—to me it seems) is an absence of complexity, a vacuum through which you are led to a state of complete relaxation of mind. After that you may return to the complexity of life again, it may not be the same, or it may be, or you may never return, but that is your problem."

Yoko had discovered almost all the intellectual raw materials that would provide for fifty years of hectic art making in multiple mediums: metaphysical art and music, the nature of reality and the mind, and the purpose and function of existence, if either can be even determined. But the difference between her and so many other youthful philosophers, as Alexandra Munroe points out, is that her works engage metaphysical questions on an immediate, perhaps even a visceral level that is almost impossible to ignore: "Provoking, upending, mirroring our received notions so as to incite a new encounter with one's self and the nature of being. These encounters, which she called events, were designed to break through banal reality to recover, in an often deceptively simple act, a moment of emptiness which she calls 'wonderment.'"

The artist herself characterized the urge this way: "After unblocking one's mind, by dispensing with visual, auditory and kinetic perceptions, what will come out of us? Would there be anything? I wonder. And my events are mostly spent in wonderment."

Wonderment would then become Ono's own personal signature state for many years to come. In fact, she would become a global apostle of wonderment.

Yoko was now slowly being recognized for the seminal activities she helped to organize and in which she participated as a member. Her associations and affiliations gained her access to the stellar reaches of the avant-garde, a place where the air was exceedingly thin, but few art critics of the time recognized the depth of her innovations, even though many now consider them to be a watershed in the history of conceptual art. Her shows were better received in Tokyo, but she did not feel accepted. Writes Curator/historian Jon Hendricks: "Always working out the odds of her Japanese and American identity, Yoko personally found her years back 'home' among her most isolated and difficult."

Some of this is attributable to Yoko's complex personality. Rebellious and experimental, she loved being on the edge, and making art and music on the edge. She was just the sort of unexpected persona that cultures seldom know what to do with: the representative of an endlessly broken boundary, a person with no apparent limits, both in her art and her personal life. She also possessed a difficult personal energy that could make her hard to be around. Fiercely independent, refusing to be bound by a particular movement, school, or, for that matter, religion (Buddhist or Christian) or nation (Japan or America), she was a perpetual outsider. This fit her fascination with personal and cultural fracture, but the cost of her stance was that she appeared abrasive to those who did fit, including the referees of culture, who could dismiss her as an outlier, if not a turncoat, to their pure cause.

Her gender also made life difficult for Yoko: there were few roles for women in the supposedly progressive art scene, especially women who rejected customary domestic life and motherhood. "Society's myth," she would later tell *Rolling Stone*, "is that all women are supposed to love having children. But that was a myth. I was struggling to get my own space in the world. I felt that if I didn't have room for myself, how could I give room to another human being?"

Despite her parents' best efforts, Yoko's marriage with Toshi Ichiyanagi was finished. The emotional and existential restlessness at the core of Ono's spirit caused her to make frequent and abrupt shifts in both her professional and personal lives. As soon as she achieved a momentary sense of balance, something would always seem to arise, within or around her, to precipitate another of the persona-shudders so dangerous to relationships or marriages.

Around the same time, a Tokyo reviewer accused Yoko of stealing ideas. There is no evidence that she was guilty of anything but the usual influence-sharing common among artists at all times throughout art history, but the charge hit her hard. Yoko swallowed sleeping pills in an attempt at suicide, not for the first time, she said: "As a teenager, I was always trying to cut my wrists or take pills. And later, even though my . . . husbands were terribly supportive of my work, I was always feeling frustrated as an artist. I felt I was not being accepted by society work-wise."

Suffering from exhaustion and depression, overwhelmed by frustration with the art scene and the limits she perceived in her life—"the whole avant-garde world seemed bourgeois to me. Who was I beyond Toshi's wife and John Cage's friend?"—she either checked into a sanatorium or, more likely, was committed to a mental hospital by her parents.

Still concerned for her, Toshi asked his friend the American musician and art promoter Anthony Cox to help coordinate her release from the facility, a rather draconian institution given to massively overmedicating the confused souls in its wards. That's one version of the story. Another has it that Cox became interested in some of Yoko's avant-garde art pieces that he'd seen in a catalogue. He was so enamored of her work that he tracked her down at the hospital and helped to get her released. Whatever happened, Yoko would wind up with the man who helped liberate her from institutional care, just as she had previously fallen in love with Toshi, the man who helped her escape the often oppressive clutches of her parents.

# CHAPTER FOUR

# Across the Great Divide

ANTHONY COX IS A MYSTERIOUS individual who appears to have possessed a singular ability to discover and multiply trouble. For a short time, he would be Yoko's new impresario and her second husband. The relationship would be even more problematic than Yoko and Toshi's, but all indications are that both parties entered into it with the best of intentions. They first married in late 1962, a union they had to annul because Yoko was not yet formally divorced from Toshi Ichiyanagi.

Initially happy together in Tokyo, Cox and Ono nevertheless perceived themselves to be stranded in Japan. They were anxious to return to New York. Indeed, joint reminiscing about New York life and the city's art world was part of what encouraged their intimacy to develop. Cox's attachment to the art scene was social as well as aesthetic. "I grew up with the whole scene," he says. "I was a beat, then I was a beatnik, then I was a hippie. I went through the whole drug trip. I was taking acid when you could get acid for free. I took my first mescaline and acid before one word had been written about it. I took a lot of acid thinking this was going to improve my mind, and it took me years to discover the opposite was true."

He is not exaggerating. Cox is considered to be instrumental in the early introduction of lysergic acid (LSD) into the ultra-hip communities of America's West Coast and the cultured classes of London.

Before they had a chance to do anything about their country of residence, Yoko discovered she was pregnant. Her friend Nam June Paik, not a fan of the second Mr. Ono, has suggested that he got her pregnant in order to force a marriage and gain a residential visa for himself. Whatever the father's motivations, this time Yoko chose not to abort. She and Cox married again, this time legitimately. Kyoko Ono was born on August 8, 1963.

To his credit, Anthony Cox, at least for a time, was devoted to promoting Yoko's career and helping her reach a broader audience. He was instrumental in the publication of the single piece of work for which Ono would be best remembered in this period of her life: a collection of her edited instruction paintings, first as a one-of-a-kind art object, and then in 1964 as a limited-edition book entitled *Grapefruit*.

Included in the collection are *Painting to be Stepped On*, *Painting to be Constructed in your Head*, and *Tunafish Sandwich Piece*, the latter comprised of the following instructions:

> Imagine one thousand suns in the
> sky at the same time.
> Let them shine for one hour.
> Then, let them gradually melt
> into the sky.
> Make one tunafish sandwich and eat.

(1964)

*Painting to See the Sky III* offered this set of instructions:

> See the sky between a woman's thighs.
> See the sky between your own thighs.
> See the sky through your belongings
> by making holes in them.
> i.e.: pants, jacket, shirt, stockings, etc.

(1962)

Many of the instruction paintings collected in *Grapefruit* identify a sensory act of everyday living as a means of encountering the self, emptied of identity. Destined to become a rare collectible, the book was called *Grapefruit* because Yoko considered the grapefruit a cross between a lemon and an orange, and thus a reflection of her own mixed identity. The book was published in an edition of five hundred under her own imprint, Wunternaum, which translates from the German to "Wonder Space." It would later be reprinted in a mass market edition with an introduction by John Lennon.

"*Grapefruit* was like a cure for myself without knowing it," Yoko later told the *New York Times* in her inimitable fashion. "It was like saying, please accept me. I am mad. Those instructions are like that: a real need to do something to act out your madness. As long as you are behaving properly, you don't realize your madness and you go crazy."

It is a significant collection, wrote the critic David Bourdon in the *Times*: "*Grapefruit* is one of the monuments of conceptual art of the early 1960's. [Ono] has a lyrical poetic dimension that sets her apart from the other conceptual artists. Her approach to art was only made acceptable when white men like [Joseph] Kosuth and [Lawrence] Weiner came in and virtually did the same things as Yoko, but made them respectable and collectible."

The new family did eventually make its way back to New York in the mid-1960s, not long after Yoko joined John Cage onstage for a performance at Sogetsu Hall—she lay on her back across an open grand piano as he hammered keys.

Over the two years Ono had been in Japan, Fluxus had gained international attention. Nevertheless, the movement's impresarios, including George Maciunas, Norman Seaman, and Charlotte Moorman, had kept up with Yoko's work and were quick to include her again in their concerts, festivals, and publication projects. From late 1964 until her departure for London in 1966, she presented several events and her earliest conceptual films at such legendary venues as the Judson Gallery, Judson Memorial Church, Carnegie Recital Hall, and Cinematheque at East End Theatre.

One of her new projects was *Draw Circle Event*. Yoko mailed hundreds of cards with an invitation to draw a circle and return it to her. Another was *Part Painting Series 5*, which involved a white paper square attached by glue to a sheet of red paper. The red sheet was numbered. A text indicated that it was one of 10,000 similar parts to be assembled in the future. Yet another, destined to become a recurrent piece, was *Self Portrait*. Writes Jon Hendricks: "The version made by the artist consisted of a small mirror signed on the back and placed in a manila envelope that was rubber-stamped with the title and date and bore the handwritten notional '(framed) imaginary' and Yoko's signature."

At a Fluxus Festival in the summer of 1965, Yoko presented an evening of works including *Bag Piece (no. 31)*, in which two performers walked onstage, took off their shoes, and climbed into a large burlap bag. Once inside, they took off their clothes and moved around before getting dressed and exiting the bag. The idea was to liberate both participants and audience from preexisting notions of appearances.

This was followed by *Beat Piece*, in which she and Anthony Cox and a handful of other performers lay onstage beside and on top of one another, listening to one another's beating heart. According to Yoko, Fluxus founder George Maciunas also performed her *Wall Piece for Orchestra*, with its simple instruction "Hit a wall with your head." She remembered him nearly killing himself.

One of the most memorable events from this stay in New York was a Fluxus concert in a recital room at Carnegie Hall. Writes Jon Hendricks:

> The admission tickets for the concert were imprinted balloons that had to be inflated and were popped for entry. The programs were folded into paper airplanes and sailed into the audience by the performers. Ono's "Touch Poems" were exhibited in the Carnegie Recital Hall reception room, which was momentarily turned into a Fluxshop. The Fluxus Orchestra members wore t-shirts decorated with silkscreened images of hairy chests or bare breasts. The evening was conducted by La Monte Young . . . Ono and the orchestra performed "Sky Piece for Jesus Christ." This piece calls for a chamber group to perform a piece by Mozart or other classical composer and to continue playing as long as they possibly can, while other performers wrap the musicians in gauze bandages, continuing to wrap the entire bodies of the musicians with their instruments until they cannot play. They are then led off the stage.

Fluxus was changing as the 1960s progressed, increasingly radicalized by the many social and political crises befalling the US. From the Bay of Pigs and the Cuban Missile Crisis, through the assassination of John F. Kennedy to campus turmoil, racial unrest, and rising protests against the

Vietnam War, America's streets were becoming a kind of living theater. Ever the organic mirror of her times, Ono was politicized in this intense social milieu. She deepened her commitment to art as an agent of social change and began evolving into a radical activist-agitator par excellence. She developed what performance historian Kristine Stiles calls "a utopian social program of love envisioned in the imagination and enacted before the world." Ono cheekily derailed McLuhan's famous precept, pronouncing that "the message is the medium." The implied message, says Stiles, "was world pacificism realized through feminine thought and culture."

She presented a video of her performance work *Cut Piece* at another Carnegie event in 1964. It showed her sitting vulnerably onstage, knees beneath her, as members of the audience took turns snipping away her clothes with scissors. The video was produced by the then-fledgling documentary filmmakers Albert and David Maysles, who would become famous for filming the disastrous Rolling Stones' Altamont Concert five years later. As usual, Yoko worked with them first, just as she had done with so many other future luminaries.

In her film, writes Alexandra Munroe, Yoko achieves "a new level of psychological unveiling, an intimate and painful sensation of self that the public can encounter, watch and feel. Cut Piece expressed an anguished interiority while offering a social commentary on the quiet violence that binds individuals and society, the self and gender, alienation and connectedness."

Ono also restaged in New York a work that had earlier been performed on the roof of the Naiqua Gallery in Tokyo. *Morning Piece* consists of a collection of fragments of a broken glass milk bottle, each labeled with dates and times of future mornings. Yoko sold the fragments to buyers who then personally "owned" their designated piece of morning; the buyers received a handwritten notice of their ownership and how much they paid for it. Yoko's friend the video artist Nam June Paik was registered as the buyer and owner of the morning of September 8, 1995, for five hundred yen.

The piece from this period that perhaps best demonstrates the crystallization of Yoko's style and the emergence of her mature preoccupations is a five-minute film entitled *No. 4*, and known informally as "Bottoms." Created with the help of Cox, the film, one of sixteen she would shoot in the late sixties and early seventies, consists entirely of close-ups of the bottoms of famous people as they walk on a treadmill. The subjects, including Ono, Cox, Kyoko, the composer Philip Corner, and artists Carolee Schneemann and Bici and Geoffrey Hendricks, are interviewed as they are filmed. The piece is intended to encourage a dialogue for world peace.

Yoko's relationship with Cox had begun to unravel almost as soon as they returned to New York, although he continued to help her conceive, plan, and execute her work. None of the men in her life would ever cease to be champions of her work. In 1966, she traveled to London to participate in the Destruction in Art Symposium (DIAS) organized by German artist and activist Gustav Metzger, whose work was often projected at concerts by the Who and Cream. The symposium attracted a diverse lot of international artists and intellectuals. Its stated objective was to "focus attention on the element of destruction in Happenings and other art forms, and to relate this destruction in society."

As a meeting between the artistic avant-garde and the underground, DIAS had more of an edge than many of the events in which Yoko took part. The conceptual artist John Latham famously constructed three large towers of books outside the British Museum and set them on fire. Brooklyn-born Raphael Montañez Ortiz and an accomplice picked up axes and hacked to pieces a freshly tuned piano that had been owned by the lyricist Fran Landesman (the remains of the piano are held to this day by the Tate Britain). Ono again performed Cut Piece at the Africa Center, helping that performance to gain what has been called its "iconic stature in the history of performance art for its proto-feminist conceptualism."

It had been more than a decade since Yoko had made her debut as a performance artist, sitting beside a piano, lighting matches one after the other and watching them burn to her fingers. She was still engaged in a larger project of aesthetic subversion and cultural transgression, hallmarks of her personal and professional agenda, but her ideas were at once sharper, more whimsical, and more provocative. Yet even with her own exhibition at DIAS, she was concerned that she was not being given the kind of serious attention she deserved, something she referred to as her Van Gogh complex. She was largely unknown, like most of the other artists in Fluxus and similar conceptual art camps, except to a handful of art critics and aesthetic philosophers whose task it was to explore the fringes of the culture for hints at future directions.

Had her career ended in London, the general public might never have known her name. Not being of one nation, or one movement, and not being male, her place in the history of conceptual art was to that point ambiguous. As it happened, she was about to receive more attention than anyone could reasonably want, although not of the kind she sought. Anthony Cox temporarily slipped out of her personal life at DIAS, while still remaining a supporter of her work, and John Lennon slipped in, assuming both roles.

It was not only art that had drawn Yoko to London. She also had accepted the invitation to DIAS in hopes of affecting a break with the increasingly volatile Cox. But he insisted on joining her, and bringing Kyoko. After DIAS, the still nuclear family took a flat in Hanover Gate

Mansions, not far from Abbey Road. Yoko painted every wall white and furnished the apartment with nothing more than a handful of brocaded cushions, much to the astonishment of the family's babysitters.

They stayed in London rather than return to New York because Yoko had been invited to exhibit her work at the new Indica Gallery in Mason's Yard. The leading force behind the gallery/bookstore was John Dunbar, a former art history student at Cambridge and the son of British filmmaker Robert Dunbar. He had recently made himself famous by marrying the British singing sensation Marianne Faithfull. Dunbar's partner in Indica was the bookseller Barry Miles, a childhood friend of Rolling Stones guitarist Brian Jones. Paul McCartney, who had been introduced to hash brownies by Miles's wife, Susan, took a keen interest in Indica, even helping to paint it for its opening. He also contributed funding to Miles's new underground newspaper, the *International Times*, which shared a building with the Indica Gallery. It went without saying that a show at Indica would bring Yoko and her work right to the heart of Swinging London.

In addition to his own involvement, McCartney had asked Miles to let his bandmates know of anything happening at Indica. John Lennon would occasionally browse its book collection, and on one visit had read the whole of Timothy Leary's *The Psychedelic Experience* on a gallery couch. In the fall of 1966, he received a catalogue for a show entitled *Yoko at Indica*.

"Dunbar told me about this Japanese girl from New York, who was going to be in a bag, doing this event or happening," said Lennon. "I thought 'hmmm' . . . 'Sex.'"

Dunbar agreed to show Lennon the exhibition on the evening of November 9, a day before its official opening. Lennon remembers showing up "in a highly unshaven and tatty state," having been high and awake for the previous three days.

Yoko was still setting up her show and uninterested in having visitors. She had painted the exhibition space white, like her flat, and was displaying her pieces on clear acrylic. Various versions of her instruction paintings were on display, as well as an array of minimalist sculptures consisting of everyday articles: "Works such as 'Pointedness (no.12)' and 'Forget It (no. 16),'" writes Alexandra Munroe, "used readymade things—a white sphere and a sewing needle, respectively—attached on Plexiglas pedestals inscribed with their titles and instructions. 'White Chess Set (no. 25)' presented Ono's first all-white chessboard and men."

Angry that Dunbar was bringing in guests before she was ready, Yoko was nevertheless too busy to complain. She did not recognize Dunbar's visitor, never mind that Beatlemania was then in full swing. "He was an attractive guy," she says. "That's all that passed through my mind. Up to then, English men had all looked kind of weedy to me. This was the first sexy one I met." She recalled that he was shaved and wearing a suit, and that he had a tan (he had just returned from Spain where he'd been shooting the movie *How I Won the War* and vigorously, perilously experimenting with LSD). "I thought he was rather a dandy kind of person. I called it clean-cut; that's what we used to say at Sarah Lawrence. John hated that expression when I told him later how he looked to me that evening. 'Clean-cut!' he said. 'I was never clean-cut!' But he was going to a gallery in London, and he'd taken trouble to look good. He could do that dandy thing very well when he wanted to."

Unfamiliar with anti-art, Lennon's initial response to Yoko's work was skepticism. "There's a couple of nails on a plastic box. Then I look over and see an apple on a stand with a note saying 'apple' . . . I was beginning to see the humour of it.

"I said, 'How much is the apple?' '$200.' 'Really? Oh, I see. So how much are the bent nails?'

"Then Dunbar brings [Yoko] over, because The Millionaire is here, right? And I'm waiting for the bag. Where's the people in the bag? So he introduced me, and of course there was supposed to be this event happening, so I asked, 'Well, what's the event?' She gives me a little card. It just says 'Breathe' on it. And I said, 'You mean [he exhales]?' She says, 'That's it. You've got it.' . . . I got the humour—maybe I didn't get the depth of it but I got a warm feeling from it. I thought, 'Fuck, I can make that. I can put an apple on a stand. I want more.'"

Yoko remembers the meeting differently. "I showed him the sign that said 'Breathe.' When he breathed out, he did it really hard and he came so near to me, it was a little bit flirty in a way. Then he went to the apple and just grabbed it and took a bite. I thought, 'How dare he do that?' I thought it was really gross, you know; he didn't know manners. He must have noticed I was so angry because he put it back on the stand."

Looking at her *Painting to Hammer a Nail (no. 9)*, Lennon asked Yoko if he should, in fact, follow the instruction. She was reluctant, wanting everything saved for the opening. When he persisted, she said he could hammer a nail in the painting for five shillings. "I'll give you an imaginary five shillings," he said, "and hammer an imaginary nail in."

"And that's when we really met," said Lennon. "That's when we locked eyes and she got it and I got it and that was it."

He noticed another of the artist's pieces and this time followed the written instructions, climbing to the top of a ladder and looking at a framed piece of paper attached to the ceiling. Feeling a bit silly, and afraid of falling, he used the magnifying glass attached to one side of the frame to peer at the paper. He saw a single word written in tiny letters: "Yes."

"I felt relieved," Lennon said afterward. "It's a great relief when you get up the ladder and you look through the spyglass and it doesn't say *no* or *fuck you*. It says *YES*."

Yoko didn't think her exhibit had made much of an impression on her guest. "He came back down the ladder again, said 'Mm' or something and just left. I went downstairs, where there were several art students who were helping us. And one said, 'That was John Lennon . . . One of the Beatles.' I said, 'Oh really? I didn't know that.'"

PART TWO

# WORLDS IN COLLISION: ENDURING THE LIVING MOVIE

*"When two great saints meet, it is a humbling experience."*
Paul McCartney, liner note to the album *Two Virgins*, 1968

# CHAPTER FIVE

# Baby's in Black

Y OKO ONO WAS AN unusual presence in London in 1966, a city with few Japanese and strong memories of the Pacific War, which had ended only twenty-one years before. She was a small woman with long, black unruly hair that tended to obscure her face. Her clothes were typically loose-fitting clothes of funereal black in an age of miniskirts and Day-Glo colors. No one was sure what to make of her. Most seemed to simply ignore her or suspect her.

However enigmatic this outsider was to the average Londoner, she was immediately and warmly embraced by the city's art scene. It was the third international capital, after New York and Tokyo, in which she'd earned the respect of avant-garde tastemakers. She seemed on the brink of a breakthrough as an artist. But it didn't happen. As the critic Robert Palmer wrote in the liner notes to a later collection of Yoko's music: "It is quite likely that having John Lennon fall in love with her was the worst thing that could have happened to Yoko Ono's art career. By the time she met the then-Beatle, she was controversial but internationally known and recognized for her work in music, film, and the kind of conceptual presentations a later generation would dub 'performance art.'"

Yoko's relationship with Lennon was unlikely in several respects. To begin with, he was married to Cynthia (née Powell), the mother of his first child, Julian. They had met in a calligraphy class at the Liverpool College of Art before the Beatles were fully formed, and married when the band returned from its long sojourn in Hamburg. Beatles manager Brian Epstein tried to keep both the marriage and the child hidden from fans. The Lennons moved from Liverpool to London in 1963, and Cynthia joined the band on its triumphant North American tour that year. She was by 1966 expert at fending off the legions of devoted young women who wanted a piece of her husband. Yoko, of course, was still married to Anthony Cox, however frayed their relationship.

Also arguing against Yoko becoming involved with John Lennon was the fact that Paul McCartney was the Beatle with whom, on paper, she had most in common. It was Paul who was interested in contemporary art. It was Paul who had helped the Indica Gallery get off the ground, giving Yoko a reason to stay in London, and who had funded Barry Miles's underground newspaper. And it was Paul, unbeknownst to most, who considered himself the Beatles' avant-garde musician, the more daring experimenter.

There have long been debates among Beatles aficionados about which of the famous songwriting partners, Lennon and McCartney, was the cutting-edge composer and cultural risk-taker. There is really no contest. Both had their genius but only one was truly comfortable with *being* a genius, and that was Paul. He has been unfairly labeled a commercial sellout over the years thanks to the scintillating perfection of his pop songs, a reputation that has obscured his experimental side, which was always stronger and more confident than Lennon's.

Both musicians were noted for their experiments in tape loops and *musique concrete*, but the most successful innovations, including the rushing tape reversals on "Rain," the wonky guitars on "Taxman," the loops on "Tomorrow Never Knows," and, of course, the *Sgt. Pepper* excursions, to name but a few, were all generated by the open confidence of McCartney, not the notorious insecurities of his brilliant but tortured songwriting partner.

It was also McCartney who knew and loved the new music compositions of two of Ono's creative mentors, John Cage and Karlheinz Stockhausen. He was familiar with sonic landscapes that no other Beatle wanted to visit even briefly. Notwithstanding his popular fame, his avant-garde dimensions remain relatively hidden. Some of that concealment was, of course, of his own making, almost as a legacy-protecting gesture.

If McCartney was the revolutionary *artist* in the Beatles, John Lennon was the revolutionary *person*. Lennon was committed to personal and social radicalism, and his troubled and sometimes violently misanthropic personality lent him a Byronic cast that many would associate with artistic genius. In fact, he spent most of his time attempting to catch up to his relatively healthy and hugely happy writing partner's penchant for pushing artistic envelopes. Lennon's alliance with Yoko was perhaps his most blatant attempt to do so.

But if McCartney was the more obvious artistic match to Yoko Ono, Lennon shared something perhaps deeper with her. They were both children of trauma, Lennon having endured a solitary childhood in the barren and blasted landscape of wartime and postwar England, and having lost his mother at the age of seventeen. Both carried wounds within them that they came to believe could only be healed by the other. Both wore emotional armor behind which they dreamed of a destiny far beyond the one they had inherited. Both engaged in radical behavior that they romantically attributed to a shared artistic chemistry.

It must also be said that Lennon and Yoko were, in their own ways, also exceptionally talented. Lennon might not have had McCartney's outsized musical gift, but he was a brilliant songwriter, one of those examples of raw genius that occasionally pop up in the field of popular music: Bob Dylan, Joni Mitchell, and Phil Ochs, to name a couple of Lennon's contemporaries, and before them the likes of Irving Berlin, Hoagy Carmichael, Jerome Kern, and Richard Rodgers.

The sad and angry young man whose uniquely raspy, nasal voice—so powerful that it transcended normal definitions of what is beautiful—would sing, "Is there anybody going to listen to my story, all about the girl who came to stay." He was probably as shocked to discover that most of the civilized world was quite willing to listen. He had a knack for honesty and self-revelation that few could match. He so often seemed to be speaking and singing on behalf of everyone, and he was rewarded and cursed accordingly. His social awareness, blistering brilliance, and towering rage were integral to the Beatles' success. Without them, there would have been no buffer for everything cute and clever in his boyhood songwriting partner (and vice versa).

When they met, Yoko was seven years older than John Lennon, more worldly, in many ways, and more mature as an artist. She had been rubbing shoulders with John Cage and Marcel Duchamp while the Beatles were taking amphetamines and sweating all night in black leather in obscure Hamburg clubs. But he was far more famous and, in the sphere of popular music, successful. By 1966, the Beatles had exploded, achieving a level of renown that few artists in history have known, and it was wearing on them.

Three months before Ono's show at the Indica, the band had performed its final live concert on its third North American tour. Its members were by then sick of touring, sick of the crowds, and sick of the circus-like atmosphere that followed them everywhere. This disenchantment had come on rather suddenly. It hadn't helped that on the eve of the tour, Lennon had let loose a string of impolitic remarks to Maureen Cleave, a Beatles-friendly reporter at the *London Evening Standard*, who reported them in a feature entitled "How Does a Beatle Live?"

Cleave opened the article by noting that the Beatles had in three short years become "famous in the way the Queen is famous. When John Lennon's Rolls-Royce, with its black wheels and its black windows, goes past, people say: 'It's the Queen,' or 'It's the Beatles.' With her they share the security of a stable life at the top." Of Lennon, she wrote: "He is now 25. He lives in a large, heavily paneled, heavily carpeted, mock Tudor house set on a hill with his wife Cynthia, and his son Julian. . . ."

Cleave toured the house, known as Kenwood, in the suburb of Weybridge and found it filled with possessions—suits of armor, model racing cars, five television sets, a swimming pool—most of which held little interest for Lennon. He did not know the numbers of his many telephones. In addition to the Rolls, he owned a Ferrari and a MINI Cooper, all painted black, and none of which he drove himself. His general detachment from his own domestic scene was one of several clues in the article that Lennon's marriage was in trouble.

Other than reading from his large collection of books, he told Cleave, he seldom got up to much at home. He described himself as probably the laziest person in England, capable of sleeping indefinitely. "Physically lazy," he said. "I don't mind writing or reading or watching or speaking, but sex is the only physical thing I can be bothered with any more."

Cleave watched him closely throughout their time together: "He is much the same as he was before. He still peers down his nose, arrogant as an eagle, although contact lenses have righted the short sight that originally caused the expression. He looks more like Henry VIII than ever now that his face has filled out—he is just as imperious, just as unpredictable, indolent, disorganized, childish, vague, charming and quick-witted. He is still easy-going, still tough as hell."

Lennon was in a discursive mood, and Cleave let his abrasive words unspool without interruption. He described his horror of stupid people: "Famous and loaded as I am, I still have to meet soft people. It often comes into my mind that I'm not really rich. There are really rich people but I don't know where they are."

He spoke of the need to send Julian, age three, to a Lycée in London: "'Seems the only place for him in his position,' said his father, surveying him dispassionately. 'I feel sorry for him, though. I couldn't stand ugly people even when I was five. Lots of ugly ones are foreign, aren't they?'"

And then he turned his attention to his recent reading on religious topics: "Christianity will go. It will vanish and shrink. I needn't argue about that; I'm right and I will be proved right. We're more popular than Jesus now; I don't know which will go first—rock 'n' roll or Christianity. Jesus was all right but his disciples were thick and ordinary. It's them twisting it that ruins it all for me."

Lennon's words, typical of his cheeky, off-the-cuff style, were mostly intended to express his amazement at how popular the Beatles had been come, but they dogged the band throughout its American tour of fourteen shows in seventeen days. Each show was the usual mayhem, with screaming audiences and people running up onstage and throwing objects. Each city they visited also produced religious figures to damn Lennon, and protestors waving placards that said "Beatles Go Home."

On August 19, the tour reached Memphis, the heart of America's Bible Belt. A huge Christian rally was organized by a hundred fundamentalist ministers to protest the Beatles as a corrupting influence on the nation's young. Their records were burned in oil drums, the Ku Klux Klan declaimed Lennon on live television, and a bomb threat was received before one of their two shows at the Mid-South Coliseum. Due to a fear of snipers on the streets, decoy limousines were used to detract attention from the Greyhound bus that carried the band to the coliseum.

Lennon admitted to being "scared stiff" by the reaction to his words. "I didn't want to tour because I thought they'd kill me—'cause they takes things seriously there. They shoot you, and then they realize that it wasn't important. So I didn't want to go, but [manager] Brian [Epstein] and Paul and the other Beatles persuaded me."

By the time it was over, Lennon had come to detest live audiences, yet at the same time "couldn't deal with not being on stage." He had no idea what to do with his life apart from being a Beatle: "What else is there?" Living in the suburbs with Cynthia was not the answer—they were living "like brother and sister," she said—and there was only so much acid one man could drop. He couldn't imagine himself following Elvis to Vegas, or joining another musical group. He could see only "a blank space in the future." Whether he knew it or not, there was a growing hole in his life that Yoko Ono would help to fill.

Two weeks after their first meeting, Yoko visited the opening of a show by her friend the sculptor Claes Oldenburg, who was then specializing in giant foam-rubber hamburgers. She noticed Lennon standing in a corner, looking scruffy and stoned. They didn't speak.

Lennon disappeared for a time into the studio with his bandmates in a frantic effort to keep up with stunning new material produced in this period by Bob Dylan, the Byrds, and the Beach Boys. Their attempt to put together a new album floundered but they did manage to get such classics as "Strawberry Fields Forever" and "Penny Lane" on a single. Yoko, meanwhile, was smitten with the angry Beatle. She had a thing for "working-class guys," no doubt something of a reaction to her privileged upbringing. She was also in need of a new patron, with Tony Cox drifting away. She sent Lennon a signed copy of *Grapefruit*. Cynthia would later write that she showered him with letters and cards and "came to the house looking for him several times." Yoko says that "wasn't my style."

Lennon did invite Yoko to his home on at least one occasion, with Cynthia and several others present. He told her how much he had enjoyed *Grapefruit*, which he kept by his bed and studied closely, feeling that its author and he shared a wavelength. With that, he returned to the studio with the Beatles, who completed their psychedelic masterpiece, *Sgt. Pepper's Lonely Hearts Club Band*.

Yoko, too, returned to her work, including what was supposed to have been another performance of *Cut Piece* at a happening at Alexandra Palace. The event was designed to raise funds for the *International Times*, which had run afoul of the authorities by printing an interview with the American radical Stokely Carmichael in which he used the word "motherfucker." The paper's editors were charged under the Obscene Publications Act. Yoko wanted to do her part but the scene at Alexandra Palace, packed with hippies, anti-war protestors, and deranged drug trippers, was too much for her. Rarely one to back away from a challenge, she had a stand-in perform *Cut Piece* as she stood in the wings. Lennon, too, was in the crowd but they didn't find each other. "People were too high," said Yoko, "to care if a Beatle was there or not."

The counterculture was in full swing in London. Sexual liberation, protest politics, religious experimentation (especially with ideas imported from the East), all under the umbrella of what Norman Mailer described as "universal rebellion," brought the moral certainties of earlier years under constant attack. Even *Life* magazine, that bright and shiny mirror held up for popular culture to admire itself, admitted that doubt was the order of the day.

And there were drugs, plenty of them, and one drug above all: LSD. As members of the cultural and social elite of the time, the Beatles were among the first to gain access to and sample this brave new world of psychological exploration. It would prove to be the undoing of many, including Lennon, whose fragile personality buckled under the weight of drastic consciousness expansion, and whose identity was literally burned away by the torrent of acid he took, but for now it was great creative raw material. "Lucy in the Sky with Diamonds," arguably the best remembered track from the *Sgt. Pepper* album, was swiftly banned by the BBC for its obvious association with LSD.

The ban didn't stop the song from becoming a hit, however. The Beatles were doing a remarkable job of staying at the cutting edge of the counterculture while remaining enormously popular. They were alert to everything happening around them. As no less a musical maestro than the American composer Aaron Copland remarked: "If you want to know about the Sixties, play the music of The Beatles." That their more dangerous and subversive material was leavened by what the writer Ian MacDonald calls "the group's innately skeptical humour" undoubtedly contributed to their success. It was all part of what McCartney called their "creative friction" with the main countercultural currents of the sixties. MacDonald writes:

As a rebellion of free essence against the restraints of outmoded form, the Sixties began with a flood of youthful energy bursting through the psychic dam of the Fifties. The driving force of this rebellion resided in the Beatles, in their capacity—then suspected by no one, least of all themselves—as unacknowledged legislators of populist revolt.

That role put an enormous pressure on the Beatles, and Lennon, in particular, felt it keenly. He was riding the crest of the movement, determined to stay at its bleeding edge, yet at the same encouraged to rebel against the mainstream success he and the Beatles had become. Life in the band had many benefits, but there was also a certain humiliation in being what he called "a performing flea," everyone's favorite mop-topped lad. He grew his hair longer and was increasingly embarrassed by the cheerful innocence of the band's early work. It is no surprise that he would be impressed by the true radicalism and more serious credentials of an alluring avant-garde artist such as Yoko Ono.

Lennon had attended the Liverpool College of Art in his late teens. He learned to draw, more or less, but he did not excel there. He is nevertheless a classic case of what Ian MacDonald calls the "art-school type" so prevalent among English musicians of the sixties: Charlie Watts and Keith Richards; Pink Floyd's Syd Barrett, Roger Waters and Nick Mason; Pete Townshend of the Who; Ray Davies of the Kinks; Jimmy Page of Led Zeppelin; Eric Clapton, Jeff Beck, Cat Stevens, David Bowie, and the list goes on. They were all academic misfits whose creativity would eventually be channeled into their music and stage shows. "The anarchic-individualistic art school ethos brought unusual invention and articulacy to British pop," writes MacDonald, "ensuring that even when its forms cease evolving, it can still ring changes in presentation and interpretation which provide the appearance of something new . . . It was the art school background of the Beatles, the Who, the Kinks, et al, which allowed them to introduce the concept of 'concept' into pop, along with other postmodern motifs like eclecticism, self-referentiality, parody, and pastiche."

It is not a stretch to perceive the Beatles as among the first conceptual artists of rock music, and even less so to view the restless Lennon as an unconscious conceptualist waiting for either the permission or the opportunity to give freer expression to his ideas and emotions. McCartney liberated him somewhat, but it would be his exposure to Yoko Ono that crystalized his dissatisfaction and anger over his status as a popular entertainer. He believed that he could be, or should be a great artist, the kind of confident, free-spirited performer that Yoko represented in so tantalizing a manner.

Yoko was entirely wrapped up in her own creative world. She existed on a different aesthetic plane, and was absolutely committed to her work in a way that no pop musician could match. She was the first authentic artist Lennon had known since the death of the so-called fifth Beatle, Stu Sutcliffe, the band's first bass player who died in Hamburg at the age of twenty-one. Yoko also had the same preternatural confidence in herself and her aesthetic judgment that Sutcliff had possessed, and that Lennon very much wanted for himself.

In Lennon's mind and heart, artistic admiration and sexual attraction were inseparable. He'd long had a fantasy about "a beautiful, intelligent, dark-haired, high-cheek-boned artist, which morphed after the Beatle's visit to India into a vision of a "dark-eyed Oriental." He'd had affairs with numerous women, but "I'd never met anyone worth breaking up a happily married state of boredom for. Escape, at last! Someone to leave home for. Somewhere to go. I'd waited an eternity. Since I was extraordinarily shy (especially around beautiful women), my daydreams necessitated that she be aggressive enough to save me i.e., 'take me away from all this.'"

The taking would require time, and it would advance through the postal service. Yoko performed a *13 Days Do-It-Yourself Dance Festival* that was to occur entirely in the mind. Participants received cards in the mail instructing them to "Breathe" or "send something you can't count," or "measure the horizon", or "Dance." Lennon was on the mailing list.

The instructions, he remembered, "would upset me or make me happy, depending how I felt."

Meanwhile she had come across two books of light verse and illustrations he had published in 1964 and 1965 respectively: *John Lennon: In His Own Write*, and *A Spaniard in the Works*. Although consisting mostly of nonsense poems, Yoko found wit and profundity in it. She was struck by a picture of a woman whose naked body was covered in flies, and a simple evocative sentence that read, "I sat belonely."

Inspired by her now half-empty apartment, Cox having vacated with Kyoko, Yoko created a new installation entitled *The Half a Wind Show*. It featured half a chair, half a wall painting, half a bed, half a chair, half a vase of flowers, and so on. She turned to Lennon for financial backing for the piece. "I felt bad about hitting on him for money," she said, so she asked him if he'd like to contribute something to the installation. He suggested adding bottles in which the missing half of the exhibit was supposedly captured. "I thought that was great," she said. "That's when I knew we were totally on the same wavelength."

Lennon refused her offer to share credit for the installation, wanting to shield his involvement from Cynthia and the public. He was less shy about his first attempt to take Yoko to bed. He invited her to the band's studio on Abbey Road to hear a recording session, and afterward took her to a nearby flat where he unfolded a sofa bed in a practiced manner. She was offended by his presumption, and turned him down. Shortly after, she flew off to exhibit *Film No. 4*, or "Bottoms," at a film festival in Belgium, with tentative plans to bounce to Paris and show her work there.

She did make it to Paris where her work attracted the attention of the great American jazz saxophonist Ornette Coleman. He invited her to perform with him in an upcoming appearance at the Royal Albert Hall. She returned to her flat at Hanover Gate Mansions and behind the door found a pile of letters, all from Lennon. She later asked him, "When you wrote me all those letters, weren't you worried I'd run to a newspaper or something? You're a married man." He told her that he used to write similar letters to Stu Sutcliffe, which struck Yoko as "a little bit strange," but it wasn't a deal breaker.

The Beatles had been doing some traveling of their own, a bizarre group trip to India to study transcendental meditation with Maharishi Mahesh Yogi. Lennon found the holy man underwhelming but did not regret the trip. "India was good for me," he said. "I met Yoko just before I went to India and had a lot of time to think things out there."

Still, he returned home a married man, and the father of Julian, who was delighted to see his father and the presents brought back for him from India. Lennon chose this moment to confess to Cynthia his myriad infidelities. She was staggered but grateful that he was at least speaking with her. There was even discussion of another child, as a companion to Julian and perhaps a salve for their relationship. Nothing came of it.

Instead, taking advantage of Cynthia's absence (with his encouragement she was holidaying with friends in Greece), Lennon made another move on Yoko, inviting her to his house. She had come to regret her rebuff of his first effort and at his urging hopped in a taxi. "He said he'd meet the taxi at the gate and pay it off. Usually, he didn't handle money at all, so I was really impressed that he had the whole thing carefully worked out."

They were both shy on her arrival. John suggested they go up to his studios, where he played her a selection of tapes, "all this far-out stuff, some comedy stuff, and some electronic music. There were very few people I could play those tapes to. She was suitably impressed, and then she said, 'Well, let's make one ourselves . . .' It was dawn when we finished, and then we made love at dawn. It was very beautiful."

It is interesting to think what Yoko Ono would have made of her new beau's artistic secrets. He considered them far out, but as Jill Johnston had noted in the *Village Voice* six years earlier, Yoko's appetite for musical experimentation was unbounded: "Yoko Ono combines electronic sounds, vocal and instrumental sounds, body movement, in her theatre of events. I was alternately stupefied and aroused. Ono concluded the work with amplified sighs, breathing, gasping, wretching, screaming, many tones of pleasure and pain mixed with a gibberish of foreign sounding language that was no language at all." As an artist and musician, Yoko Ono could be forgiven for finding the rest of the 1960s world, and especially the youth culture out of which the Beatles sprang, merely to be catching up to where she'd already been for years.

# CHAPTER SIX

# Nowhere Plans for Nobody

CYNTHIA LENNON RETURNED FROM her visit to Greece in May 1968 to find her husband and Yoko Ono sitting on the floor in Kenwood's rear sun parlor, wearing matching bathrobes. He said, "Oh, hi." She turned around and walked out, returning several days later to find John alone and unapologetic, although he insisted that she was still the love of his life. For the first time in years, they made love, after which he turned cold again and she fled to Italy with Julian and her mother.

Yoko promptly moved into Kenwood. "We both knew this was it," she said. "We were both so excited about discovering each other, we didn't stop to think about anyone else's feelings. We just went ahead, gung-ho; what he had was more precious than anything else."

They made music together, and they made films, including *Number 5,* also known as *Smile,* which is nothing more than a close-up of a happy Lennon shot at an astonishing 20,000 frames per second. Yoko strung the frames out to fill fifty-two minutes.

The Beatles were wary of Lennon's new love. When he asked them to join him to view a new work by Yoko at the Arts Lab, a new gallery in Drury Lane, they all claimed to be busy.

Whatever the other Beatles felt, there was no avoiding Yoko. Lennon took her everywhere. The new couple made their debut as fodder for the British tabloids on a rainy June 18 when they turned up, both dressed in white, along with the other Beatles at the National Theatre for a stage play based on his published writings, *John Lennon: In His Own Write.* There were fleets of photographers and a crush of people, and catcalls aimed at Lennon: "Where's your wife?" The next morning, their affair was all over the newspapers. Beatles fans were staggered. The reaction, as the ungenerous Philip Norman put it, was "what could Lennon possibly want with a fiercely unglamorous-looking Japanese woman from the art world's lunatic fringe?"

Cynthia learned of the joint appearance while in Italy, where she had become close friends with an Italian gentleman. She returned to London, staying with her mother, and intended to confront John about his behavior but he would not take her calls. Peter Brown, a manager at the Beatles' company Apple Corps, eventually convinced him to be civil. He and Yoko moved out of Kenwood, allowing Cynthia (who had no financial resources of her own) and Julian to move back in. He also agreed to a sit-down meeting with Cythnia and then arrived at Kenwood unexpectedly with Yoko, both of them dressed in black. Cynthia was joined by her mother. The ensuing row could be heard by Lennon's driver waiting by his car outside.

It was the end of the Lennons' marriage. Cynthia would compare it, in her own memoir, to being cut off "like a gangrenous limb." She was also cut off by the rest of the Beatles and their wives. Only McCartney showed her kindness, visiting her alone one day with the gift of a red rose. He joked that they should become a couple. McCartney was also sympathetic to Julian Lennon, for whom he began to compose the song, originally titled "Hey Jules," that would become his anthemic "Hey Jude."

John and Yoko now moved into a flat owned by Ringo Starr—the same two-story flat at 34 Montagu Square that Cynthia, her mother, and Julian had fled to after she first discovered John and Yoko in their matching bathrobes. Having sorted out things on the Lennon side of the equation, it remained for Yoko to explain to Anthony Cox and Kyoko that she had a new man in her life.

It could have gone disastrously. Despite his own philandering, Lennon was possessive, so much so that he made Yoko write out a list of every man she had ever slept with; he considered each of them an enemy. Yet he got on well with Cox, and he showed an interest in Kyoko that he'd never evinced even in his own son. "He was always very sweet," she would say later. "He never lost his temper with me, though I knew he had a temper. Later on, he and my mom and dad would have very bad rows in front of me. All of them believed in really letting it go."

Lennon's jealousies were not the only thing Yoko had to accommodate in her new relationship. He wanted to spend every moment with her, and he wanted her to be completely involved in everything he did. He also expected her to perform certain domestic duties that she had to that point in her life shunned, such as making him breakfast every day.

Lennon was stunned by her unwillingness to subordinate herself to his will. He was used to being largely served by women, whether it was his aunt Mimi early on, or later, his girlfriends and wives. But he was impressed by the fact that Yoko didn't buy that scenario. She couldn't care less about the Beatles. It was totally clear to Lennon from the day he met her that she demanded equal time, equal space, equal rights. At first he was stymied and pleaded for an explanation. She clarified it, somewhat, for him, by pointing out that she couldn't really ever be with him if there was no space for her to do so. She found that kind of atmosphere so restricting that it left her unable to breathe freely. And breathing freely was a prerequisite for her.

Lennon, too, would need to make accommodations. He would later tell *Newsweek* that Yoko had saved him from the fate of Elvis, becoming a fat and pampered "king" indulged by sycophants and courtiers. "She didn't fall in love with the Beatle," he said. "She didn't fall in love with my fame. She fell in love with me for myself, and through that brought out the best in me." It was different from anything he'd known before: "This is more than a hit record," he told himself. "It's more than gold. It's more than anything."

Yoko may not have thought much of the Beatles' fame, but she did have her own insecurities about her relationship with Lennon. "I'm not an insecure artist," she said later, "but as a woman I had all kinds of hesitations about myself. When I met John, I was self-conscious about my appearance. I thought I was too short, my legs were the wrong shape, and I used to cover my face with my hair. My hands are so stringy in a way, my fingers and all that. I was always hiding my hands. John said to me, 'No, you're beautiful. You don't have to hide your hands, your legs are perfect, tie your hair back and let people see your face."

He wasn't always so conventionally complimentary. "Do you know why I like you?" he said another time, echoing his early comment that writing letters to her had been like writing letters to Stu Sutcliffe. "It's because you look like a bloke in drag. You're like a mate." Yoko's response was that he must be "a closet fag." She was teasing, although she did sometimes wonder about Lennon's relationship with Paul McCartney. She would always suspect that John's feelings for his songwriting partner were deep.

Whatever John saw in her, Yoko's appeal would remain lost on Beatles fans, the vast majority of whom would have preferred her out of the picture altogether. Says the experimental filmmaker and Ono aficionado

Kirk Tougas: "Obviously John's fascination with and love for her disturbed the popular music crowd, as she was outside of their world: an artist, a woman, a foreigner, a 'witch.' They couldn't empathize with John, who needed all of these things."

Instead, the fans blamed Yoko for violating their dreams of who he and, by extension, the Beatles, were—dreams that were mostly the manufactured products of pop culture machinery but very much alive in their minds. Female fans were particularly hostile to her, greeting her with shouts of "Chink" when she appeared with him in public. The habitually vicious British press joined in, making racist jokes about the sexual lures of Oriental women.

Even Lennon's beloved aunt Mimi, according to author Craig Brown, was nasty. "I took one look [at Ono] and thought, 'My God, what is that?' Well, I didn't like the look of her right from the start. She had long black hair all over the place, and she was small—she looked just like a dwarf to me. I told John what I felt while she was outside . . . I said to him, 'Who's the poisoned dwarf, John?'"

Yoko, for her part, had nothing but warm feelings toward Aunt Mimi. Having learned to deal with hostility when dropped by her mother in Japanese farm country during the war, she took the abuse in stride. "I'd always felt like an outsider," she said. "So this was kind of a familiar feeling." She admits there was "a narcissistic side" of her that "was totally in love with my work and had nothing to do with those pitiful people who were ignorant about me and saying things. And an incredibly romantic side of me thought, 'This is a test. Fate is testing me to see if I'm going to give up this love affair.' I thought of it almost as a Greek tragedy, because I was losing my daughter, I was losing my artistic credit, all because of my love for this man. I sensed that it would be a very difficult life for me—and I did sense that if I got involved, some terrible tragedy was waiting."

The fans were correct in thinking that she represented a threat to the Beatles, although it had more to do with John feeling he deserved a brand-new life of his own, an identity for himself apart from his famous band, than any effort on her part to steal him away. He would compare meeting Yoko to any young man's first love, spending more time with her and leaving "the guys at the bar. . . . Once I found the woman, the boys became of no interest whatever other than that they were old friends. . . . That was it. That old gang of mine was over the moment I met her. . . . But it so happened the boys were well known and weren't just the local guys at the bar."

The boys were hoping that Yoko was merely an infatuation, and they were in the recording studio, not the bar, and Lennon's comments notwithstanding, he soon joined them with Yoko in tow. "He wanted me to be part of the group," she said. "He created the group, so he thought the others should accept that. I didn't particularly want to be part of them. But by that time, he had got all the avant-garde friends of mine out of my life, so I had nobody else to play music with. I couldn't see how I would fit in, but John was certain I would. He kept saying, 'They're very sensitive guys. . . . You think they're just Liverpool gits, but no, they're very sensitive. . . . He thought the other Beatles would go for it. He was trying to persuade me."

When she joined him in the studio through the summer of 1968, sitting beside him on a stool identical to his stool, it became apparent to her that Lennon had explained her presence to the other Beatles as a necessary move to alleviate some kind of funk she was under. "So George came over and said, 'Hello, how are you?'" said Yoko. "They were all treating me like this depressed woman they had to cheer up."

The other Beatles did not want Yoko as a fifth member, and their entourage, too, was unsettled by her unprecedented intrusion into band time, but she stayed, shadowing Lennon all day, following him literally everywhere. "People said I followed him to the men's room," she observed, "but he made me go with him. He thought that if he left me alone with the other Beatles even for a minute, I might go off with one of them." She even felt justified in commenting on their music, given her classical training, and giving John much-needed assistance with his rhymes. Out of respect for Lennon, the other band members were careful in what they said. McCartney, at one point, gently tried to brush Yoko back, suggesting she "keep in the background a little more." Harrison mentioned that several people he knew in New York had confided to him that she gave off "bad vibes." Lennon was offended by both interventions. McCartney, he concluded, was scheming against him. As for Harrison, Lennon even went so far as to wonder aloud why he didn't punch his bandmate over the remark.

Ringo Starr did walk off in a huff, at least for a few days, telling the others he was finished. He jetted off to Sardinia with his family. This, at least for a time, brought the others to their senses. They sent a telegram inviting Ringo back. He returned to the studio to find his drum kit showered in flowers.

But the recording work for a new album went ahead regardless of internal tensions—something they'd been used to for years—beginning with one of Lennon's most famous tracks, "Revolution," a reflection of the civil unrest sweeping the world that year. It was first released as a B side to McCartney's "Hey Jude," which had begun life as words of consolation for Lennon's abandoned son and morphed into a love ballad. Lennon, meanwhile, wondered whether it was about him, since most things were, he ruefully surmised. "If you think about it," he later told *Playboy*, "Yoko's just come into the picture. . . . The words 'go out and get her' . . . Subconsciously he was saying 'Go ahead, leave me.' But on a conscious level he didn't want me to go ahead. The angel inside him was saying 'bless you.' The devil in him didn't like it at all because he didn't want to lose his partner.'"

Lennon and McCartney were both credited with "Hey Jude," and whoever's version of the song's origins you accept, it is clear that Yoko was now a presence in Beatles music as well as in the studio. It appears that she was now writing for the band, as well. The Lennon solo track "Julia," a song about his late mother, originated during the Beatles' trip to India. The folk singer Donovan, along for the ride, had taught John a new finger-picking guitar technique and helped him get the tune started. In 1971, speaking to *New Musical Express*, Lennon would credit the lyrics primarily to Yoko: "She had written other things, even 'Julia' back in the Beatle days."

Yoko was also influencing other aspects of Lennon's creative output, as exemplified by his first solo art exhibition at a gallery on Duke Street owned by Robert Fraser (who a year earlier had been jailed for possession with Keith Richards and Mick Jagger). As Yoko was wont to do, John painted his exhibit space white, and wore white (as did Yoko) to his opening. Outside the gallery, 365 white helium balloons were released, each with a tag inside carrying the name and address of the exhibition on it—finders were meant to return the tags with a message. "I declare these balloons high," Lennon said as he cut the strings to release them. The contents of the exhibit, dedicated "to Yoko with love," were similarly imitations of her work: a large white canvas on which tiny letters declared "You Are Here," and an assortment of charity collection boxes. Some of the balloon tags would eventually be returned with comments critical of the artist's new relationship and Yoko's ethnicity.

Back in the studio at the band's new headquarters on Savile Row, the interior of which was also painted white, work on what would become known as the Beatles' *White Album* continued. The band was not communicating well, and barely functioning as a group at all. "There was a lot of friction during that album," admitted McCartney. "We were just about to break up, and that was tense in itself." They did manage, however, to lay down thirty songs on four sides, including such classics as "Back in the USSR," "Ob-La-Di, Ob-La-Da," "While My Guitar Gently Weeps," and "Blackbird."

Perhaps the most unexpected track on the *White Album* was "Revolution #9," a sound collage created by John, Yoko, and Harrison while McCartney was conveniently out of town. It began as an extended ending for the single "Revolution" in a take that lasted over ten minutes, including feedback, discordant jamming, random voices, screams, and other sound effects. Producer George Martin, though dubious, oversaw the recording from a respectful and professional distance. The basic track was developed with multiple tape loops all running at once and mixed live in a kind of waterfall effect. It has long been understood as another instance of John being drawn away from pop and into the avant-garde by Yoko, but it is just as easily viewed as another instance of John trying to keep up with his longtime songwriting partner's daring in composition mode.

Early in 1967, McCartney had composed a musical piece for the Million Volt Light and Sound Rave, an art festival organized by the design firm Binder, Edwards & Vaughan. He attempted to capture the spirit of experimental jazz music he'd been listening to. Entitled "Carnival of Light," the piece was recorded by the Beatles. "This is a bit indulgent," McCartney had told his bandmates, "but would you mind giving me 10 minutes? I've been asked to do this thing. All I want you to do is just wander round all of the stuff and bang it, play it." The track included hypnotic drum and organ playing, bursts of guitar, whistles, fragments of conversation, Native war cries, among other sounds. It was performed only twice and afterward remained long buried in the vaults.

None of the Beatles were present at the performances, but Yoko was. The psychedelic musician Daevid Allen heard "Carnival" at the Roundhouse Theatre on January 28, 1967. He recalls Yoko's contribution as substantial, evoking what felt like a "tentative pre-echo of the new age interpersonal therapy group. She had the lights turned out and each audience member was instructed to touch the person next to them as one of the guitar solos was accompanied by a motorbike being revved wildly in energetic empathy."

While "Carnival" was a stunning new sonic landscape for McCartney and his bandmates, "Revolution #9" was the first piece of its kind to make it into the mainstream as an actual Beatles' product. It remains one of the most unusual and controversial Beatles tracks ever recorded, one capable of inciting arguments among the group's fans even until this day. For Yoko, it was old hat. She had been exploring machine noise in the tradition of Edgard Varèse since her early Fluxus days. The event at the Roundhouse, technically the first rave in history, was simply another performance art space for her.

Enthralled with this new direction, and clearly energized by his new love, John began producing experimental albums with Yoko while recording the *White Album* with the Beatles. The first of these was *Unfinished Music No. 1: Two Virgins*, the result of their all-night jam session while Cynthia Lennon had been in Greece. They decided it would be released with a nude portrait of the couple on its cover, proudly announcing both their independent arrival as artists as well as their lack of concern for public opinion. The nudity, as characterized by John, "was to prove we are not a couple of demented freaks, that we are not deformed in any way and that our minds are healthy. . . . What we did purposely is not to have a pretty photograph, not have it lighted so that we looked sexy or good. There were a couple of other takes . . . when we looked rather nice, hid the little bits that aren't that beautiful. . . . We used the straightest, most unflattering picture just to show that we were human. . . . We felt like two virgins because we were in love. So we just said 'Here.'"

It is not difficult to find in the *White Album* more evidence of Lennon gradually pulling away from the Beatles. His song "Glass Onion," contains a run of insider jokes on fans who made too much of the band's lyrics. One of the lines, "the Walrus is Paul," referred to the great mystery launched by his earlier composition, "I am the Walrus." Lennon's allowing McCartney to assume the role of the Walrus, writes Beatles chronicler Todd Compton, was "partly an act of generosity because he felt guilty that he was starting a major relationship with Yoko and leaving Paul as a creative partner." Lennon more or less confirmed that interpretation, one of the few times he ever acknowledged that his extracurriculars were forcing Paul to assume the burden of managing their band:

> At that time, I was still in my love cloud with Yoko, I thought, well, you know, I'll just say something nice to Paul, and it's all right and "You did a good job over these few years of holding us together." He was trying to organize the group and all that and do the music and be an individual artist and all that.

As they were wrapping up the album, Lennon made two appearances on the David Frost television show, the first at the end of August with Yoko. It was the first time the two had sat together for an interview. They appeared, as usual in those days, in matching clothes, black this time. Yoko brought along her *Painting to Hammer a Nail In (no. 9)*, and permitted Frost to drive his own nail and describe, in pedestrian terms, his emotions. A clip from the video *Smile* was also shown, providing Lennon an opportunity to express his personal views on the current state of art: "The thing is, there's no such thing as sculpture or art. We're all art. Art is just a tag. Sculpture is anything you care to name. This is sculpture, us sitting here. This is a happening. We are here. This is art." Alas, one response from a music critic summed up the views of many in the public: "I only wish John would stick to things he's good at."

Two weeks later, Lennon was back on *Frost*, this time with the Beatles, who performed "Hey Jude" live before an audience of about three hundred people. It was their first public show of any kind in two years. McCartney, in a red velvet jacket, stole most of the camera time, and helped reassure the vast viewing public that the Beatles hadn't entirely abandoned the songs and crowd-pleasing style that had brought them to fame in the first place. The album would be an enormous success.

As if the five-month-long process of making the *White Album* hadn't been fraught enough, Yoko unexpectedly discovered she was pregnant over the summer. John, at least, was overjoyed by the news. And then, on the morning of October 18, he and Yoko awoke in Ringo's flat to the following:

We were lying in bed, feeling very clean and drugless, because we'd heard three weeks before that they were coming to get us—and we'd have been silly to have had drugs in the house. All of a sudden a woman comes to the front door, and rings the bell and says, "I've got a message for you." We said, "Who is it? You're not the postman." And she said, "No, it's very personal," and suddenly this woman starts pushing the door. She [Yoko] thinks it's the press or some fans, and we ran back in and hid. Neither of us was dressed, really; we just had vests on and our lower parts were showing.

We shut the door and I was saying, "What is it? What is it?" I thought it was the Mafia or something. Then there was a big banging at the bedroom window, and a big super-policeman was there, growling and saying, "Let me in, let me in!" And I said, "You're not allowed in like this, are you?" I was so frightened. I said, "Come round the front door. Just let me get dressed."

There were some [police] at the front and some at the back. Yoko held the window while I got dressed—half-leaning out of the bathroom so they could see we weren't hiding anything. Then they started charging the door. I had a big dialogue with the policeman, saying, "It's bad publicity if you come through the window." And he was saying, "Just open the window, you'll only make it worse for yourself." I was saying, "I want to see the warrant." Another guy comes on the roof and they showed me this paper, and I pretended to read it—just to try and think what to do. Then I said, "Call the lawyer, call the lawyer," but [Yoko] called our office instead. And I was saying, "No, not the office—the lawyer."

Then there was a heave on the door, so I ran and opened it, and said, "OK. OK. I'm clean anyway," thinking I was clean. And he says, "Ah-ha, got you for obstruction!" And I said, "Oh, yeah," because I felt confident that I had no drugs.

They all came in, lots of them and a woman. I said, "Well, what happens now? Can I call the office? I've got an interview in two hours, can I tell them that I can't come?" And he said, "No, you're not allowed to make a phone call. Can I use your phone?" Then our lawyer came.

They [the police] brought some dogs. I'd had all my stuff moved into the flat from my house, and I'd never looked at it. It had just been there for years. I'd ordered cameras and clothes—but my driver brought binoculars, which I didn't need in my little flat. And inside the binoculars was some hash from last year. Somewhere else in an envelope was another piece of hash. So that was it.

Thanks to a tip from a friend in the press, Lennon had thoroughly cleaned the flat before the raid (notorious user Jimi Hendrix had been a previous occupant), but the eight police officers and two police dogs found the small amounts of drugs that he'd overlooked, including the hash in the binoculars case, a tiny amount in an envelope in a bedroom trunk, a bit more in a cigarette case, and traces of cannabis in a cigarette-rolling machine. John and Yoko were each charged with possession.

Lennon had been smoking pot and dropping acid for several years before the arrest. "He was on everything," lamented Yoko, by the time they moved in together. "Next to his bed, he had a huge glass jar of pills, acid, Mandrax (Quaaludes), I don't know what the blue one was called . . . In the morning when he woke up, he used to just grab a handful at random."

Yoko had avoided all drugs before arriving in Europe. While showing "Bottoms" in Belgium, she gave LSD a try. Ornette Coleman's entourage introduced her to heroin, but it had not become a habit. She resisted John's offers of quaaludes, joining him instead in other vices: his endless stream of Gitanes cigarettes, and swearing, an experimental behavior for her highly reserved demeanor. He had apparently once told her that she was too Asiatic (meaning too taciturn) and she should say "fuck" more often, claiming that a beautiful woman swearing is very attractive. She had told him that she wasn't beautiful enough to say that, but she nevertheless went to the mirror diligently, and probably very stridently, commenced practicing her newfound dirty word.

The couple were formally charged at Marylebone police station. Lennon, long paranoid about his increasingly heavy drug use becoming public, found it almost a relief, in part because police had not caught him with harder drugs, but also because he was no longer beholden to the Liverpool lads' clean image. "It was better when it happened," he said. "It was building up for years. The Beatles thing was over. No reason to protect us for being soft and cuddly any more—so bust us."

In the weeks after the drug bust, Yoko had to be hospitalized due to complications with her pregnancy. John stayed beside her night after night at Queen Charlotte's Hospital, either sleeping in another bed or on the floor, his acoustic guitar in the corner of the room. She was given blood transfusions but on November 21 she miscarried at six months. The unborn child was christened John Ono Lennon II.

They appeared in court together on November 28. John testified the drugs were his alone and pleaded guilty. The charge against Yoko was dropped, a relief to both of them as she might have faced deportation if convicted. Lennon was handed a modest fine, Yoko had her hair pulled by a jealous Beatles fan on the steps of the courthouse, and the incident blew over or, at least, was soon overtaken by what the public considered a greater outrage.

The very next day, *Two Virgins* was released in the UK. Less than half an hour long, the album consisted of a variety of tape loops with John on different instruments, sound effects, snatches of conversation, and Yoko's ad-libbing. As Ian Peel has noted, it is "a startling and unsettling voyage, showing a mid-Sixties audience the extremes that music could be pushed to." John said he believed *Two Virgins* could "change people."

McCartney contributed a liner note for the record: "When two great Saints meet, it is a humbling experience. The long battles to prove he was a saint." Barry Miles said McCartney took the words at random from a newspaper, consistent "with the avant-garde spirit that the album was made." That may be true, but it is difficult to brush aside the iceberg of psychological insight into Lennon's motives and objectives contained in the last part of the quote. Lennon's passionate, one might almost say desperate, need to outdo his creative partner in pursuit of abstract and non-pop music formats could not have been lost on McCartney.

Retailing in a brown paper wrapper due to its nude cover shot, *Two Virgins* did not perform well in either England or the US, despite a lot of people buying the record just to see John and Yoko nude.

Lennon's adoring fans could not adapt to the drastic changes that he so obviously needed and wanted. Instead, the album confirmed for many of them that either John was abandoning the Beatles, or Yoko was infiltrating them. Either way, in the minds of many confused fans, Lennon the pop star had been kidnapped or otherwise hypnotized away from them by this supposedly evil woman, as if he really belonged to them and them alone.

While different from his previous work, *Two Virgins* was intended as a heartfelt and sincere expression of the union of John and Yoko, and the couple had hoped, in a naive and romantic way, that the public would join them in celebration. "We felt, John and I, that we had created a whole new sound, a new world," said Yoko. "Even though most people were busy throwing our records into the trashcan. We didn't expect that—we actually thought that the whole world would recognize that this was a brand new sound."

She considered *Two Virgins* "so reckless that it's great." Sure, she told the *New Zealand Herald* in a rambling interview, "the stuff we were doing was a little too soon, a little too early, I think. But you know, we suffered, we really suffered for not being able to communicate. But that kind of suffering was probably very good for us because we were both very strong-headed people and had very high opinions about ourselves. It's good to learn a lesson that way. But we were totally, totally naïve as well. I think that because it was us, the combination of . . . the Western hero, so to speak, John Lennon, and he decided to get together with an oriental woman. That whole combination made people angry, I think. I wasn't prepared for it. I was really surprised by it, but so was John. We went through that and it was a learning process. Also, I think it was a learning process for John's fans." Indeed, many people are still learning.

Yoko's pregnancy and miscarriage appear to have spurred John and Cynthia to drop their divorce petitions against each other. John gave her a settlement of £100,000, and she retained custody of Julian, for whom a similar amount was put in trust (with the proviso that it would be shared with any future Lennon children).

Yoko, for her part, formally ended her relationship with Anthony Cox, aided by a cash settlement of £6,000, ostensibly for loss of income. They shared custody of Kyoko, although she continued to live with Cox, who always had been her primary parent. Cox thought Lennon should cover his legal expenses. Lennon refused.

As 1968 came to a tumultuous close, Yoko and John Lennon belonged finally and exclusively to each other alone. At a Christmas party for the families of Apple employees, they appeared as Santa and Mrs. Claus. George Harrison had also invited some Hells Angels friends who were visiting London from San Francisco at his suggestion, and living at the Beatles' 3 Savile Row headquarters. Drink flowed and the Angels were soon out of hand: "We wanna eat!" Frisco Pete, one of their members, demanded. "What's all this shit about havin' to wait until seven? There's a 43-pound turkey in that kitchen and I want some of it now."

Lennon, according to one Apple employee, knew nothing of the scheduled release of what had been billed as the largest turkey in Great Britain and "looked up at the frightening figure of Frisco Pete in total bewilderment." The food was promptly served. "A huge turkey came in on a big tray with four people carrying it," said Apple Music President

Neil Aspinall. "It was about ten yards from the door to the table where they were going to put the turkey down, but it never made it." The Hells Angels just went 'Woof!' and . . . by the time it got to the table there was nothing there. They ripped the turkey to pieces, trampling young children underfoot to get to it. I've never seen anything like it."

# CHAPTER SEVEN

# Help Me If You Can

THE *FROST* APPEARANCE IN the autumn of 1968 and another live performance of the song "Revolution" had convinced the Beatles that they could once again perform in public without having to face hordes of screaming teenaged girls. At the start of 1969, they agreed to work toward some vague notion of a live show, and also to make a documentary of themselves rehearsing new material. Paul suggested that Yoko direct the film, which was probably both a sign of his regard for her talents and an effort to regain Lennon's full attention in the studio. The mind reels to think what Yoko might have made of the opportunity but she had no interest in the conventional documentary format. The New York–born Michael Lindsay-Hogg, director of a number of British pop music series, was handed the job instead.

The footage shot and edited by Lindsay-Hogg shows an uptight group of Beatles frequently at odds with one another in the studio, and ultimately performing their last live appearance together in daylight on the roof of the Apple building. Entitled *Let It Be*, the film was almost claustrophobically intense, funereal in tone, and compact at eighty minutes, in part because the Beatles insisted on edits. "There was much more stuff on John and Yoko," said Lindsay-Hogg, "and the other three didn't really think that was appropriate because they wanted to make it a nicer movie. They didn't want to have a lot of the dirty laundry, so a lot of it was cut down."

*Let It Be* was released in 1970, after the band had broken up, and none of the Beatles attended the premiere. Despite receiving an Academy Award for Original Song Score, the film's reception was cool, and Yoko's omnipresence at Lennon's side fed the narrative, adhered to by many Beatles fans, that she was a major cause of in-studio tension and the band's ultimate demise. *Esquire* magazine would months afterward publish the blatantly racist article "John Rennon's Exrusive Gloupie, which purported to tell the story of the Yoko nobody Onos." Sadly, it featured a disturbing cartoon by David Levine of a gigantic Yoko leading a tiny cockroach-like Lennon on a leash.

Lindsay-Hogg's film has been buried by Apple Music since its initial release, although he believes it deserves to be seen by new generations of fans. "When I finished filming it at the end of January 1969," he told the *New York Times*, "the Beatles had not broken up. I now recognize that my cut is a very accurate, enjoyable cinema verité of what it was like to work with the Beatles for a month."

It took another half century for McCartney, Starr, George Harrison's widow, Olivia, and Yoko Ono to hand Lindsay-Hogg's fifty-five hours of film, most of it never-before-seen, and an additional 140 hours of audio to Oscar-winning director Peter Jackson. His eight-hour documentary, *The Beatles: Get Back*, presented in three parts in November 2021, is a far loftier take than Lindsay-Hogg's. An almost operatic work of auto-nostalgia, it injects considerable humanity, insight, and even joy into what might otherwise have been an endless stream of rehearsal scenes, some of which amounted to actual on-the-spot hit-music composition.

Each of the Beatles makes his own contribution to the drama of Jackson's film. Ringo comes across as a cheerful and generous figure and perhaps the most important unifying force in the band. Paul, more committed to the Beatles project than any of the others, was urging the live performance (the rest weren't keen). Anxious to rekindle the group's creative spark, he also reluctantly assumed the role of leader in the absence of Beatles manager Brian Epstein, who had died a year earlier. Harrison temporarily quits the group in protest of McCartney's disinterest in his songwriting and corrections of his playing. Lennon sometimes shows up on time, sometimes late, and sometimes not at all. Yoko is never more than a few feet from his side, watching, sewing, reading, feeding John tea, cigarettes, and chewing gum, and occasionally, during breaks, howling into microphones.

Yoko is the revelation of Jackson's film, first because his cut explodes the charge that Yoko destroyed the Beatles. She is at all times a benign presence in the studio, never expressing opinions or trying to direct what the boys are doing. McCartney, in particular, seems to get on well with her, and jokes at one point at how silly it would be for anyone to think the Beatles would collapse "because Yoko sat on an amp."

But that's only the beginning of Yoko's performance. As Amanda Hess wrote in the *New York Times*, "At first I found Ono's omnipresence in the documentary bizarre, even unnerving. The vast set only emphasizes the ludicrousness of her proximity. Why is she there? . . . But as the hours passed, and Ono remained—painting at an easel, chewing a pastry, paging through a Lennon fan magazine—I found myself impressed by her stamina, then entranced by the provocation of her existence and ultimately dazzled by her performance. My attention kept drifting toward her corner of the frame. I was seeing intimate, long-lost footage of the world's most famous band preparing for its final performance, and I couldn't stop watching Yoko Ono sitting around, doing nothing."

Dressed in black, her long wild hair parted in the center and tightly framing her face, Ono appears as Ono is: a full-time artist whose life is one extended performance. "She seems to orbit Lennon," writes Hess, "eclipsing his bandmates and becoming a physical manifestation of his psychological distance from his old artistic center of gravity."

She also appears to have opened a window for the Beatles, who are no longer an exclusive quartet, excluding everyone else as they smother one another. Her presence during the *White Album* recordings permitted Harrison to invite Eric Clapton into the lair to play on the track "While My Guitar Gently Weeps." The brilliant keyboardist Billy Preston, who had first met the Beatles in Hamburg, visits the band in the studio during the *Let It Be* sessions and ends up staying to play joyously on "Get Back" and other tracks. More startlingly, McCartney begins showing up daily with his new girlfriend Linda Eastman. This was the same McCartney who had earlier said of Lennon's inseparability from Yoko, "I'm glad I'm not in love like that." Eastman would occasionally bring along her young daughter, Heather. She can be seen riding on McCartney's shoulders and giving the studio an unaccustomed big-happy-family vibe. None of this would suffice to save the Beatles, but it may well have extended the band's life.

The final live rooftop performance almost never came off. "About ten minutes before we were due to start, all the Beatles were in a little room at the top of the stairs and it still wasn't certain they'd go ahead," said Lindsay-Hogg. "George didn't want to, and Ringo started saying he didn't really see the point. Then John said 'Oh fuck—let's do it.'" It is now probably the best known of all the Beatles performances, with Yoko enjoying the show off to the side with Linda Eastman and Ringo's wife, Maureen.

A month after the *Let It Be* sessions, Paul married Linda Eastman, prompting John, as part of his ongoing efforts to keep up with his songwriting partner, to tell Yoko that they, too, must wed. "I'd never really wanted to be married the other two times," recalled Yoko. "It was just something I'd fallen into. Having a child wasn't something I'd wanted either, but had all come from Tony. I didn't particularly like the thought of limiting myself to one guy again. And I still had that strange thought at the back of my mind that if I stayed with John, some terrible tragedy was waiting."

Lennon first insisted they get married that day, at sea. A Liverpool native, he knew that ships' captains were qualified to perform nuptials. Tickets were bought for a P&O cruise ship leaving Southampton for the Bahamas that evening. John then thought it would be easier to take a shorter trip from Southampton across the English Channel to France. There were problems with Yoko's passport, however, and they were turned back by a diligent official.

John dropped the idea of marriage by sea captain and decided they would take a private plane to Paris and find someone to perform a ceremony there. Apple's Peter Brown, in Amsterdam for the weekend, was enlisted to help with their plans. The only location he could find that didn't require at least two weeks of advance residency was the island of Gibraltar. On March 20, 1969, John and Yoko flew from Paris by private plane to Gibraltar and proceeded directly to the British consulate. They were met by Peter Brown and a photographer and wed in a short ceremony, afterward posing for photos, Yoko in a short white dress and a floppy white hat, and John in white slacks and a white jacket over a white turtleneck. "Intellectually," said John, "we knew marriage was a stupid scene, but we're romantic and square as well as hip and aware."

They honeymooned in Amsterdam, checking into the presidential suite on the ninth floor of the Hilton hotel. Word of their wedding had reached the press and was all over the front pages, an inevitability that Yoko had somehow not anticipated. The thought that Kyoko would see them led to tears. She quickly recovered, however, and in her own inimitable style, the honeymoon was transformed into performance art. The newlyweds announced a weeklong "bed-in for peace" and invited the world's press to attend. "Yoko and I decided that we knew whatever we did would be in the papers. We decided to use the space we would occupy anyway with a commercial for peace. We sent out a card 'Come to John and Yoko's honeymoon. . . .' The press seemed to think we were going to make love in public because we made an album with us named—so they seemed to think anything goes."

The reality was much tamer than expectations. Reporters and photographers did find the couple in bed, but propped up with pillows, clad in pajamas buttoned to the neck, surrounded by flowers, and ready to be received as the Ghandis of their time. "Marching was fine and dandy for the Thirties," said John to journalist Howard Smith. "Today you need different methods—it's sell, sell, sell. If you want to sell peace, you've got to sell it like soap. You have war on every day, not only on the news but on the old John Wayne movies and every damn movie you see, war war, war, kill, kill, kill. We said, 'Let's get some peace, peace, peace in the headlines, just for a change."

If the invocation of Ghandi wasn't enough, Lennon added, "We're trying to make Christ's message contemporary. What would he have done if he'd had advertisements, records, films, TV and newspapers?" (It's an intriguing question indeed, as is: what would Yoko and John have been able to do in the age of Twitter, Facebook, TikTok and Instagram?)

On it went for seven days, with Yoko sitting, mostly quietly, as John talked nonstop about the futility of violent protest, the war in Vietnam, and how he was hijacking the media that had hounded him through his whole career for his own purposes. "I mean, it's a funny world when two people going to bed on their honeymoon can make the front pages in all the papers for a week. I wouldn't mind dying as the world's clown. I'm not looking for epitaphs."

Because John did most of the talking, the happening seemed to be his production. He had once commented that his wife was the most famous unknown artist in the world, and it was true. As the *Nation's* art critic Arthur C. Danto wrote, "The art for which she was unknown could not conceivably have made her famous—although even the most famous of artists would be obscure relative to the aura of celebrity surrounding the Beatle of Beatles and his bride. As part of an avant-garde art world itself, very little known outside its own small membership, the most robust of her works were subtle and quiet to the point of near-unnoticeability. We are not talking about anything on the scale, of say, Les Demoiselles d'Avignon, Picasso's early 1907 masterpiece, for example, we are speaking of things one would not see as art unless one shared the values and ideologies of Fluxus."

But anyone who had been watching Yoko knew that the bed-in was entirely consistent with her work over the previous decade. She already had a long history of turning trouble, frustration, and trauma into compelling conceptual art, almost as though she were rising above her troubles. Now, hounded by the press, criticized incessantly for her looks, her race, and her relationship with Lennon, she turned the world's attentions to her purposes. The cause—peace—was one Yoko had adopted long before she'd moved to London and met Lennon. The bed-in was a late Fluxus performance piece par excellence. The clues were staring the world right in the face. Affixed to the windows over the couple's bed were two placards, one reading "Hair Peace," the other "Bed Peace." Mistaken as political slogans, they were in fact puns on Yoko's usual manner of naming her performances (for instance, *Cut Piece*). As her fellow performance artist Lisa Carver writes, the world assumed that Yoko was with John in the Hilton when, in fact, *he* was there with *her.*

We are now entirely accustomed to seeing popular musicians, from Bob Geldof to Bono to Pussy Riot, using their high-profile personas to advance causes. They all walk, usually less artfully, in Yoko's footsteps.

Of course, nothing material came of the bed-in. Yoko would later say that she and John hoped they might be able to spark successful negotiations to end the war in Vietnam: "How naïve we were, you know? But the thing is, things take time. I think it's going to happen. I mean, that I think we're going to have a peaceful world. But it's just taking a little bit more time than we thought then."

Making the most of their moment, John and Yoko engaged in an astonishing months-long spree of releases and performances. The day after the bed-in they debuted the seventy-seven-minute film *Rape (Chase)*, credited to both of them, but shot from a script Yoko had written a year earlier. The script follows the brief format of her earlier "instructions" pieces: "The cameraman will chase a girl on a street with a camera [i.e., the rapist] persistently until he corners her in an alley, and, if possible, until she is in a falling position."

Funded by an Austrian public broadcaster and starring the young Hungarian actress Eva Majlata, the film was shot in the weeks after Yoko's miscarriage using the newly invented handheld "éclair" camera. Majlata is friendly toward the camera at first, but soon it is chasing her through the streets, a cemetery, and into traffic until she is cornered in her own apartment. With tears in her eyes she begs the camera to leave her alone.

But for some effects added during editing, said Yoko in Goldmine, the film was entirely candid:

It was just a filmic idea about just following a girl and keep following and filming her and what would happen to somebody who is totally exposed all the time. That filmic idea was something I thought before John and I really got together. It's interesting because in a way, the Beatles were in that position and John was obviously in that position constantly being followed by a camera. We arranged to get a key to the girl's apartment (from her sister) and she didn't know anything about this. Guys are still filming her, so she freaked out. There's just a beautiful scene where she is saying, "Why are you doing this, why are you doing this? Why is this happening to me?" and she's hiding her face. The biggest riot they ever had about a film thinking it was sexual. There is no sex in the film but this girl is being followed and is cracking under the strain of the camera crew stalking her.

Yoko had pushed the cameraman, Nic Knowland, to be as aggressive with the actress as he could manage. "I kept saying he could do better than that, that he actually had a personal problem doing the film because he was a Buddhist and a peacenik—he didn't want to intrude on people's privacy. I remember John saying later that no actress could have given a performance that real." It is a harrowing, eerily prescient film about an increasingly suffocating media environment. It is difficult to watch without feeling both seduced and shamed by the intense scrutiny of the unknown woman.

On the evening of March 31, the day of the film's release, Yoko and John held court for the press once more, this time in Vienna's nineteenth-century Hotel Sacher, a five-star institution famous for its chocolate torte. Adopting another of Yoko's conceptual theater devices, they hid themselves in a giant white sack and refused to show themselves to the assembled reporters and photographers. "This is a Bag Event," John explained to the press assembled, "Total communication. . . . [We] can communicate from one room to another and not be confused by what color your skin is or how long your hair's grown, or how many pimples you have." He repeated his anti-war messages message as the press tried to lure him out with chocolate torte and cheekily asked if it was hot inside the bag.

Less than two weeks later, on April 11, the Beatles released the single "Get Back" as recorded during the rooftop concert. On the B side was Lennon's "Don't Let Me Down," a passionate declaration of his feelings for Yoko:

> I'm in love for the first time don't you know it's gonna last
> It's a love that lasts forever it's a love that had no past

As "Get Back" climbed the charts, the couple returned to London and, this time dressed in matching black, climbed back onto the roof of the Apple building for an intimate ceremony in which John changed his name by deed poll from John Winston Lennon to John Ono Lennon. He had never much liked his middle name anyway, a wartime tribute to Churchill. Yoko Ono Lennon, he told the newspapers, had "changed her name for me, I've changed mine for her. One for both, both for each other. She has a ring, I have a ring. It gives us nine 'O's between us, which is good luck. Ten would not be good luck." It was left for others to point out that under British law, which does not permit the renunciation of birth names, his official name was now John Winston Ono Lennon, which of course has ten Os.

As all this was going on, Lennon was still writing songs, including a satirical account of his wedding and honeymoon to which he'd give the title "The Ballad of John and Yoko."

From Paris to the Amsterdam Hilton talking in our beds for a week
    Say what you doing in bed I said we're only trying to get us
some peace

For a man who genuinely felt hounded by the press, he did a fine job of maintaining a self-deprecating sense of humor at least, observing that the newspapers claimed that Ono had gone to his head and that they resembled gurus in drag.

Anxious to put the song on vinyl, Lennon once again turned to McCartney. Harrison was out of town and Ringo was busy with another project. They sorted out the approach to the new track while walking in the garden at Paul's house and cut the record the same day at Abbey Road, dividing up the instruments between them. The chorus "Christ! You know it ain't easy" and the prophecy "They're gonna crucify me!" got the song banned from many radio stations in the US but it still reached the Billboard top ten, and hit number one in the UK.

On May 9, Yoko and John released another experimental album: Unfinished Music No. 2: Life with the Lions. There was no nudity on the cover of this record but rather a sedate portrait photograph of Ono in bed at Queen Charlotte's Hospital around the time of her miscarriage, with Lennon sitting on the floor beside her (the back cover is a photo of the couple leaving Marylebone police station after John was convicted on drug charges). The first side contains material from a free concert she had performed earlier at Cambridge University, with Lennon (back to the audience) playing guitar as she screamed and vocalized. The flip side, recorded at Queen Charlotte's, contains Yoko and John singing news clippings about themselves, and the recorded heartbeat of the baby they lost. It was a brave and astonishing way to exorcise the negative energies of the miscarriage.

The album was released by Zapple, a minor subsidiary of Apple run by Barry Miles of Indica Gallery fame, and dedicated to recorded poetry and experimental music. Rolling Stone magazine called it "utter bullshit" yet it still spent eight weeks on the Billboard 200 chart, peaking at 174, because it was John Lennon, after all.

Yoko and John had planned to perform another bed-in in the US in late May 1969. Tickets were purchased for the Queen Elizabeth II. Ringo, Peter Sellers, and the author Terry Southern (with whom Lennon had collaborated on a film) agreed to join the entourage but the trip was called off when the US refused John a visa, a consequence of his drug conviction. "The States are afraid we're going to go over there and rouse the kids up, which we don't intend to do at all," said John. "We intend to calm it down, you know. I think the States needs us, and we can help."

New plans were hatched, with the couple first flying to the Bahamas. The Sheraton Oceanus Hotel proved hot and uncomfortable so they moved on to Toronto, Canada, and from there to Montreal (not as staid as Toronto and more convenient for New York–based media) where they occupied four rooms at the Queen Elizabeth Hotel. Once again surrounded by flowers and sitting under the "Hair Peace" and "Bed Peace" placards, they entertained a steady flow of reporters, photographers, and celebrities, including Timothy Leary, Allen Ginsberg, and Tommy Smothers, among others, in a raucous sing-along.

During an interview with a journalist, Lennon offered a cogent summary of his objectives: "All we are saying is give peace a chance." Yoko urged him to write those words into a song, and he did. In a matter of hours, he had scribbled lyrics on paper, mostly quasi-nonsense rhymes with the sentence Yoko had liked serving as a chorus. He picked up his guitar, an eight-track recording device was set up, and the whole room began to sing, Yoko using her natural voice, in time and in tune:

Ev'rybody's talking 'bout Bagism, Shagism, Dragism, Madism, Ragism, Tagism

This-ism, that-ism, is-m, is-m, is-m, all we are saying is give peace a chance

The food served in the suite was macrobiotic, mostly vegetables and fish. The entire floor of the hotel reeked of marijuana. Once again, John talked endlessly about world peace, and the need to advertise the cause, and this time Yoko had more to say. When the Montreal Gazette asked if it was really possible to bring about peace through advertising, she responded: "Definitely. Because, you know the Blue Meanies, the ones that are selling evil, poisonous stuff, violence, etc. are advertising as much as possible, so if we are going to sell peace, we have to at least push it as much as they are doing . . . peace talk has got to be just as loud as Marilyn Monroe, or whatever."

A reporter covering the bed-in for the Gazette later described the scene as "surreal." He knew he was being used for the couple's perceived publicity stunt but didn't really mind: "Truth is, nobody quite knew what to make of these freaks and their bed-in for peace, but there was an underlying sense of awe, nonetheless. Hey, we're talking 1969 here, and this guy's a Beatle. Let him preach about World Peace and Blue Meanies and we'll write it down. They were just really human. I was surprised how nice they were, how easy to get along with."

Yoko's memories of the second bed-in were fond. "After we finished doing interviews and talking to people and everyone else had gone away, it was the nicest time in our lives. One night, there was a beautiful full moon in the sky and no clouds and John said, 'Well, we're going to keep on writing songs together and our songs are going to be played all over the world. That's our life. That's how it's going to be.' It was just the moon and us. It was great."

The song "Give Peace a Chance" was originally credited to Lennon-McCartney, perhaps out of habit, or to thank Paul for his help on "The Ballad of John and Yoko" but on its release as a single in July, it was attributed to the Plastic Ono Band, which gave Yoko some much deserved recognition.

The Plastic Ono Band originally started life as a multimedia piece of conceptual art conceived by Yoko for a Berlin art show in 1967. It was comprised of four large pillars or containers made of clear acrylic, each containing pieces of electronic equipment—a tape recorder, a turntable, a TV screen, a closed-circuit camera, a loudspeaker—and wires. Images of people looking at the installation were captured by the camera and played on the screen, providing a Fluxus-style interactivity—"You are the Plastic Ono Band," read a caption.

Naturally, or so it seemed at the time, the four containers were read as representations of the four Beatles, and the whole project as a sort of protest by Lennon against what the Beatles had become. The Plastic Ono Band was to be more organic and easygoing, less manufactured and fractious. There's also an obvious shared vibe with Andy Warhol's 1966 project, the Plastic Exploding Inevitable, designed to showcase the Velvet Underground.

The Plastic Ono concept would expand from the four-pillared exhibit to an actual band that would share none of the formulaic pop values or rigid membership of the early Beatles. It would be like the impromptu, freewheeling, everybody-join-in assemblage in the Queen Elizabeth Hotel. "The Plastic Ono Band is going to be pretty flexible," said Lennon, "because it's plastic. The Beatles playing live is a different matter—we've got that great thing to live up to; it's a harder gig—but just for Yoko and me to get out there, we can get away with anything."

Simply *getting away* seems to have been almost as important to John as what he could get away with. The photographer Ethan Russell, a favorite of Lennon's in part because he had a knack for capturing good images of Yoko, spent a lot of time with the couple during these years. "John wanted only to be with Yoko," he observed, and the resentment she stirred in the Beatles' universe hurt them both. Russell once drove out to their home and, finding the front door open, walked right in. "Yoko came down first, in this black cape, and said she wanted to show me something. She had got this brown parcel in the post and inside it was a doll with long black hair. It was dusted with charcoal and had pins viciously stabbed into its torso. There was a note that said, 'Leave John alone!'"

John took the pins out of the doll before throwing it away. "Look," said Russell. "They had the greatest love story of the twentieth century. At a time of enormous sexism and racism, they managed to block it all out and create their own universe."

Exasperating as he found Beatles fans at times, Lennon's attitude to them was fiercely ambivalent. He was also capable of great generosity toward them. To celebrate their relationship, he and Yoko released the third of their series of deeply personal and unapologetically experimental records, *Wedding Album*, in October 1969. It had been recorded in room 902 of the Amsterdam Hilton during the first bed-in and "edited" by John. Side one features them calling each other's names in a variety of tempos and tones, from whispers to screams, over the sound of their heartbeats, which Lennon likened to "African drums." The opposite side consists of Lennon's interviews on peace and snatches of conversation and random sounds from the hotel room, interspersed with songs and guitar playing. Yoko and John are pictured on the cover in their white wedding outfits. The album was released in an elaborate package including drawings, photographs, a picture of a slice of wedding cake, and a copy of their marriage certificate.

"It was like our sharing our wedding with whoever wanted to share it with us," said Lennon honestly, expressing the ambivalence he had toward his audience. "We didn't expect a hit record out of it. It was more of a . . . that's why we called it *Wedding Album*. You know, people make a wedding album, show it to the relatives when they come round. Well, our relatives are the . . . what you call fans, or people that follow us outside. So that was our way of letting them join in on the wedding."

Perhaps not surprisingly, except to the besotted couple, those who did join the wedding were not thrilled with what they found. Ono later shared her bewilderment with the world's responses with the *Independent*: "We felt, John and I, that we had created a whole new sound, a new world. Even though most people were busy throwing our records into the trashcan. We didn't expect that—we actually thought that the whole world would recognize that this was a brand new sound."

Richard Williams, a writer for *Melody Maker*, received a promo copy of *Wedding Album* that somehow contained two discs. The two extra sides were merely test patterns. Williams gave them the same attention he brought to what the performers had intended to offer, and the result was published on the magazine's front page: "Constant listening reveals a curious point: the pitch of the tones alters frequency, but only by microtones or, at most, a semitone. This oscillation produces an almost subliminal, uneven 'beat' which maintains interest. On a more basic level, you could have a ball by improvising your very own raga, plainsong, or even Gaelic mouth music against the drone."

Reading what amounted to the most positive attention received by the album, the charmed artists sent Williams a telegram of thanks: "Dear Richard Thank You For Your Fantastic Review Of Our Wedding Album Including C-And-D Sides. We Are Considering It For Our Next Release. Maybe You Are Right In Saying That They Are The Best Sides Stop We Both Feel That This Is The First Time A Critic Topped The Artist. We Are Not Joking. Love And Peace Stop John And Yoko."

# CHAPTER EIGHT

# I'm Looking Through You

O ne of the ironies of the Lennon-Ono outburst of creative
expression in 1969 was that it happened while John was
developing a raging heroin addiction. He had been fascinated
by Yoko's experimentation with the drug while in Paris with Ornette
Coleman. Yoko recalls him reading Jean Cocteau's *Opium: The Story of a
Cure*, and being "fascinated" by the author's experiences with the drug and
his efforts to get clear of it. "The story was all about Paris in the Twenties,
Picasso, Diaghilev, Eric Satie and people like that," as she described it.
"John couldn't put the book down. . . . He started asking me again what
taking heroin was like, saying how interesting it must have been." Perhaps
it was, in Paris of the 1920s.

Eventually he began experimenting on his own, encouraged to some
extent by the already addicted singer James Taylor who was then in
London, one of the first non-Beatle artists signed to the Apple label.
"I was a bad influence to be around the Beatles at that time," said Taylor.
"I gave John opiates."

When Lennon decided to use heroin, he naturally demanded that
Yoko join him. Both found it a better high than weed or LSD, allowing

them to feel sharper and continue working. It also helped with the hurt. "We sniffed a little when we were in real pain," admitted Lennon to *Rolling Stone*. "We got such a hard time from everyone, and I've had so much thrown at me and at Yoko, especially at Yoko. . . . We took H because of what the Beatles and others were doing to us."

Heroin, writes Beatles historian Kenneth Womack, was yet another significant contributor to the decline of the band. "The end of the group is often unfairly blamed on Yoko Ono, but from what I found . . . John's heroin addiction was key. What the group was dealing with was a person with an opioid addiction. They were a quasi-family, like many families suffering today in the world from our opioid crisis. It was a serious problem and a distressing part of the story. There was a suffocating sadness that all of this was on its way. . . . It was hard enough to work through their interpersonal problems, and when a person has an addictive behavior that was not treated, as it wasn't, that only makes it double, tenfold, really the kind of problem to deal with."

Lennon was not good at hiding his drug problem, and despite his output of happenings and experiments with Yoko, his creative contributions to the Beatles were waning. He was not nearly as prolific a songwriter as he had been in the past. "It's really quite harrowing," writes Womack. "He has moments of lucidity but this was a full-blown addiction."

Peter Jackson's edit of Lindsay-Hogg's film from early 1969 does not allude to heroin but Lennon's problem is obvious. "He is in immediate, terrifying danger of death or mental decomposition throughout the first part of the documentary," writes Colby Cosh in the *National Post*. "When George Harrison walks out on the group toward the end of Part One of the series, it's treated as an inconvenience. When John Lennon fails to turn up the next day, Paul McCartney suffers a total emotional collapse on camera, and even the unflappable Ringo Starr is notably upset.

"[Lennon's] sheer inability to get a grip on new songs leaves a crater in the work schedule. He's so unhealthy looking that you wonder at times why an ambulance wasn't called. Performances and conversations get constantly derailed by Lennon's pun-filled Liverpudlian babble, which has by now tipped over from shared private band language to insane static."

In light of his addiction, John's need to have Yoko constantly at his side suggests more than love at play. He was dependent on her to function "as a human being," writes Cosh, "let alone an elite musical performer. . . . Remember, this is a famous avant-garde artist—was she excited or happy to become a human security blanket?"

Since the Beatles were formed, Lennon was their de facto leader, even if much of the group's management had been handed off to Brian Epstein early on. With Epstein out of the picture and Lennon barely functional, the Beatles were rudderless and Apple was wildly disorganized, despite a lot of money flowing into their asylum's headquarters. The band desperately needed to hire someone to lead its business affairs. Unfortunately, Lennon and McCartney couldn't agree on a candidate. McCartney was keen to hire Lee Eastman, his father-in-law and a reputable New York show business lawyer. Lennon considered Lee Eastman just another suit. He and Yoko had meanwhile arranged a secret meeting with the Rolling Stones' rough-and-tumble manager, Allen Klein, a New Jersey accountant with a long history of artist management and a plaque on his desk reading: "Yea, though I walk through the valley of the shadow of death, I shall fear no evil for I am the biggest motherfucker in the valley." John was impressed that Klein could quote all of his song lyrics. He told the other Beatles on the day of the rooftop concert that Klein was getting all his personal business.

With McCartney casting his lot with the Eastmans, and them reluctant to work with Klein, a business rift now joined the long list of the Beatles' troubles. Both of the new management groups moved into Apple headquarters. Their meetings frequently ended in shouts and acrimony. When the other Beatles tried to coax McCartney into dropping the Eastmans and signing with Klein, Paul, after a long argument, told them all to "Fuck off." He eventually relented and Klein was hired, but the damage to the Beatles' comity was lasting. "It was like a crack in the Liberty Bell," said McCartney. "It never came back together after that one."

During this difficult stage, Lennon's former family was also on the receiving end of his increasingly erratic behavior. After the Montreal bed-in, he suddenly decided that he wanted his all-but-forgotten son Julian back in his life. He communicated his intentions to his ex-wife, Cynthia, then in a relationship with Roberto Bassanini, and before long Julian was being transported by Rolls-Royce on weekends to John and Yoko's temporary lodgings, the ironically named Sunny Heights.

Their drug bust had publicized the address of John and Yoko's home in London, prompting them to start looking for a place of their own. Ringo, who had just abandoned Sunny Heights in favor of Peter Sellers's sixteenth-century mansion in Surrey, allowed John and Yoko to stay there as they looked for a property of their own. After an extensive search that took them through an estate once owned by David Lloyd George and an empty church in Hertfordshire, they found a stately seventy-two-acre home near Ascot, Berkshire, owned by chocolate magnate Peter Cadbury. It featured behind its imposing wrought-iron gates a white Georgian country house, a mock-Tudor villa, servants' cottages, and extensive landscaping with famous rhododendrons. Called Tittenhurst Park, it set them back £145,000 but gave them all the privacy they desperately wanted and also accommodated the professional amenities they needed, including a recording studio, editing facilities, art workshops, and darkrooms.

One weekend, John decided that Yoko, Kyoko, and Julian needed to see the Scottish Highlands, where he'd spent vacations as a child, and insisted on driving them himself in an unfamiliar Austin Maxi. Before hitting the highlands, they toured Liverpool and visited some of Lennon's relatives, none of whom were comfortable with his thin-and-hairy appearance, or with Yoko, or with the couple's exotic macrobiotic diet. Proceeding north, Lennon promptly drove his car into a ditch near the town of Golspie. All four of the vehicle's occupants were taken to hospital. John, Yoko, and Kyoko suffered cuts to the face and required stiches. Julian was uninjured but treated for shock. When Cynthia, who hadn't been informed of the trip, joined them at the hospital, John refused to explain what happened or even to speak with her.

He did, however, manage to get himself back to London and into the studio for the recording of the Beatles' *Abbey Road* album within days of the ordeal. He bought a bed at Harrods and had it set up in the studio for the comfort of Yoko, who had hurt her back in the accident. Their drug use continued. "The other Beatles had to walk on eggshells just to avoid one of [John's] explosive rages," wrote Barry Miles in *Many Years From Now*. "Whereas in the old days, they could have tackled him about the strain that Yoko's presence put on recording and had an old-fashioned set-to about it, now it was impossible because John was in such an unpredictable state and so obviously in pain."

Due largely to the guidance of producer George Martin, the *Abbey Road* sessions were smoother, more enjoyable, and more fruitful than *Let It Be* had been at the start of 1969. The band members managed to leave all of their troubles outside the studio and made music as only they could. "We all knew this was the end," said George Martin. "There was an unspoken feeling of 'Let's make it the best we possibly can.' I'm sure that's why John was so collaborative." And indeed, they did manage to make a singularly marvelous final album together, largely due to the steady presence of Sir George.

In that spirit of collaboration, Harrison's efforts were also given far more attention than in albums past. His "Something" is one of the best songs on the record, and "Here Comes the Sun," which struck Lennon as something Buddy Holly might have written, wasn't far behind. Ringo Starr pitched in with the sing-along tune "Octopus's Garden." McCartney contributed "Maxwell's Silver Hammer," pointing to the kind of work he would eventually do outside the Beatles format, and "Oh, Darling," which Lennon, in his classic grouch mode, would later claim he could have sung much better.

His new wife inspired one of John's offerings, "Because." "Yoko plays classical piano and she was playing one day and I don't know what she was playing," he told journalist Tony McCarthur. "I think it was Beethoven or something so I said give me those chords backwards." The Beethoven in question was "Moonlight Sonata," and the chords are not strictly reversed, but Lennon made them work well for "Because" with some excellent and haunting three-part harmony sung with McCartney and Harrison, and a distinctive harpsichord riff played by George Martin. "Between us," remembered Martin, "we also created a backing track with John playing a riff on guitar, me duplicating every note on an electronic harpsichord, and Paul playing bass. Each note between the guitar and harpsichord had to be exactly together, and as I'm not the world's greatest player in terms of timing, I would make more mistakes than John did, so we had Ringo playing a regular beat on hi-hat to us through our headphones."

Inspiration for another Lennon track on the album came from the bed-ins. Timothy Leary, the former psychologist, acid champion, and prospective governor of California, had visited the Queen Elizabeth in Montreal and asked his host to write a theme song for his political campaign, the slogan of which was to be "Come Together." Lennon obliged, although the funky and satirical result was useless for Leary's practical purposes and the two never met again. "It was gobbledygook," admitted Lennon. "You can't have a campaign song like that, right?" "Come Together" did become a hit, however, and is frequently cited as one of the Beatle's best ever. It definitely delivers a punchy grandeur.

Meanwhile, Lennon's drug use continued unabated. His skin was increasingly pale and his speech sometimes slurred. In January 1970, he excused himself from a television interview with a Canadian film crew and vomited off camera. His cousin Leila Harvey, a doctor, saw him around this time and recalled that "he looked about ninety, his eyes were staring. He was a sick boy."

Yoko maintains that it was discussions of having a child together that convinced them to go clean. "Right, that's it," John said. "We cut it here," she said. And they did, at least for a time. "We were very square people in a way," said Yoko. "We wouldn't kick it in a hospital because we wouldn't let anybody know. We just went straight cold turkey. The thing is, because we never injected, I don't think we were sort of—well, we were hooked, but I don't think it was a great amount. Still, it was hard."

Legend has it that Lennon wrote his song "Cold Turkey," with its lyrics "temperature rising/fever is high," about their withdrawal but his former personal assistant, Fred Seaman, later claimed that the real inspiration for the song was an actual meal of Christmas leftovers that made them sick. In any event, Lennon offered to record the song with the other Beatles and when they responded without much enthusiasm, he enlisted Eric Clapton and then released it as a Plastic Ono Band single. A few days later, he played the song for Bob Dylan and started using smack again. "We were both in shades," opined Lennon, "and both on fucking junk."

On the other side of "Cold Turkey" was one of the most remarkable recordings attributed to either John or Yoko in their lifetimes. "Don't Worry Kyoko (Mummy's Only Looking for Her Hand in the Snow" was conceived by Yoko while in hospital recovering from her miscarriage. She and Lennon recorded a demo of the song from her bedside, with John on acoustic guitar, and mailed it to Kyoko care of Anthony Cox, along with a private letter explaining her long absence and that she hadn't forgotten her daughter. A hard-rocking version was later recorded with Eric Clapton on lead guitar and Ringo Starr on drums, with both those artists delivering some of the boldest and most startling performances of their careers.

Among the many milestones represented by "Don't Worry Kyoko" is Yoko's graduation from avant-garde music to rock. "When John and I got together I was not thinking pop music so much as rock," she reported to BBC Radio. "I was interested in that strong heavy beat, which I equated with the heartbeat. I thought avant-garde music is mainly for the head— mostly male avant-garde composers avoided the voice because it's too animalistic—they were into very cool instrumental kinds of things. Cool was in, and by using my voice I was uncool in their eyes. Strange, isn't it? The sound of my voice was too human and emotional. Because of that, I kind of rebelled against the avant-garde tendency and I went even more animalistic. When I heard the rock beat, I thought, this is what I was looking for, and I never looked back."

It did qualify as rock, but Yoko's vocal performance on "Don't Worry Kyoko" was something never before put on a record. It was a physical and mental storm, an aural hurricane of screams, vocalizations, and the words "don't" and "don't worry" frantically chanted over and over against driving, bluesy guitars and some of the fiercest drumming Ringo ever managed. The stripped-down song was liberating and fresh. It packed a visceral impact that anticipated punk by some seven years, not to mention grunge and trance dub, then both some twenty years away. Nothing in the Beatles oeuvre pointed so directly to the future of popular music. The best description of it was probably from Lennon himself when he introduced it before its first live performance at Toronto's Rock and Roll Revival festival in the autumn of 1969: "Now Yoko's gonna do her thing all over you."

Yoko could have chosen many other modes of expression. She spoke excellent Japanese and English, and she had been trained in voice and told by her instructors that she had the talent to make it as an alto or mezzo-soprano. "I was supposed to go to music school to study voice, and then eventually go to Italy. I thought, there's something wrong with it." She didn't enjoy singing other people's songs. She had an urge to compose—to find an honest way to express what she felt.

The avant-garde men with whom she broke into the art world had no higher value than "cool," and she had tried that approach in her very first performances, for instance, sitting quietly beside an unplayed piano. There were no notes or lyrics. It was so-called music of the mind, with the artist and everyone in the audience imagining sounds. It was about controlling rather than releasing the voice. Yoko found it stifling. She wanted a musical approach to abstract expressionism that was about unleashing rage: "I was dying to scream."

Her operatic training had taught her to bring her voice up from her stomach, carry it, and hold it. These techniques, along with her comprehensive study of the "many styles of how the breath hits inside of your body and makes different sounds—the French way, the German way, the Italian way, the Chinese way, and the Japanese way"—were all brought to bear on this new purpose; she told *Rolling Stone* magazine, "I wanted to throw blood."

There was something of a precedent for her style in hetai, a vocal technique used in Kabuki theater that involves deliberate straining of the vocal cords to express extreme emotion. "When I performed at Carnegie Recital Hall in 1961, and performed subsequently in Sogetsu Kaikan in Tokyo in 1962, I took and morphed my vocalization, consciously, from Kabuki," she said. "It was a very early avant-garde musical attempt made only by me at the time, and I was conscious of presenting something that had a familiar reference to it, to be understood more clearly. Otherwise, I usually fly away from all references. Therefore, I am not aware of what I am doing with my voice in terms of where it stems from. Some people told me that it was very close to the Spanish vocalization which couples their classic dance. Well, it's quite possible, since we/I have had many lives, I'm sure. I might have been Spanish in one life."

Whatever its origins, Yoko's aural assaults enabled her to release her emotion as directly and sincerely as possible. "I think I'm just expressing something that is desperate. That is something that you can't express in words because it's too desperate. Just like you scream when you are just drowning and just like you're stuttering in your mind all the time before you talk . . . I want to deal with the world that is in subconscious. Not the world in consciousness but underneath the consciousness. That is where I am."

As she expressed it to Jonathan Cott of *Rolling Stone*, "The older you get the more frustrated you feel. And it gets to a point where you don't have time to utter a lot of intellectual bullshit. If you were drowning you wouldn't say: 'I'd like to be helped because I have just a moment to live.' You'd say, 'Help!' but if you were more desperate you'd say, 'Eioughhhhhh,' or something like that. And the desperation of life is really life itself, the core of life, what's really driving us forth. When you're really desperate it's phony to use descriptive and decorative adjectives to express yourself."

At the time "Don't Worry Kyoko" was released, Yoko had yet to explain herself so fully. Many listeners greeted the song with utter incomprehension, appalled by what sounded to them like a lot of random shrieking over a stubbornly unvaried two-bar blues riff. It would take decades for it to be recognized as "Yoko Ono's finest recorded moment" and gain the status of a much-covered classic. No less than Malcolm McLaren, the Sex Pistols' manager, would call it "the first punk record."

The year 1969 was something of a watershed for music festivals. Woodstock, of course, was the most famous, and Altamont the most notorious, with its stabbing and three accidental deaths. The Isle of Wight Festival, headlined by Bob Dylan and the Who, was well-managed and legendary in its own right. The Beatles rejected their invitation to Woodstock and were falsely rumored to be joining Dylan onstage at Isle of Wight. Lennon tried to get the Plastic Ono Band onto the bill at Woodstock but wasn't wanted. Toronto was more accommodating. Its organizers had asked Lennon if he would appear as master of ceremonies. Stirred by the thought of sharing the bill with a lot of his early rock-and-roll heroes, including Bo Diddley, Junior Walker and the All Stars, Chuck Berry, and Little Richard, he offered the Plastic Ono Band and was accepted.

The Toronto version of the band was put together almost overnight. It included Clapton, Klaus Voormann, a Beatles friend from Hamburg, and drummer Alan White. Their only rehearsals, unamplified, were on the flight over. "Cold Turkey" was also performed live for the first time at the festival, along with "Blue Suede Shoes" and a few other rock classics. In addition to "Don't Worry Kyoko," Yoko performed a stylistically similar twelve-plus-minute version of "John John (Let's Hope for Peace)," which had no lyrics other than the words in the title. The whole set was recorded. Lennon mixed it in a day on his return home and released it as an Apple record in December, the first time either the Beatles or any one of the band's members had produced a full live album, *Live Peace in Toronto 1969.*

Capitol Records was reluctant to distribute *Live Peace* in the US. As Lennon recalled, "They said, 'This is garbage, we're not going to put it out with her screaming on one side and you doing this sort of live stuff.' And they refused to put it out. But we finally persuaded them that . . . people might buy this." It reached number ten on the Billboard 200. Yoko's contributions once again baffled critics. "Side two, alas, was devoted entirely to Ono's wailing, pitchless, brainless, banshee vocalizing on "Don't Worry Kyoko" and "John John (Let's Hope for Peace),"—the former backed with plodding rock rhythms and the latter with feedback," wrote the Editors of *AllMusic*. The great Carl Perkins, however, told Lennon that the Plastic Ono Band's show was "so beautiful you made me cry," which made it all feel somehow worthwhile.

Lennon returned to London for a final showdown with his fellow Beatles. He had talked on the flight to Toronto of finally leaving the band, and suggested to Eric Clapton and Klaus Voormann that they join forces. He hadn't quite worked out the practical details of how to accomplish this mission, or whether it was to be a permanent group or an occasional pickup band. In the end, he gave up on the idea, reluctant to "get stuck" with another group of people, regardless of who they were.

On September 20, 1969, the four Beatles met in Apple's boardroom. Lennon unburdened himself, complaining that Paul had been dominating the Beatles in recent years and writing most of the songs on their albums. McCartney admitted that he had "come out stronger" in the studio but noted that Lennon hadn't been as productive as in the past. No one dared raise Lennon's drug use, although he was comfortable taking shots at his partner's occasionally cute and cloying "granny music." Still, McCartney urged them all to let bygones be bygones and return to form, pointing out that whatever stresses there were, once they were all in the studio, even on the worst day, they were still "there" together creatively, with George's guitar, Ringo's drumming, and his bass playing all merging seamlessly, or almost.

Lennon said he was out. "I started the band," he said later to Jann Wenner. "I disbanded it. It's as simple as that. When I finally had the guts to tell the other three . . . they knew it was for real. . . . I must say I felt guilty at springing it on them at such short notice. After all, I had Yoko; they only had each other." Even Yoko was surprised by the announcement. "He hadn't even told me he was going to do it. Paul was saying 'Why don't we do it this way and that way.' John said 'You don't seem to understand, do you? The group is over. I'm leaving.'"

She was disconcerted by the news and its implications for their relationship. When they were alone together, John told her the Beatles were over, and from now on it was just the two of them. It occurred to her that replacing everything the Beatles had meant to John over the years would be a heavy load.

That load, as the 1960s came to an end, involved an endless series of interviews, public statements, campaigns, and performances on behalf of a wide range of causes. Peace remained a top priority, but California migrant workers, Britain's Roma population, and the accused murderer James Hanratty, hanged in 1962, all received support from John and Yoko. When Hanratty's father made a plea in Hyde Park for an inquiry into his son's execution, they sat quietly at his side in a white sack (DNA evidence would later prove conclusively that Hanratty was indeed guilty of murder). In the weeks before Christmas 1969, they erected large white billboards in New York, London, and nine other cities stating "WAR IS OVER if you want it, Happy Christmas, John and Yoko."

Prior to meeting Yoko, Lennon had been casually racist in the manner of many of his countrymen. Those attitudes evaporated as he watched with horror the abuse flung at Yoko simply for the color of her skin. "Racism is a hard thing for whites to understand," he said. "It takes a lot to open your eyes. But I see it now because I'm married to a Japanese." When anti-apartheid protesters were arrested at a match between a Scottish team and an all-white side from South Africa, Lennon paid their fines.

John and Yoko were by now two of the most famous people in the world and a focal point of the many decade-ending retrospectives on television and in the press. In an interview with ATV, John professed himself optimistic about where youth culture was headed: "Not many people are noticing all the good that came out of the last ten years," he said, citing Woodstock, "the biggest mass of people ever gathered for anything other than war," as a highlight. "I'm full of optimism . . . I'm not insane and I'm not alone. That's on a personal level and of course the Woodstock, Isle of Wight, all the mass meetings of the youth are completely positive for me . . . And this is only a beginning. The Sixties bit was just a sniff. The Sixties was just waking up in the morning and we haven't even got to dinner-time yet and I can't wait, you know. I just can't wait."

At the same time, it was clear Lennon was anxious to make a break from the decade. He was severe about "people who are hung up on the Beatles and the Sixties' dream," and unable to let it all go. Soon enough, he would be dramatically demonstrating what letting go might look like.

Yoko Ono at two years of age in 1935, with her mother Isoko and father Eisuke. This was the first time she actually met her father, who left for America two weeks before she was born.

Yoko in 1940, age seven, traveling to America for the second time.

Yoko with her
first husband, the
avant-garde Japanese
composer Toshi
Ichiyanagi (left), with
their musical colleague
Toshiro Mayusumi, in
Tokyo in 1961.

Yoko captured on stage
during her seminal
performance art work
"Cut Piece", 1964, at
Carnegie Hall in New
York.

Yoko and her second husband, the American artist/curator Anthony Cox, during an exhibition installation in London, 1966.

Yoko assisted by Anthony Cox during the filming of her controversial *Film #4* (aka *Bottoms*) in 1966 in London.

The portrait of Yoko used on the book jacket for her book *Grapefruit*.

Yoko during the installation of her "Ceiling Painting" at Lissom Gallery, 1966. This is the sculptural ladder piece that John Lennon famously climbed to discover the word "Yes" printed on the ceiling.

Portrait of the recently introduced and soon besotted couple at Yoko's Lissom Gallery reception, London, 1966.

Yoko with her new boyfriend and his chief songwriting partner Paul McCartney, 1966. McCartney is holding an apple with a bite mark in it to playfully commemorate the action that John had taken when he encountered Yoko's apple sculpture.

Portrait of the artist as a newly famous celebrity, on the occasion of her second Lissom Gallery installation, Half a Wind, 1967.

"Lion Wrapping Event" in Trafalgar Square, 1967.

The notorious back cover of 1968's *Unfinished Music #1* (aka *Two Virgins*) concept album collaboration, which required a brown paper cover so it could be distributed.

Yoko with their young son Sean Ono Lennon, in 1985.

Yoko relaxing with a later reiteration of her Plastic Ono Band, 1985.

Yoko publicity image for the *Starpeace* album tour, 1985.

"Untitled" (aka "Unnamed") a pen and ink drawing
by Yoko on paper, 11 × 17 cm, executed in 2000, and
reminiscent of some of her "Grapefruit" drawings.

Later pensive portrait image of Ono ca. 2000.

Yoko in full flight during her 80th birthday celebration in Frankfurt for a reprised "Half a Wind" installation, 2013.

# CHAPTER NINE

# Cross Purposes

WHILE YOKO'S ART PROJECTS stemmed purely from an urge to create, John's frequently had a more commercial impetus, as one might expect of one of the world's most popular music stars. Tipped by his art adviser, Anthony Fawcett, to a potential market for limited-edition Lennon lithographs, he went to work in late 1969, drawing a series of fourteen pictures. They began innocently enough with a representation of himself and Yoko on their wedding day and another at a bed-in, and then quickly devolved into studies of Yoko's naked body in a series of erotic poses, including one of her spread-eagle and another with his head between her legs. The drawings were printed with soft covers in a limited edition of three hundred, priced at £550, signed by John and packaged in a white envelope labeled "Bag One."

To promote the venture, a show was arranged on January 15, 1970, at the London Arts Gallery, with follow-up exhibitions planned for Paris and New York. The lithographs had just gone up on the wall in London when police arrived to seize them, and the London Arts Gallery was charged under the Obscene Publications Act. Several months later, Eugene Schuster, the gallery's American owner, appeared in court. He was exonerated and on leaving the courthouse gave the press his personal review of Lennon's work: "I think some were bad art, some mediocre, and some showed good draughtsmanship."

Still anxious to drive his musical career in directions distinct from the Beatles, Lennon aimed to make something lighter and more spontaneous than the heavily rehearsed music he was accustomed to. He invited George Harrison to join him in studio on January 27: "I've written this tune and I'm going to record it tonight and have it pressed up and out tomorrow. That's the whole point—Instant Karma, you know." Klaus Voormann was recruited to play bass with Alan White on drums and Billy Preston on electric piano. They all arrived to find the famed American producer Phil Spector had come out of retirement to man the control room.

It was a light song, as intended, with a catchy chorus: "And we all shine on / Like the moon and the stars and the sun." Yoko sang backup. The recording session took just ten takes, with a group of people hastily recruited from a nearby club to add strength to the chorus. The song reached record stores ten days after it was written and hit the top five as a single on both sides of the Atlantic. Lennon and the band performed it live on the BBC's Top of the Pops, with Yoko sitting on a chair beside his piano, wearing a white blindfold and knitting with white wool.

Early in the New Year, the publisher G. P. Putnam's Sons mailed to Lennon a new book by the California therapist Arthur Janov entitled *The Primal Scream: Primal Therapy, the Cure for Neurosis*. "John got his copy about two weeks ahead of publication," the author told *Rolling Stone*. "He read it, and he came to me."

That a book on primal scream therapy would pique his interest is unsurprising given his attraction to a woman who had made an art of screaming. "He passed me over this book," said Yoko, "and said, 'Look . . . it's you.'"

Janov's theory was that by reliving our primal pains we can eliminate their effects on our daily lives. Primal scream is about facing shadows and demons, and attempting to transcend the limits imposed on us, whether by things inside or outside of ourselves. Both Yoko and John had shadow sides, histories of personal trauma, that made them strong candidates for Janov's methods. John seems to have understood this intuitively. He was soon on the phone to Janov, arranging for the therapist to travel to London for a session.

Janov found that his new client was a handful. "The level of his pain was enormous. . . . As much as I've ever seen. He was almost completely nonfictional. He couldn't leave the house, he could hardly leave his room. He had no defenses . . . he was just one big ball of pain. This was someone the whole world adored, and it didn't change a thing. At the center of all that fame and wealth and adulation was just a lonely little kid."

It is unclear whether or not Janov understood that his client was still using heroin, which could easily have contributed to his unease. Yoko was using, too, and sometime in March was an inpatient at a clinic in Harley Street where many of London's medical specialists are clustered. "She's a junkie, you know," John reportedly told a nurse. She was also pregnant again.

Lennon found Janov's treatment helpful, and would later continue it for four months in California. Yoko, too, tried primal scream therapy— John wouldn't have had it any other way—but her relationship to the scream was far more complex. She had been using primeval vocalizations to exorcise demons, repair herself, and make art long before Janov came along. She was a virtuoso of scream, having discovered an ability, which she attributed to a pea-sized growth on one of her vocal cords, to scream in two or three notes simultaneously. "If you listen," she said, "you'll hear the voice going like a harmonica, you know, three sounds."

She not only found screaming "extremely expressive of our emotional life," but a source of empowerment. "We sort of censor that, especially women. People don't want to hear women screaming. They want to hear women sing a pretty song. That's the idea in the male society. But we're the ones who have babies, we're the ones who created the human race. So naturally women have big power, but we're supposed to hide that power." Primal scream therapy seemed to be, for a time anyway, a means of unleashing that power.

In an interview with *Arthur* magazine, she compared herself to a warrior, "a warrior with one sword, which was just my voice. I could go anywhere. I felt if you wanted me to do something with you, then let's do it. And I'll do it with my voice. That's how I was when I arrived places. And when I met John . . . I was trying to create a new sound. The reason you create a new sound is because you're not that interested in the sounds that are around you."

It would take therapy with Janov and a couple of years of exposure to Yoko's thinking and methods to bring Lennon up to speed, but by 1970 he was not only including her pure, visceral expressions in his music but joining her in them. Lennon's song catalogue had long given expression to his own troubles, fragility, and pain, from the earliest Beatles tunes about romantic insecurities such as "In My Life," "Hide Your Love Away," "Help!" on through to "Strawberry Fields," "I Am the Walrus," and all of the *White Album* songs. Now in the fall of 1970, returning to London from California where he'd had to cut short his sessions with Janov because of visa issues, he and Yoko returned to the Abbey Road studio and took things to a new level.

The result was a deeply personal album, *John Lennon/Plastic Ono Band*, that explored his abandonment by his father, the early death of his mother, and other childhood trauma. The making of it felt to him like a rejection of rock music as he had played it in the sixties. He worked with other musicians, including Ringo and Voormann, but no band per se, just him and his primal therapeutic voice and the producer Phil Spector, who stripped down his famous "wall of sound" for the occasion. Lennon's voice is raw and anguished throughout the sessions. The first track, "Mother," is an indictment of both of his parents: "Mother, you had me / But I never had you," followed by "Father, you left me / But I never left you." It builds to Lennon chanting, Yoko style, the words "Mama don't go, daddy come home" over and over with increasing urgency until he screams the line at the song's conclusion.

The song "Look at Me," with its plaintive questions—"What am I supposed to be?" and "What am I supposed to do?"—is another example of him turning himself inside out in public to express his pain. It finds a measure of resolution that put still more pressure on his relationship with Yoko: "Just you and me."

Ringo would later recall Lennon being unusually emotional in the studio, occasionally bursting out in tears in the middle of a song. "The old John was gone," said Starr. "It was a different John." Lennon himself attributed his demeanor to the absence of the other Beatles, who he said could be emotionally inhibiting, but it still wasn't a particularly happy time for the couple.

Yoko had become pregnant again, the baby was due in October, and both the mother and father were temporarily off heroin again, but Yoko fell ill one evening and an ambulance was called to Tittenhurst Park. It took her to King's College Hospital in Dulwich where, after another blood transfusion, she miscarried again.

John's long-absent father, Alfred, chose that moment to make one of his rare appearances in his son's life. He showed up at Tittenhurst with his new wife, Pauline (she had been eighteen, and he fifty-three when they met), and their year-old son. The meeting, on the occasion of John's thirtieth birthday, did not go well. According to a statement later produced by Alfred Lennon's solicitor:

> [John] launched into an account of his recent visit to America, and as the story unfolded, so the self-inflicted torture began to show in his face, and his voice rose to a scream as he likened himself to Jimi Hendrix and other pop stars who had recently departed from the scene, ending in a crescendo as he admitted he was 'Bloody mad, insane' and due for an early demise. It seemed he had gone to America, at great expense to have some kind of treatment through drugs, which enabled one to go back and relive from early childhood the happenings, which in his own case, he should have been happier to forget. I was now listening to the result of this treatment as he reviled his dead mother in unspeakable terms, referring, also, to the aunt who had brought him up, in similar derogatory terms, as well as one or two of his closest friends. I sat through it all, completely stunned, hardly believing that this was the kind considerate 'Beatle' John Lennon talking to his father with such evil intensity . . .

Lennon senior would also claim that his son was homicidal, and that he had left his account of the visit in the hands of his lawyer "to be opened only if I should disappear or die an unnatural death."

It was also in these months, April and May 1970, that Paul McCartney released a self-titled solo album. The Beatles' *Let It Be* record, produced all those months ago, was finally made available to the public, and the world learned that the Fab Four were permanently finished. McCartney, who had always hoped that Lennon's earlier departure might be reconsidered, called up his songwriting partner and according to his friend Barry Miles said: "I'm doing what you and Yoko are doing and putting out an album. And I'm leaving the group, too." That he insisted on releasing his own record almost in competition with *Let It Be* did not sit well with the other Beatles, but McCartney was adamant on his release date. He also released a press statement that mentioned his "break with the Beatles." He said he had no plans of either producing another Beatles record or writing again with Lennon. "I couldn't just let John control the situation and dump us as if we [were] the jilted girlfriends," he confided later.

The breakup made headlines around the world. "The event is so momentous that historians may, one day, view it as a landmark in the decline of the British Empire," ventured CBS News. Lennon, for his part, was philosophical, sharing with one news reporter that, "It's not a great disaster. People keep talking about it as if it's the end of the earth. It's only a rock group that split up. . . . It takes a lot to live with four people over and over for years and years, which is what we did. We'd called each other every name under the sun. . . . We'd been through the mill together for more than ten years. . . . It's just that you grow up."

It was clear to the public that at least some members of the band were reluctant to see its demise. George Harrison, interviewed in the US not long after McCartney's statement, said it would be "selfish" of the Beatles not to find a way to work together again. Music journalists were quick to point out that individual band members had been doing their own thing since at least the *Abbey Road* album yet always managed to get together again. This would be enough fuel to sustain a decade's worth of speculation that the band would reunite, but there was considerable acrimony behind the scenes.

McCartney wanted out of Apple records, and was demanding access to the company's accounts. The others weren't keen to see him go and were worried about tax liabilities should Apple wind down. Their disagreement eventually wound up in court where the old enmities between the Eastmans and Allen Klein bubbled over, with Team McCartney portraying Klein as a reprobate unfit to manage the company's affairs. McCartney eventually succeeded in dissolving the partnership but the lawsuits and personal recriminations would plague everyone associated with the band through the 1970s.

*John Lennon/Plastic Ono Band* was released on December 11, 1970. It hit number eight in the UK and number six in the US, and received a mixed reception overall. "Lennon's album makes a deep impression, if more on him than us," wrote Geoffrey Cannon of the *Guardian*. "He screams and cries, desolation, bitterness, anguish. This is the album of a man of black bile. This is declamation, not music." *Creem*, on the other hand, said it was "totally enthralling to see that Lennon has once again unified, to some degree, his life and his music into a truly whole statement." It would eventually be considered Lennon's best solo album, and stand thirty-third on *Rolling Stone*'s 500 Greatest Albums of All Time.

No album comes out of nowhere. The music critic Robert Palmer has written about the avidity with which musicians in the late sixties were attacking the boundaries of their craft. "Music in a Jam," he writes. "The Sixties were a period of feverish experimentation and exploratory mixing of media in all the arts. In pop music—cutting edge records, by the Beatles, Yardbirds and Jimi Hendrix—often topped the charts, a situation that has not really been duplicated before or since. The audience for rock music was willing to sit still while artists searched, groped or noodled their way toward the occasional epiphany."

The tape loop/sound collage mania that struck with "Revolution #9" and spun off in various new directions through to *John Lennon/Plastic Ono Band* "wasn't just the byproduct of LSD trips," writes Palmer. It was part of an experimental ethos running through the music world. Lennon was motivated to keep pace with his Beatles bandmates and the many other talented bands and solo artists who were making hits at the time, but no one was fueling his expansive artistic efforts more than Yoko Ono. Far from a being strange and unpredictable Japanese avant-garde artist who was ruining him, as some of her critics supposed, she was clearly more his mentor and inspiration, not to mention his actual reason for living, or at least surviving: "Just you and me."

While Lennon was recording his album with the Plastic Ono Band, Yoko wound up working at the same studio on a record of her own with a similar title, *Yoko Ono/Plastic Ono Band*. It started by accident, as she characterized it to *Rolling Stone*:

When John was recording, I was mostly in the control room and John was making his music and sometimes he had to fool around a bit just to get inspired. He just kept on jamming and then suddenly I realized it was just really beautiful jamming, he'd started something very unusual with the guitar. I was listening to what they were doing and I just couldn't help it. I thought, "well, I just have to join them. This is great!"

The kind of improvisation that I was doing by myself only had to do with my body rhythm, when you just totally rely on your body and let your body take you to wherever the body wants to go, it seems like all the strange things come out. I'm letting my body do it and that startles me too. It's almost like the primal therapy thing and like the Japanese kind of vocal, or the operatic vocal, all the moaning and groaning and screaming, all kinds of things that I experienced in my life came out.

Klaus Voormann and the other musicians in the room didn't know quite what to make of what she was doing, but they had heard her Royal Albert Hall recording with the master avant-jazz composer Ornette Coleman, "AOS" (included on her album), and valiantly tried to pick up where Coleman's band left off. And they did a stellar job of it, too.

*Yoko Ono/Plastic Ono Band* consists of six songs. One track, "Greenfield Morning I Pushed an Empty Baby Carriage All Over the City," has Harrison on sitar and no lyrics beyond the words in the title, alluding to her recent miscarriage. It ends in birdsong.

The first song on the album, "Why," is an extended vocal exercise in which Yoko screams, cackles, howls, and laughs the title word over and over, with John playing a haunting slide guitar in the background. "Even we didn't know where Yoko's voice started and where my guitar ended on the intro," he shared. "It became like a dialogue rather than a monologue and I like that, stimulating each other."

Captain Beefheart guitarist Gary Lucas was most impressed with Lennon's musicianship on the album: "[He] was always able to make his guitar talk. He was one of the most visceral from-the-gut rock guitarists of all time. But never more so than on "Why," where his guitar spits lovely, processed shards of metal to inspire Yoko Ono's uninhibited caterwauling. This is some of the most radical guitar soloing of the era, rivaling Lou Reed's "I Heard Her Call My Name," Syd Barrett's "Interstellar Overdrive," and Robert Fripp on "Cat Food" for sheer conic bravado." But Yoko's voice is without a doubt the star of her album.

She does much more than scream, using voice in a manner that recalls the free jazz movement of the era, including influential figures such as John

Coltrane, Sun Ra, Miles Davis, and the Art Ensemble of Chicago. "The rock audience seemed to be tolerant concerning the eccentricities of a few cherished performers who were virtually brand names," writes Robert Palmer. "This tolerance had its limits. Yoko exceeded those limits . . . Going into the studio with a rock band and little or no preparation, as Yoko did, may have been a risky proposition. But this strategy eventually yielded some of [her] most intense and prescient performances."

The music press, not to mention the record-buying public, were cool to the album, although several gave it tentative praise, including the legendary Lester Bangs in *Rolling Stone*. And *Cashbox* magazine also effused: "Yoko Ono sums up the philosophy of the age as succinctly as anybody yet has in her first two sides here, "Why" and "Why Not." Mrs. Lennon's voice is the most interesting new instrument since the Moog Synthesizer and she uses it throughout."

"Yoko Ono has produced a real weirdie," wrote Duncan Fallowell, partially dismissive yet also supportive, in the *Spectator*. "The first track is the most ferocious and frantic piece of rock I've heard in a long time and sets the pace for much of the rest. The most extraordinary feature of all is Yoko's high-pitched voice which she uses not for singing but for producing stream of vocal effects. This produces a whole new territory of sound which, in pop, she is alone in exploring with any thoroughness, and unless her voice has been fed through electronic modulators she has quite remarkable tonsils. But I doubt this album will receive the attention it deserves, such is the antipathy toward Yoko Ono that she can do no right. Yet why she should be the object of such derision and plain insult I have never been able to understand. A couple of odd films and odd records hardly explains it."

"Yoko breaks through more barriers with one scream than most musicians do in a whole lifetime," said the *Record Mirror*. "Yoko's album, if you like melody and what we recognize as logical form, is much harder to take. Most people will write it off as just weird and not worth listening to, but it has its value. Yoko takes music beyond its extremes, into the realms of non-music. But suffice it to say that if you can use your imagination then the sounds do mean something, much as ink blots appear as different objects to people's eyes. Think to yourself: is Yoko's voice any different from a lead guitar? Can it not convey equally well (better I would say) different emotions? She can be the wind blowing across close cropped grass of terror scavenging the night. It just depends on what she wants to be, and what you want her to be."

Again, it would take decades for the pop music world to catch up with what Yoko was doing on that debut solo album, but it would catch up eventually, and with a vengeance, influencing performers from the B-52's to Wu-Tang Clan. Said the *New York Times* as recently as 2016, Yoko Ono/Plastic Ono Band "still sounds like the future."

Released on the same day as *John Lennon/Plastic Ono Band*, *Yoko Ono/Plastic Ono Band* barely touched the charts in the US and did not chart at all in the UK. Both records were overshadowed by George Harrison's six-sided masterpiece *All Things Must Pass*, which came out at the same time to near universal acclaim. Led by the hit "My Sweet Lord," the first solo effort of a former Beatle to reach number one, it spent two months at the top of the album charts on both sides of the Atlantic. Until, that is, he was sued for borrowing too much of the melody from a 1963 song called "He's So Fine" by the Chiffons.

Harrison would be the first of the old bandmates to establish himself independently of the Fab Four, something Lennon had desperately wanted to do. "Every time I put the radio on, it's 'Oh My Lord,'" he complained to Jann Wenner of *Rolling Stone*. "I'm beginning to think there must be a God." Refusing to give the album any better assessment than "all right," Lennon nonetheless couldn't help but claim some credit for it: "[George's] talents have developed over the years, and he was working with two fucking brilliant songwriters and he learned a lot from us. And I wouldn't have minded being George, the invisible man, and learning what he learned. And maybe it was hard sometimes for him, because Paul and I are such egomaniacs, that that's the game."

It was still better than what Lennon had to say—"Rubbish"—about McCartney's first solo effort. He claimed his former partner, by recording with Linda Eastman, was imitating John and Yoko: "They're imitators, you know," he said, seemingly forgetting that he had rushed to marry Yoko in the immediate wake of Paul marrying Linda. Lennon claimed to hope that *John Lennon/Plastic Ono Band* would "scare [Paul] into doing something decent, and then he'll scare me into doing something decent, and I'll scare him, like that. I think he's capable of great work. I think he will do it. I wish he wouldn't, I wish nobody would, Dylan or anyone. I mean in me heart of hearts I wish I was the only one in the world." John was always one to drastically overshare his feelings (that was one of the things that made him such a brilliant confessional songwriter), and especially so to journalists from *Rolling Stone*.

The interview with Wenner, conducted during his first trip to New York with Yoko, clearly demonstrates how much more healing Lennon's fragile psyche required. He veered from competitively vaunting himself over other performers to self-pitying threats to swearing off art altogether: "If I could be a fuckin' fisherman, I would. If I had the capabilities of being something other than I am, I would. It's no fun being an artist. You know what it's like, writing, it isn't fun, it's torture. . . . I'd rather be in the audience really, but I'm not capable of it. . . . I know it sounds silly, and I'd sooner be rich than poor and all the rest of that shit. But the pain . . ."

The pain did not stop Lennon from continuing to make art with Yoko. While in New York talking to Wenner, they also co-directed the twenty-five-minute film *Fly*. Formally known as *Film No. 11*, it is based on an original Yoko concept: "About a fly going from the toe to head of a lying naked body, crawling very slowly."

And that's exactly what happens. The camera follows at close range a housefly crawling on the honey-covered naked body of actress Virginia Lust, to the "tune" of Yoko's bleating, gasping, orgasmic breathing. The background is whitewashed. The soundtrack again features Lennon on guitar and Yoko's vocalizations. "Here," wrote filmmaker Matt McKinzie, "our housefly, gargantuan in close-up, pitter-patters over the model's arm, then her nipple, then her stomach. Ono's filmic cuts vanish into her vocal cords—two mediums coalescing into a combined mode of expression—and she now seems closer to the unfolding action than ever before. Via voice, the artist fuses herself (invisible amid the off-camera blackness) into the illumined world captured on-screen. Similarly, her housefly fuses the model's limbs, scattered by that very screen, rethreading them at the insistence of Ono's cries. Here, she posits the body as its own landscape, and offers a female participant as witness to the meditation on, and fragmentation of, her soma." Towards the film's end, the fly is joined by several other flies, all recruited from a nearby restaurant and gassed to keep them from flying off, which they eventually did, sailing into the sunrise as the script outlined.

Shown at Cannes, the film received a standing ovation. As the artist Sam Taylor-Wood saw it, "Perhaps what's most remarkable of Ono is that her ideas are based on the simplest, most banal, everyday things. But when *she* focuses on them, she makes you see the world differently. A fly flitting about on a woman's body isn't an irritation: it can be the most beautiful thing in the world."

In 1971, the couple took another trip, this time to Japan to introduce John to Yoko's parents. Her father, Eisuke, had retired from the bank and returned with Isoko to Tokyo. Always dismayed by their daughter's lifestyle, they had watching with growing alarm her antics with Lennon over the previous two years. After the release of the *Two Virgins* album, with its nude cover photo, the Yasudas, Isoko's side of the family, had stated publicly that they were "not proud" of the display. Her mother blamed Yoko for her father's ill health, and refused to have her name mentioned at family gatherings.

John was traveling to Japan with prejudices of his own. He believed that all Japanese men were short, and expected to tower over Yoko's father. (He didn't.) "He just went to my parents' place unshaven, and wearing an army-surplus coat," she said. "Just the most hip outfit, very rock'n'roll! I mean, rock'n'roll can be a performance in a theatre, a beautiful, gorgeous thing. But he was just looking like a bum. This kind of 'here I am' attitude. My family was not enamoured. If some families had a son or a daughter involved with the Beatles, maybe they would say, 'We'd like to meet that guy, we'd like to be invited to a Beatles concert.' There was none of that, of course."

Eisuke turned out to be slightly taller than Lennon. Even more surprisingly, they all got along. "He said, 'Just leave it to me,'" said Yoko. "And my mother adored him. There are pictures of her holding his arm and gazing adoringly into his eyes." Her father, dressed for the occasion in a velvet smoking jacket, was less impressed. "The other one," he said, referring to Anthony Cox, "was better looking."

Lennon found much to identify with in Yoko's great-grandfather Yasuda Zenjiro, who was born in rural Japan and rose to riches by his own talents. As a banker, he had been generous to victims of financial depressions and, preferring to remain a commoner, had refused honors from Japan's emperor. Lennon looked at a portrait of Yasuda and saw his own reflection: "That guy is me in my past life."

"He just said that out of the blue," said Yoko. "And I said, 'Don't wish for that. Because he was assassinated." Yasuda was murdered in 1921 by a sword-wielding socialist, Heigo Asohi, who approached him about a bank loan. Yoko finished the story at a later date: "Afterwards, Asahi killed himself and left a letter to the world, saying that he's assassinated this capitalist. But some people believe that he had asked my great-grandfather for money and he was refused, and others still believe that he was just a very enthusiastic socialist."

Returning to London, John continued to grant interviews, including one to the radical *Red Mole*, in which he discussed another area of his life where Yoko had been transformational. "We can't have a revolution that doesn't involve and liberate women," he said. "It's so subtle, the way you're taught male superiority. It took me quite a long time to realize that my maleness was cutting off certain areas for Yoko. She's a red-hot liberationist and was quick to show me where I was going wrong even though it seemed to me that I was just acting naturally. That's why I'm always interested to know how people who claim to be radical treat women. How do you talk about power to the people unless you realize that 'the people' is both sexes?"

Yoko was indeed a staunch feminist, both in reaction to the Japanese society into which she'd been born and the male-dominated art scene in which she'd made her career. Some of her early works, such as *Cut Piece*, are now recognized as major statements of proto-feminist ideas, but she was seldom explicit about her own feminism. One startling exception was when she gave an interview to a journalist and made her famous off-hand statement "Woman is the N****r of the World."

The statement was received with knowing nods by white liberals and denounced by white conservatives as well as some voices in the Black community who found it dismissive of their experience. Both Yoko and John stood by the statement. "When I went to London and got together with John, that was the biggest macho scene imaginable," she said later. "That's when I made the statement." John appeared on *The Dick Cavett Show* to read a statement by the chair of the Congressional Black Caucus, Ron Dellums: "If you define 'n****r as someone whose lifestyle is defined by others, whose opportunities are defined by others, whose role in society is defined by others, the good news is that you don't have to be black to be a n****r in this society. Most people in America are n****rs."

Doubling down on the statement, John and Yoko took it into the studio and recorded a five-minute song entitled "Woman Is the N****r of the World." Paradoxically perhaps, it won them a "positive image of women" award from the National Organization for Women, and was even performed by staunch Ono-admirer Patti Smith at a Lennon tribute as recently as 2017. A year after that, days before the Senate confirmation of supreme court justice Brett Kavanaugh, who had been accused of sexual assault, the actress Bette Midler took to Twitter and quoted Yoko's exact phrase. The extreme reaction against her—"Bette Midler is the Clueless White Lady of the World," wrote *Huffington Post*—brought an immediate apology. Times had changed.

# CHAPTER TEN

# The Expanding Field

GROWING UP, YOKO ONO had often felt like a stranger in her own family. As the music journalist Jerry Hopkins wrote, she had "a father who was married to his job and a mother divorced from mothering." Yoko would often speak of the hurt she had felt at home yet she was often absent for long periods of time from her own daughter's life. Her daughter, Kyoko, lived with Anthony Cox through most of her childhood, although her parents technically shared custody. Even when they were together, Yoko tended to look at Kyoko as an object of artistic potential rather than as a child, sharing with *Playboy*: "When she was not even a year old, I took her onstage as an instrument, an uncontrollable instrument, you know. My communication with her was on the level of sharing conversation and doing things. She was closer to my ex-husband because of that."

On the whole, the arrangement seemed to work well for all concerned, until it didn't. Yoko unquestionably loved her daughter. Cox and Kyoko were even routine visitors at Tittenhurst. Lennon, however, still considered Cox something of a grifter. The mistrust was strong enough that he forbade Yoko from attending a birthday party for the seven-year-old Kyoko because he didn't want to deal with Cox. "Can you imagine how I felt," reflected Yoko. "I heard that Kyoko had been watching the door all afternoon, waiting for me to arrive."

Lennon's misgivings about Cox weren't misplaced. He did seem to view his ex-wife, Yoko, as something of a meal ticket, and he had a history of involvement in shady organizations, including a cult in Denmark through which he relived past lives and communicated with extraterrestrial life. More recently he'd become close to Maharishi Mahesh Yogi, whom Lennon, after an initial infatuation, dismissed as a fraud. Cox also had his own misgivings about Lennon and the life he led with Yoko. He was around them often enough to at least have suspicions about their drug habits, and he was apoplectic about Lennon's car accident that left his daughter with cuts to her face. He began withholding access to Kyoko and in April 1971 the two of them abandoned their London flat and simply disappeared.

Yoko learned through Cox's friends that he had decamped to Majorca, where the Maharishi kept a house. She and John flew to Spain, checked into a hotel under assumed names, pulled Kyoko out of a kindergarten class, and tried to leave the country with her. Cox, who had been in a meditation session while all this was happening, received a call from the school and in turn alerted the police, who dramatically arranged checkpoints at all exits from Majorca.

Officers found Yoko, John, and Kyoko at their hotel and led them to a police station to make a statement. A photo of Lennon carrying a barefoot Kyoko to the station made newspapers around the world. All parties next appeared before a Spanish judge who asked the girl which parent she wanted to live with. Kyoko chose her father, leading to a second widely circulated picture of Cox carrying Kyoko on his back out of the courthouse.

In the days that followed, everyone returned to London and some sort of truce was arranged among the adults. Kyoko was even allowed to visit Yoko at Tittenhurst. And then Cox and his daughter disappeared again. Yoko launched a massive search but this time was unable to pick up their trail. There was a hint that Cox might have flown to America. Yoko and John dutifully hurried off to New York, but found nothing and no one.

Cox, his new wife, Melinda, and Kyoko were indeed in the United States though, and traveling under assumed names. They would eventually join another cult, this one of a pseudo-Christian variety, based in Iowa. It would be nine long years before Yoko heard from her daughter again.

While all this was going on, Paul and Linda McCartney were putting the finishing touches on *Ram*, his second solo album. It was ripped by critics on release in May, with *Rolling Stone* calling it "monumentally irrelevant" and suggesting that McCartney without the Beatles had nothing to offer but "cutsie-pie, florid attempts at rock muzak." It sold well, nevertheless, hitting number one in the UK while the single "Uncle Albert/Admiral Halsey" topped charts in the US. It also won a Grammy Award for best arrangement and accompanying vocalists. It has since come to be regarded as something of a cult classic, especially with its parallel Thrillington version in creative tow.

McCartney's success followed on the heels of George Harrison's massive breakthrough with *All Things Must Pass*. Ringo Starr, too, had launched himself, albeit less grandiosely, as a solo artist. His song "It Don't Come Easy," written with George Harrison and recorded with Stephen Stills on keyboards, reached number four in both the US and the UK and number one in Canada. People always seemed to love Ringo, no matter what he did. He was just lovable.

Lennon was disconcerted by the ability of his fellow bandmates to find their way forward, creatively and commercially, without him and was furious at McCartney for a perceived dig in his track "Too Many People." The lyrics are not crisp or obvious, and Lennon isn't mentioned by name, but he was sensitive enough to McCartney's ways to appreciate that lines such as "You took your lucky break and broke it in two" and "Too many people preaching practices" were aimed at him. McCartney later admitted as much: "He'd been doing a lot of preaching, and it got up my nose a little bit."

In fact, Lennon believed that several of the songs on *Ram* were about him, and he returned to the studio determined to get even. "How do You Sleep?" was a vicious and misguided riposte to McCartney in the shape of a break-up song:

A pretty face may last a year or two but pretty soon they'll see what you can do

The sound you make is muzak to my ears you must have learned something in all those years

Ringo and others in the studio tried to convince Lennon to tone down the attack and they apparently did manage to trim its excesses. He remained unapologetic, however, claiming that he wasn't really feeling that vicious at the time, as unlikely as that seems, and that it was not the horrible vendetta people portrayed it to be. Perhaps struggling to justify the truly mean-spirited song, he claimed that he was merely using his resentment over withdrawing from Paul and the Beatles to write a song. "I don't really go round with those thoughts in my head all the time," he demurred, which was partially true: he only had them while writing his songs.

As he exorcised McCartney, Lennon leaned still more on Yoko, as he admitted in another track on the album, "Oh, Yoko!," a jaunty love song that gently mocks his need to be around her every minute of the day: "In the middle of a shave / I call your name."

Yoko had not merely replaced McCartney as Lennon's muse and the most important person in his life. She was coming into her own as his musical partner as well. "Yoko was an incredibly positive influence on the whole album," said Dan Richter, an American actor who was close to the couple and a regular at Tittenhurst Park during the recording of the album. "She wasn't just sitting in the background and yowling occasionally. She could read and even write musical notation. If there was ever a problem, say over harmonies, Yoko as likely as not would come up with the solution."

She also provided the inspiration, content, and even some of the lyrics for the most famous song Lennon would ever write as a solo artist. Back in 1964, when John was still singing "Yeah, Yeah, Yeah," Yoko had published *Grapefruit*, with its more than a hundred instruction paintings. One of those was *Cloud Piece*, the instructions for which were: "Imagine the clouds dripping. Dig a hole in your garden to put them in. (1963, Spring)." Another, *Pencil Lead Piece*, asked readers to "Imagine your head filled with pencil leads / Imagine one of them broken." Lennon, a fervent fan of the book, had lately also written a short introduction to its 1970 commercial reprinting. He overlooked the subversive nature of some of the conceptions—there is no other way to read "Smoke everything you can. Including your pubic hair"—which was odd for a man known for his withering wit. He saw them as therapeutic pieces employing the power of imagination as a survival tool: "I think this is an important book to help people act out their madness. If you do some of the things in it, you stop going crazy in a way. This Yoko book has changed some people's lives."

Lennon reworked Yoko's poetic instructions into the piano ballad "Imagine," his effort to keep up with the spiritual turns of both Harrison's

"My Sweet Lord" and McCartney's "Let It Be." Forgetting for a moment that he'd just slammed the door on all 1960s idealism, John writes what is probably the most wide-eyed and wistful song of the period:

> Imagine there's no countries
> Imagine all the people living life in peace

It would take a decade for him to acknowledge his creative debt to Yoko, notwithstanding his early claim to being a feminist. "[Imagine] should be credited as a Lennon-Ono song because a lot of it—the lyric and the concept—came from Yoko," he told the BBC. "But those days I was a bit more selfish, a bit more macho, and I sort of omitted to mention her contribution. . . . If it had been a male, you know—Harry Nilsson's 'Old Dirt Road,' it's Lennon-Nilsson. But when we did [Imagine] I just put Lennon because, you know, she's just the wife and you don't put her name on, right." It had been John, of course, who had insisted after their wedding that they both shared the Ono and Lennon names.

The song was rehearsed with Yoko and producer Phil Spector sitting in the studio making occasional suggestions for different words and sounds. Released in the US in October 1971, it reached number three on the *Billboard* charts in the US and number six in the UK, the bestselling single of Lennon's solo career. Lines such as "Imagine there's no heaven" annoyed religious groups but, on the whole, the reception was exceptionally positive considering the radicalism of the song's message. "Anti-religious, anti-nationalistic, anti-conventional, anti-capitalistic, but because it is sugar-coated it is accepted," said Lennon sarcastically. "Now I understand what you have to do. Put your political message across with a little honey."

The *Imagine* album reached number one in the UK. It was accompanied by an eighty-one-minute documentary of John and Yoko rehearsing, talking, and puttering around Tittenhurst in the company of an odd assortment of celebrities, from Andy Warhol and George Harrison to Jack Palance and Fred Astaire. Both John and Yoko sport new looks in the film. His hair has grown back over his ears. His granny glasses have yellow lenses, and his face looks healthier than it had during the *Let It Be* sessions. His sideburns are long, in part to cover a scar left by his car accident. Yoko's hair has grown back down to her shoulders and she dresses more provocatively than ever before, appearing frequently in tight hot pants, with lacy tops and plunging necklines, and leather boots. Her hair is often pulled back, revealing her full face, often framed by chokers and headbands. She and John both look younger than they had only a few years before.

The documentary is now largely forgotten but the song "Imagine" would go on to have an astonishingly long and successful life. Among its many honors: one of the 100 most performed songs of the twentieth century; number 30 on the American recording industry's 365 songs of the century; number 3 on *Rolling Stone*'s 500 greatest songs of all time (2004), and a Grammy hall-of-fame award. It would be covered by more than 200 artists, including a who's who of popular music: Elton John, Stevie Wonder, Neil Young, Madonna, and Lady Gaga. It would be featured at five separate Olympic opening or closing ceremonies and year after year at Times Square on New Year's Eve. Yoko Ono would only receive official credit for her crucial co-authorship of the song in late 2018.

Ironically, just after the recording of "Imagine," Yoko and John separated for the first time. George Harrison was arranging his Concert for Bangladesh, a fundraiser for the war-torn country. He invited Lennon and other musical friends to join him onstage in New York on August 1. Yoko, presuming she had been invited along with John (she wasn't) was naturally excited. "It's a charity event," she told John. "We should do it."

After all, they were already in New York when Harrison called with his bad news, quite the contrary to their innocent assumptions. Lennon got angry and eventually stormed out of their hotel room. "I didn't realize at the time he was so angry and worried by the thought that my feelings would be hurt," she said. "Later he told me he hoped I would chase after him, saying, 'Oh, please don't go,' but I'm not like that."

Lennon showed up at the doorstep of Dan Richter. "He couldn't swallow the idea that Yoko wouldn't be allowed to appear with him. And anyway, he was terrified the other Beatles were out to trap him. He thought he'd be onstage with George and Ringo, and then Paul McCartney would walk on, and headlines all over the world would say 'Beatles Reunion.'" Lennon left Richter's place for JFK airport and flew to Paris that very night.

The next day, Allen Klein called Yoko to tell her John was on his way to Tittenhurst and that she should follow him. "Suddenly my brain, which had always tried to make myself so small in this relationship, opened up," she said. "I said 'Listen, I'm getting a rest from it, okay? He was the one who left me."

She stayed in New York until repeated calls from Klein finally prompted her to move. She flew to London and was met by Lennon's chauffeur. She expected John to be waiting for her at the front door. He wasn't. "I went upstairs to our bedroom," she said. "I opened the door, the bag from my "Bag Piece" was on the floor and John was inside it. 'I'm sorry Yoko' was all he said. And in Paris he had got me a heart-shaped diamond necklace. I thought it was so touching and sweet, because the heart was so small. He knew I didn't like anything too big and ostentatious. And so we got cozy in bed, and that was that."

It was perhaps inevitable that Lennon's animosity toward everything Beatles oriented would eventually drive him away from London, the once-swinging city with which they were so closely identified, but in the end, his departure happened almost by accident. Yoko and Anthony Cox had finally been divorced in the U.S. Virgin Islands. Her lawyers advised her that her best shot at winning full custody of their daughter, Kyoko, would be to apply in the same locale. So she did. The court granted her wish with the proviso that she raise Kyoko in the US. It followed that she needed to move to America to have any hope of regaining custody of her daughter, and New York was really the only home she'd known there. For his part Lennon was only too glad to escape from Britain, the locale of too many fraught memories.

After some initial difficulty, she and John were both granted visitor visas. Their gigantic estate, Tittenhurst Park, was simply abandoned, with all seventy-four acres left untended. It would be sold in a couple of years to John's old pal Ringo for a song, almost literally, with the drummer assuming responsibility for taxes and repairs as part of the deal. John and Yoko checked into two suites at the St. Regis hotel on August 31, 1971, determined to live for the foreseeable future on her turf.

"It was Yoko who sold me on New York," John said to *Playboy* magazine. "She'd been poor here and she knew every inch. She made me walk around the streets and parks and squares and examine every nook and cranny. In fact, you could say I fell in love with New York on a street corner." He found welcome echoes of Liverpool in Manhattan: "There's the same quality of energy, of vitality in both cities. New York is at my speed . . . I like New Yorkers because they have no time for the niceties of life. They're like me in this. They're naturally aggressive, they don't believe in wasting time." Before long, Lennon was telling everyone he met how he preferred New York to London. Its food, its newspapers, its Chinatown, its galleries, its bars, its people, were better than everything at home. "If I'd lived in ancient times," he said, "I'd have lived in Rome. Today, America is the Roman Empire and New York is Rome itself."

From the St. Regis, they moved to the West Village, leasing an apartment there from Joe Butler, the drummer for the Lovin' Spoonful, who was off touring a rock opera. Yoko's old friend John Cage lived next door. They bought a building farther downtown on Broome Street, intending it as a replacement for the old Apple headquarters on Savile Row.

Yoko wasted no time reintroducing herself to the American art scene. I. M. Pei's Everson Museum of Art in Syracuse hosted *This Is Not Here*, a major retrospective of her work, in October. The title, she said, was inspired by a flat she had occupied in London: "I had a room . . . extremely small, and there was this huge, huge, some kind of closet—not exactly a closet but this huge thing was right in the middle of it and you couldn't move it because it was so heavy. So I just put (a note on it saying) 'This Is Not Here.' And then I thought 'Wow, this is great . . . That's how the Instructions developed.'"

She and John had used the line as a welcome sign at Tittenhurst, and Yoko repurposed it for the Syracuse exhibit, which had her usual anti-art dimension. As she explained to critic Emily Wasserman in their interview at the time: "I was trying to get across the idea that the art is in the people who come to see it. It's like saying, 'You're important, not the objects.' I'm not saying, 'Come and look at these beautiful things on pedestals.' I'm saying that whatever is important is in your head. It's your reactions that count.'"

A poster for the retrospective was designed by Fluxus founder George Maciunas. He also helped Lennon produce a catalogue for the occasion. Over eighty works were displayed, including a transparent acrylic maze with a toilet in the middle, Yoko's homage to Fluxus hero Marcel Duchamp's 1917 R. Mutt urinal.

For another piece, *Water Event*, Yoko invited one hundred and twenty participants to bring objects or ideas of objects into which she could pour water to complete a sculpture. "It was a Zen joke," she said. "Jokes and laughter are very important elements in Zen. This particular joke is that I get all the containers from the artists to fill them with water, and the water I supply is conceptual. Meaning that I never fill them with actual water. I like that bit." Dan Richter brought a cup of instant soup. Andy Warhol met the conceptual challenge, bringing a film of a water cooler with a recording of people speaking.

As far as attendance, the Syracuse event was a smash, with six thousand people visiting on opening day (rumors of a Beatles reunion no doubt helped, although only John and Ringo were present). "The whole atmosphere was so festive and noisy," said Yoko, wearing a black velvet hot pants suit for the occasion, "that anybody who was seriously interested in my work would have had a hard time to find it even. I started to feel guilty that I wasn't presenting Ringo, George and Paul. I felt discouraged from doing anything like that again. It just didn't work."

The *New York Times* covered the opening, asking the question, "Is Syracuse ready for Yoko Ono and John Lennon?" An editorial in a local newspaper had accused Everson, which according to the *Times* saw itself "as a bastion of the avant-garde set down in a cultural wasteland," of seeking to attract publicity and crowds by hosting Yoko. People might show up, ventured the editorial, but only at "a tremendous loss of good taste and of respect in the art world." The whole of the museum's staff had signed a letter of protest defending the retrospective.

The *Times* itself seemed puzzled by the exhibits, particularly items such as "a real apple on a pedestal baldly labelled 'Apple,'" and "'Imagine the Flowers,' a row of empty flower pots." It noted that *Painting to Let the Evening Light Go Through*, a clear Plexiglas sheet, was a favorite of Lennon, who celebrated his thirty-first birthday at the show. The paper overlooked his contributions (he was listed as a guest artist), including a pale red plastic bag that he'd titled *Napoleon's Bladder*.

Seeming to agree with Yoko that the atmosphere at the Everson was a little too festive, the *Times* reported that someone ate Yoko's apple, a Venetian vase sent by Peggy Guggenheim as her contribution to *Water Event* was smashed, and "an antique eyeglass case and a set of false teeth were missing from their vitrines."

Back in Manhattan, John and Yoko continued their publicity binge for the *Imagine* record and documentary. They bought bicycles and toured around the West Village. John launched into a theatrical phase of volatile and occasionally ill-advised political radicalism, rubbing shoulders with the Yippies Jerry Rubin and Abbie Hoffman, Black Panthers Huey Newton and Bobby Seale, the poet and White Panther John Sinclair, and David Peel, a musician whose hippie band performed regularly in Washington Square Park (Lennon would eventually produce Peel's widely banned album, *The Pope Smokes Dope*). He supported the Attica Prison riots and deplored the imprisonment of feminist Angela Davis. By January 1972, the FBI would be closely following the activities of John and Yoko, whom they believed to be seditious radicals.

The FBI's interest in the couple dated back to the naked cover photo on the *Two Virgins* album, which was brought to the attention of J. Edgar Hoover by an indignant congressman. One of the undercover agents who routinely showed up at Lennon's rallies and concerts claimed he was "a strong believer in the . . . overthrow of the present society in America today." There was talk of deporting Lennon on the grounds that he was conspiring to disrupt the US electoral process, which led to their telephones being bugged and confrontational meetings with the Immigration and Naturalization Service. America was never in any danger from either of them, and the INS eventually was eventually ordered to back off by a federal judge who said "the courts will not condone selective deportation based upon secret political grounds."

In later years, Lennon would often wax rhapsodic about the innocence he demonstrated on arriving in New York, wanting to fit in with the locals and the times. He sometimes even categorized his behavior as a guilt-driven outcome of his royal status. Roy Carr, author of *Century of Jazz,* counters with a sobering assessment of the ex-Beatle's initial American period: "Lennon was living in a New York radical-chic ghetto surrounded by committed political figures and a fair percentage of the usual big city cultural vampires. Having deliberately rejected world leadership as a Beatle, Lennon freely allowed himself to be manipulated as John Lennon, ex-Beatle."

Yoko engaged in some activism of her own, writing an op-ed piece for the *New York Times* entitled "The Feminization of Society." She warned that the recent vogue for talk about female liberation was in danger of leading to "dead-end cynicism. Public fuss over the issue is all right as long as it does not divert one's attention from the real effort to gain freedom. The feminist movement faces this danger now. The majority of men greeted the movement with a condescending and receiving smile, while the newspapers picked up the issue as an ideal space filler. Unless women become more strongly aware of what is really happening and start to transform the issue into a serious revolution, the movement will fade away as another happening of the decade. We must not let it die. We have to keep on going until the whole of the female race is freed." Her byline on the piece read "Yoko Ono, artist and composer, is author of *Grapefruit.*"

And still the music kept coming. Yoko released *Fly,* her second album, which had been recorded in between the *Imagine* sessions, with Eric Clapton, Klaus Voormann, and Ringo Starr among its musicians. Like *Yoko Ono/Plastic Ono Band, Fly* features a sometimes harrowing soundscape, far ahead of its time. Among its notable tracks are the soundtrack to the film of the same name, "Don't Worry, Kyoko" and "Mrs. Lennon," a ballad intended as an expression of anxiety about losing her identity, although the lyrics are typically enigmatic:

Husband John extended his hand, extended his hand to his wife
And he finds, and suddenly he finds that he has no hands

Yoko was in her customary Fluxus-like mode when she characterized "what happened with Fly." She had casually created a few songs, recorded them, and then she and Lennon shelved them in their voluminous library of material. After a time, John suddenly suggested it was a good time for her to release a new record, and rather than going into the studio in a formal sense with that intention, she went to her archive and fished out the content that evolved into her masterpiece. This method of letting pieces accumulate until it seemed logical to assemble them into an album format appealed to both John and especially Yoko as an alternative to consciously controlled creative exercises. As always, the key was letting go of conscious decisions in favor of pure intuition.

The notes on *Fly*'s album sleeve resemble a series of Fluxus drawings, poems, and gestures and contain her reversal of Marshall McLuhan's famous statement "The medium is the message": "Message is the medium." There are also photographs of mechanized musical instruments designed by Fluxus artist Joe Jones, a classically trained musician who ran the Tone Deaf Music Store in New York. These repetitive drone contraptions were built so that anyone could press a button and produce sound. Yoko used them on several songs. As she explained in her liner notes, "I was always fascinated by the idea of making special instruments for special emotions— instruments that lead us to emotions arrived by their own motions rather than our control. With those instruments I wanted to explore emotions and vibrations which have not been explored yet in music. I thought of building a house on a hill which makes different sounds on a windy day by the wind that goes through different windows, doors and holes. Then I met Joe Jones who's been making such instruments for ten years almost unnoticed. Joe built me eight new instruments specially for this album which can play by themselves with minimum manipulation." The phrase "almost unnoticed" could stand for a lot of Fluxus artists, and probably would have described Yoko, too, had she not met Lennon.

Robert Palmer makes a strong argument for *Fly*'s prescience. "Yoko's arrangements have elements that anticipate ensuing developments in rock. At a time when only a few bands used percussion instruments other than a standard drum kit, the assimilation of ethnic percussion and rhythms was well underway in Yoko's music, beginning with the *Fly* album. One of a kind percussion instruments made of metals and other materials that Fluxus artist Joe Jones brought to some of the sessions. Sparser percussion is also heard on several other pieces. If Yoko's emotional intensity dominates, she also reveals an affinity for an almost Miles Davis-like pacing of sounds and silences in the disc's quieter moments."

It should also be noted that Yoko's work with her live musicians in the studio had creatively evolved into an approach quite similar to that used by some of the most innovative musical artists of the time. Bob Dylan and Miles Davis, for instance, were both known for keeping their studio players in the dark about what they were going to be playing until about ten minutes before recording started. The idea was to knock them out of their well-worn grooves. In Yoko's case, though, it was often mistakenly viewed as unprofessionalism, yet another sign of the misogyny and racism she so routinely encountered during her career.

Toward the end of John's first year in New York, he and Yoko jointly dropped *Some Time in New York City*, a four-sided record combining studio material and live recordings, including a blistering sixteen-minute live version of "Don't Worry Kyoko" from a 1969 UNICEF benefit with George Harrison, Keith Moon of the Who, Delaney & Bonnie, and Billy Preston, among others. Another four songs had been performed in June 1971 with Frank Zappa and the Mothers of Invention at Fillmore East, an exotic partnering apparently suggested by Andy Warhol. The couple's activism is made explicit in every track on the first two sides of the album, including "Attica State," "Born in a Prison" (a critique of the education system), "Sunday Bloody Sunday" (the Irish troubles), and "Angela," a tribute to the aforementioned Ms. Davis. Yoko even sang harmony with John on a number of songs, just as McCartney used to do, almost.

Backing John and Yoko on a number of songs are Elephant's Memory, a Greenwich Village street band that had contributed to the 1969 soundtrack for the movie *Midnight Cowboy*. Yoko was so impressed by their untutored rawness that she would include them on another double album release, her 1973 dark bluesy romp *Approximately Infinite Universe*.

*Some Time in New York City* was both a commercial and critical flop. Lennon's emphasis on getting songs out as quickly as possible had caught up with him, resulting in manifestly substandard material. The album reached only forty-eight on the *Billboard* chart, and *Rolling Stone*'s Stephen Holden described it as "incipient artistic suicide." The songs are "shallow and derivative and the words little more than sloppy nursery-rhymes that patronize the issues and individuals they seek to exalt. Only a monomaniacal smugness could allow the Lennons to think that this witless doggerel wouldn't insult the intelligence and feelings of *any* audience." Time has done nothing to improve the album. In 2014, Garry Mulholland of *Uncut* called it "a contender for the worst LP by a major musical figure, its list of '70s left-wing clichés hamstrung by the utter absence of conviction within the melodies and lyrics."

Even with all this going on, Yoko never gave up on her search for Anthony Cox and Kyoko. In December 1971, they learned that Cox had surfaced in Houston, where his wife Melinda lived, and was challenging Yoko's custody award, hoping to regain equal access rights to Kyoko. Yoko and John flew to Texas for a court appearance. A judge ordered Cox to produce Kyoko but he repeatedly refused (she was staying at an undisclosed location with members of Melinda's family). His obstinacy earned him five days in jail for contempt of court. Yoko meanwhile had found a teacher who testified that the eight-year-old Kyoko had fallen years behind in her education. The judge ordered that the girl live with Yoko in anticipation of a final ruling. Instead of complying, Cox once again disappeared with Kyoko.

While Yoko remained largely silent about her daughter, John used their joint appearance on *The Dick Cavett Show* to launch a lively appeal to Anthony Cox's conscience. They sat side by side, he in his mock army tunic, she in a copper hot pants ensemble and black beret and choker. John, as usual, did most of the talking, urging Anthony Cox to return Kyoko, and promising that access would be shared between the parents. "All Yoko wishes is that now and again, Kyoko could be brought to [Tittenhurst] to spend some time with her mother," he said. "Yoko's going mad, as any mother would because her daughter is being withheld from her."

In fact, Yoko was unsure what to do. Part of her, however heartbroken, thought, "Leave them alone." At the same time, she felt that a good mother would do all she could to find her daughter. So Yoko and John hired private detectives to chase Kyoko, which turned out to be a disappointing experience. "One guy came to report, 'It was great! We almost had them. We were just behind them in a car, but they sped up and got away,'" recalled Yoko. "I went hysterical. "What do you mean you almost got them? We are talking about my child!"

While Yoko was coping with these personal agonies, it was John who was unraveling. The failure of *Some Time in New York City* cut him deeply. He buckled under the barrage of negative criticism, something he was far from accustomed to receiving. He wrote angry letters to editors of music magazines to complain of perceived slights by writers, or by George Martin, or by Paul McCartney. His former songwriting partner was also struggling post-Beatles, drinking heavily in response to unaccustomed press criticism of his attempts to launch a band with wife Linda. John and Paul did meet briefly in New York in 1972, but failed to make themselves or their relationship feel better. They at least managed to agree to quit insulting each other through the press and their music.

On the night of the 1972 election, Yoko and John joined a late party at Jerry Rubin's home. By the accounts of several in attendance, John was totally out of his head with drugs and pills and drink because he couldn't stand the fact that George McGovern lost. Yoko was stunned by what next occurred, as witnessed by the whole party, regardless of the reason, as Lennon appeared to approach the first woman he came across (or so it seemed) and pull her into the bedroom. Someone kindly put an album on to drown out the ensuing groping and groaning sounds (Yoko recalls it possibly being a Dylan record). Due to the fact that all the coats were piled in that bedroom, no one could go in to retrieve theirs so they could leave the party, and were thus forced instead to be innocent bystanders to a rather guilty betrayal.

She and John had occasionally discussed the cooling down of their love life and, after all, how could it go anywhere but down after having reached so incendiary a height? He was also utterly unable to reconcile his love for her with the fact that he was still so strongly attracted to other women. Yoko had begun to think that he was somehow repressed but the election night debacle was a wake-up call to be sure. "What am I doing here?" was her chief reaction to their joint dilemma, pondering that it was worth all their sacrifices if they were still totally in love with each other. If not, why continue? In this regard, they were not unlike any other couple entering a domestic doldrums. But hers was obviously much more public, and thus more painful.

As always, she turned her personal trauma into art. Her 1973 double LP *Approximately Infinite Universe* is a departure from her earlier experimental records. Using her normal voice and playing piano, she covers a lot of genres, from ballads to hard rock to funk and calypso. She also covers a lot of subjects, starting with the feminist themes she had advanced in her *New York Times* piece. The point of the song "Woman Power" is obvious but its hard-edged guitars, bass-heavy bottom, and funk groove seem to anticipate the mind of heavy-metal-rap crossovers that would become popular in the mid-1980s.

The title track is a chilling semi-autobiographical account of her loneliness and heroin use:

> In this approximately infinite universe I know a girl who's in constant hell
> No love or pill could keep her cool cause there's a thousand holes in her heart

"Now or Never," the first song recorded for the album, is a straightforward (for her) political song that joins the utopianism of "Imagine" to a protest of the Vietnam War and a bracing call for her adopted country to come to its senses:

> Are we gonna keep pretending things are alright?
> People of America when will we see it's now or never we've no time to lose

But the most stunning song on the album is the second track, "Death of Samantha." It is Yoko's processing of John's infidelity. She has characterized how it "came to her" in the studio on the morning after the notorious Rubin party, where she wrote it down quickly, described the key to her musicians, and they launched into what is indeed a harrowing dirge. Lennon reportedly came in from the rear room and declared that he couldn't listen to it because it was too painful. Maybe it was, but being Yoko, she included it on her new album. The most telling lyrics:

A friend lent me shades so I could hide my eyes that day
But something inside me something inside me died that day

"I think if I didn't put out *Approximately Infinite Universe* John would have been a very difficult person to deal with because I would have been very irritable or something like that. And I think that instead of resolving my emotions by going to a shrink or by talking with my partner, by making them into songs, that made it easier for me. I mean, it made my life easier."

Her son, Sean, always a passionate supporter of his mother's art and music, explained to *Hyperallergic* in 2017: "Yoko can pack a lot into a lyric. Approximately infinite? What does that mean? It helps to set up the contrast between the vastness of someone's potential experience in life and the more limited, painful situation of the woman who is the subject of the song."

# CHAPTER ELEVEN

# Honeymoon with History

ARLY IN 1973, Ono and Lennon moved from Bank Street
to a new apartment in the fading but still elegant Dakota
on Central Park West. A favorite of New York's cultural
community, home to Leonard Bernstein, Roberta Flack, and Lauren
Bacall, the nineteenth-century building featured spectacular views of the
park and a well-protected entrance behind a large black iron gate. Much
to the surprise of their real estate agent, the Dakota's board lifted its
prohibition on rock stars to allow John and Yoko to occupy apartment
72. They painted the walls white, shipped in some of their white carpets
from Tittenhurst, swore off all drugs, including weed, and tried to move
forward in their relationship as best they could.

At the same time, she felt the spark between them had gone out, and
she began to wonder if they were just going to stay together out of habit
and become one of those conservative couples who are together only due
to the circumstantial fact that they were married. "I said, 'Look John, it's
getting a little bit like we're not passionate about each other. Are we just
going to be one of those old conservative couples who are together just

because we're married?" Wouldn't that make marriage itself just another drug?"

They agreed to an open marriage but had no idea how to go about it. John spoke of a musician he knew who would casually walk up to the bar at the Plaza Hotel whenever he wanted company and wait only a few minutes for some random woman to pick him up. His nervous wife asked whether he wanted her to call the Plaza for him, but he was taken aback by the prospect of 'Mrs. Lennon' resorting to something as crass as that. Yoko was left to ponder his often wayward and mercurial intentions, and to wonder just what it was he really wanted from her.

As if to emphasize the new distance between them, John went back into the recording studio alone, without either Yoko or the Plastic Ono Band. Departing from his recent public causes, he sought a gentler tone that he hoped would help him reconnect with his familiar audiences. The title track was vaguely inspired by the self-help book *Mind Games: The Guide to Inner Space* by Robert Masters and Jean Houston, which Lennon had read. Yoko may not have been in the studio with him but she was clearly on his mind. The song's chorus "Love is the answer" is transformed at last singing to "Yes is the answer," a muted reference to her art installation at the Indica Gallery that had brought them together seven years before.

It was, in the end actually Yoko herself who suggested he spend some time away from her in Los Angeles, and also famously even chose his mistress. May Pang was the couple's twenty-two-year-old production assistant, and was both able, efficient as well as attractive. She had previously worked on their films as well as in Allen Klein's management office. She might indeed be a youthful Yoko surrogate during a time of travails for the troubled couple.

She approached the pretty girl with the chic New York hippie look and explained that John had never traveled by himself. He needed someone to look after him and Yoko asked if May would accompany him to the West Coast. "I have things to do here," she said, "and I'm not a very good wife, you know." She didn't intimate that part of May's job would be to potentially also sleep with her husband. But she likely knew what might happen, since she was well aware of his inability to be alone. Yoko did not appear to know that John and May had already hooked up behind her back.

For his part, the formerly possessive John suggested it was only fair that Yoko have an affair of her own, and proposed she sleep with David Spinozza, a guitarist who had played on *Mind Games*. "David's so beautiful," he said, "I wouldn't mind having sex with him."

John and May, carrying $10,000 in traveler's cheques, boarded a flight to LA on September 18, 1973. They were picked up at the airport by the disc jockey and their future publicist/spokesperson Elliot Mintz, and dropped at an apartment in West Hollywood owned by a legal associate of Allen Klein. John told Mintz that Yoko had kicked him out, they were taking a break from each other, and he didn't know if their relationship had a future. That would be the story he told anyone who asked for the duration of the trip, which was supposed to last two weeks and stretched on for fourteen months. "We're just playing life by ear," he said to *Melody Maker*. "And that includes our careers. We occasionally take a bath together and occasionally separately, just how we feel at the time."

Lennon later told *Playboy* he thought he was in for a great time in California. "I'd never been a bachelor since I was twenty or something, and I thought, 'Whoopee!' . . . And then I woke up one day and I thought, what is this? I want to go home! But she wouldn't let me come home . . . We were talking all the time on the phone and I would say, 'I don't like this, I'm getting in trouble and I'd like to come home, please.' And she would say, 'You're not ready to come home.' So what do you say? OK, back to the bottle."

From the very beginning, he could think only of returning to Yoko. "He called her every day," said his associate Mintz. "She'd also call me every day to see how he was doing and check that he wasn't harming himself or making a fool of himself, though at that stage she certainly wasn't looking for steps to get him back. Most of the time, John was in denial. But when he got drunk or high, he couldn't stop talking about Yoko and how much he needed her. The sense with him all the time was, 'What do I have to do to get out of here and back to her?'"

Nor was it easy for Yoko. On the one hand it was a relief to be out of the limelight that followed her husband everywhere, as she shared with *The Telegraph*: "I needed a rest. I needed space," she said. "Can you imagine every day of getting this vibration from people of hate? You want to get out of that." At the same time, she admitted to suffering marital-withdrawal symptoms. "For the first two weeks, my whole body was shaking. I couldn't stop. Because before that I was never without him, and now I was alone . . . But I didn't want to tell that to John because then he would have come back. I thought, 'I have to get over this because I can't be in a position where my existence relies on being with somebody.'"

The one member of the trio who seemed to adjust to the new circumstances well was May Pang. She accompanied Lennon everywhere in what he was soon calling "Lost Arseholes" and was universally considered kind and likable and a good influence on him. He sometimes treated her as a gopher, and sometimes as a lover, one of many he encountered on the trip. "May talks about that period as if it was her time with John," said the photographer Bob Gruen, a Lennon intimate, "but there are dozens of other women who can dispute that."

There were parties with his new friends Elton John, Warren Beatty, and Jack Nicholson, expensive weekend jaunts to Vegas, and endless drinking. "The guys were all drinking," May Pang reported in her own memoir. "And John was being one of the guys. Everyone was as blitzed as he. One of the bass players got into a car wreck. We got kicked out of A&M [studios] when someone threw a bottle of liquor down the console." John and Harry Nilsson were ejected from the Troubadour in West Hollywood for heckling the Smothers Brothers. "It was my first night on Brandy Alexanders," explained Lennon, while also claiming Nilsson encouraged him. He also said, more accurately in all likelihood: "I usually have someone there who says, 'Ok, Lennon. Shup up.'"

Lennon was a mean and sometimes violent drunk. "When we were out and about together and John was in that state, it used to be quite pitiful if a fan spotted him and came over for an autograph," said Elliot Mintz. "This was the Beatle who had made us all think, the John Lennon who lifted us onto a higher place of consciousness with his lyrics, who was always so witty and apropos. And here he is spilling a drink on his pants and not able to form a coherent sentence."

His famous "lost weekend," as he dismissed it in a sardonic reference to the 1945 noir classic about an alcoholic writer trying and failing to kick his addiction and regain his creative powers, would last until the beginning of 1975. While his substance abuse was notorious, his other serious problem at the time was his apparent addiction to his wife. Alcohol would frequently spike his pain over Yoko. "We had to hold him down in the back of the car to stop him kicking the windows in," said the drummer Jim Keltner. "He was lashing out . . . pulling my hair and screaming Yoko's name."

Lennon would later admit to *Playboy* his self-destructive bent, and that he and Nilsson were essentially trying to drink themselves to death. "It was 'let's all drown ourselves together. From where I was sitting, it looked like that. Let's kill ourselves but do it like Errol Flynn, you know, the macho, male way. It's embarrassing for me to think about that period because I made a big fool of myself. But maybe it was a good lesson for me. I wrote 'Nobody Loves You When You're Down and Out' during that time. That's how I felt."

Despite all the insanity, certain parts of Lennon's life improved during the Lost Weekend. One was his relationship with Paul McCartney, who was also in LA for a time, riding high on the success of his excellent *Band on the Run* album. Their business disputes were behind them, and their personal animosities had to some degree abated. They got together twice for jam sessions, including a magical one at a crowded Santa Monica beach house. "There were about fifty people playing," said John, "and they were just watching me and Paul. "

Also improved was Lennon's relationship with his son Julian, who at Pang's instigation saw his father for the first time in four years. John bought him a guitar and a drum machine and taught him a few tricks. "Dad and I got on a great deal better then," said Julian. "We had a lot of fun, laughed a lot and had a great time in general when he was with May Pang. My memories of that time with Dad and May are very clear—they were the happiest time I can remember with them."

As Lennon was acting out in LA, Yoko also kept herself busy but with considerably more creative aplomb. *Approximately Infinite Universe* had been released at the beginning of 1973. While more conventional than anything she'd done before—"She's not screaming, she's really trying to sing," observed Mick Jagger (who played a bit of guitar on the album) without sarcasm—it was nonetheless challenging to conventional pop sensibilities, both for its enthusiastic genre-hopping and Yoko's habit of subverting each genre with either musical departures, thematic contrasts, or unpredictable vocals. It enjoyed a better response than her earlier records. "It's easy to poke fun at Yoko Ono," wrote the *Evening Standard*. "Or at least it was for me until I'd heard this album and let its effect soak in. Yoko has more than a dilettante interest in the Women's Liberation movement but her strange ways of communicating have sometimes disguised her sincerity. But here . . . her lyrics cut through with stark simplicity. . . . The album is quite an achievement, managing as it does to be both musically satisfying and mentally stimulating."

Yoko followed that achievement with her fourth studio album, *Feeling the Space*, the title of which makes explicit reference to John's absence. She demonstrates a vastly more sophisticated awareness of the studio as a laboratory, which was perhaps easier for her without Lennon's huge aura always looming nearby. Her work with guitarist David Spinozza, a regular collaborator with James Taylor, is sparkling and liberated. Feminist themes prevail from track to track: "Women of Salem," "She Hits Back, and "Angry Young Woman." It was originally intended as another double album but the record label told her "a message album" needed to be brief and insisted it be edited. The record was released with liner notes that parodied personal ads at the back of magazines: the male band members are identified with birthdates, phone numbers, and vital statistics. Apart from some Lennon guitar on two songs, *Feeling the Space* is totally Beatle-free, and as a result, much more of a personal revelation.

The nature of Yoko's relationship with Spinozza is unclear, but *Rolling Stone* believes she followed John's own quirky instructions and became involved with him, perhaps mostly to assuage her husband's own guilt. A reporter for the magazine visited Yoko in the studio while she was working with the guitarist and pronounced her unusually happy. Spinozza had a reputation as one of New York's leading ladies' men, with several Balanchine ballerinas among his conquests in his past. Indeed, *Rolling Stone* heard Yoko's overtly sexy "Men Men Men" on *Feeling the Space* as an authentic account of their love affair:

Men, men: your pants are never tight enough, boots never long
enough

Your skin is never young enough, I want you to hold your
rightful position

In January 1974, *Rolling Stone* continued its ongoing Yoko-watch with the
following: "Reports persist that John and Yoko are at the grim and bear it
stage, all because she's in love with her session guitarist David Spinozza."
A slightly rare foray into the gossip-tabloid realm on their part. Yoko did
invite Spinozza to join her and the Plastic Ono Super Band on a tour of
Japan in 1974 but he backed out at the last minute for reasons that are
about as unclear as the rest of their relationship.

It was nevertheless a refreshing trip for her personally and professionally.
No one in Japan blamed her for breaking up the Beatles. They really
didn't care who broke up the Beatles or even that they had broken up at
all. She was appreciated as an artist in her own right. When she landed at
Tokyo's Haneda airport on August 9, she was warmly greeted by throngs
of journalists, photographers, and fans. Her half dozen art shows were
well attended. She looked more like her pre-Lennon self throughout
the ten-day stay, with her hair once again long and wild. The hot pants
were gone; she wore relatively demure white pantsuits and dresses. In
her interviews, she implored the people of Japan to "dream and project
something higher than just being economic animals." Asked about
Lennon on rare occasions, she was characteristically blunt: "When a thing
is over, it's over."

In the summer of 1974, Lennon and May Pang moved back to
Manhattan. The return has not been properly explained but it wouldn't
be wildly off base to assume that one day John woke up with a heroic
hangover and realized that he was going to die if he continued making

a comedy show of his decline in the company of equally self-destructive neurotics such as Keith Moon and Harry Nilsson. He stopped drinking and began work on what would become *Walls and Bridges*. May Pang was a large presence on the album: the subject of "Surprise, Surprise (Sweet Bird of Paradox)," a whispering voice on "#9 Dream," and production coordinator in the credits.

A selection of golden oldies Lennon had recorded with Phil Spector in chaotic Los Angeles sessions formed the basis of another album, *Rock 'n' Roll*. May was again credited as production coordinator. She also found the old photograph of a younger, leather-jacketed John in Hamburg that was used on the record's cover.

The two albums were released five months apart, in September 1974 and February 1975 and went a little way toward rehabilitating Lennon musically. *Walls and Bridges* hit the top ten in the US, and its initial single "Whatever Gets You Thru The Night" made number one on the *Billboard* Hot 100, the only Lennon song to do so in his lifetime. *Rolling Stone* said *Rock 'n' Roll* "lends dignity" to such classics as "Peggy Sue" and "Be-Bop-a-Lula," and described Lennon's singing as "tender, convincing and fond." The record reached number six in both the US and the UK, and John's evocative version of "Stand By Me" became a standard in its own right.

Yoko was in the studio at the same time, working on the album *A Story*, on which Spinozza has equal billing with Yoko as a producer. It is an intensely personal rumination on her childhood, girlhood, and womanhood. It features some of her most intriguing and powerful work to that date, and a further therapeutic working through of her relationship with Lennon. As she writes on "Heartburn Stew": "I threw my woman power in a pot of stew and waited for my love to come / But not a single word did i hear from him." The album is held in high regard today, and is indeed one of her finest. As the music critic Jake Cole, of *Spectrum Culture*, has written:

It's hard to say if *A Story* might have changed the public perception of Ono. There's no world in which she would have become a chart figure . . . but much like Lou Reed's own 1974 opus, *Coney Island Baby*, the record might have shown an avant-garde artist flexing her capabilities as a songwriter. As it stands, the album still sounds ahead of its time. In the odd embellishments of lush, baroque pop are sounds that Kate Bush would arrive at independently, while Ono's half-earnest, half-ironic lyrics, as smitten with lovers as they are ferociously critical of them, foresee the entire career of Fiona Apple. As fascinating a glimpse into Ono's powers as her own version of Plastic Ono Band . . . *A Story* is a curio that deserves wider exposure, and it may well be the best starting point for exploring Ono's solo discography.

It wasn't released because Lennon was on his way back into her life. The finality she had expressed toward him in Tokyo did not hold. She had begun to think life with John hadn't been as bad as she remembered. "It slowly started to dawn on me that John was not the trouble at all," she said to *Playboy*. "John was a fine person. It was society that had become too much. We laugh about it now, but we started dating again. I wanted to be sure. I'm thankful for John's intelligence . . . that he was intelligent enough to know this was the only way that we could save our marriage, not because we didn't love each other but because it was getting too much for me."

John would drop in on Yoko at the Dakota and tell her what he was up to and who he'd been dating. "I was telling him what happened to me because both of us had very bad times dating-wise, and we'd be laughing like crazy. I thought, 'This is great. We're just going to be great friends.'" He encouraged her to have sex with other men, but at the same time made clear that he didn't want her to fall in love with another man. He also asked repeatedly for permission to move back into the apartment. He was obviously as ambivalent and conflicted as he'd always been but, then again, that's part of what made him a uniquely brave and vulnerable artist.

Elton John, who was to popular music in the early 1970s what the Beatles had been in the early 1960s, would play a major role in their reconciliation. He had met Lennon in Los Angeles, and in between wild party sessions, they wound up in the studio together, with Elton playing a wicked piano and singing hot harmonies on Lennon's "Whatever Gets You Thru the Night." Elton, who had great confidence in the song's potential, made Lennon promise that if it became a number one hit, they would appear together onstage at some future concert. The song topped the charts and Elton invited Lennon to join him for the final show of his American tour at Madison Square Garden on November 28, 1974.

It was a sold-out date, with a screaming, amped-up audience that reminded Lennon of the Beatles' early tours. Before the curtain went up, a messenger arrived backstage with boxed white gardenias, one for Elton, the other for Yoko's estranged husband, and a note reading "Best of luck and all my love." She had also arranged for good seats for herself and Spinozza, although off to the side so Lennon would be unable to see her, knowing that her presence would throw him off. It was a good decision. Lennon was heard to say: "Thank goodness Yoko's not here. Otherwise, I know I'd never be able to go out there."

So nervous about the performance that he was sick before going onstage, actually a rather common pre-gig occurrence for him, he initially looked awkward to Yoko's eyes, bowing too quickly, and too often before the audience. He then settled in, performing "Whatever Gets You Thru the Night," "Lucy in the Sky with Diamonds," and "I Saw Her Standing

There," a brilliant McCartney pop bouncer, to an overwhelming response. Yoko caught up with him backstage afterward. They were photographed holding hands as May Pang and David Spinozza waited in the wings, presumably anxious for the historic moment to pass.

"Backstage at the Elton show, John was like he wanted to eat me up or something," said Yoko later. "But I said, 'Oh, please don't start this again.' I really didn't want to come back together so much because I thought it would be the same thing all over again. The entourage. People being so jealous, whispering to him. And the whole world hating me. And also, I lost my artistic credit. I couldn't make anything without people attacking it. My career was killed and my dignity as a person was totally gone."

She wasn't even sure she still loved him, or that he was still the man she had known. He'd "lost credit too, because people are saying he's crazy. I was thinking it's like a doomed love affair that could kill both of us. I thought we could be friends, though that never happened with either of my other ex-husbands."

On one of his visits to the Dakota, ostensibly to help him quit smoking as she had done, they reconciled. "We were in our bedroom and John said, 'So I really burnt the bridge, right? You won't let me come back.' And it was said in such a sad way that I said, 'Okay, you can come back.' I was thinking to myself, 'What am I saying?' but I couldn't help it."

In theory, that put her *A Story* album on the shelf, and for a very very long time. "It was all done and mastered and it was there, and then John and I came back together again. And I felt that I didn't want to go through the flack of people and reporters asking me, well you made this album, what's this song about. I thought, I'm not doing that to John, or to me, or to us. And it was great that I didn't. It was fine."

Of course, their reconciliation also spelled an abrupt end for May Pang. One moment she and John were considering buying a house in the

Hamptons. The next he was back with his wife, although she saw met him on and off for brief trysts until 1979, apparently with Yoko's liberal-minded permission. Such was life in Lennon-land. The photographer and friend Bob Gruen recalls John never being terribly serious about May: "But she was the one who ran his life, made all his arrangements. As he told me, 'I don't know how to get rid of her 'cause she's my phone-book.'" Lennon would later claim to have fond memories of Pang: "I may have been the happiest I've ever been . . . I loved this woman, I made some beautiful music and I got so fucked up with booze and shit and whatever."

It came as no surprise to anyone when Yoko and John renewed their vows in a ceremony in their candlelit apartment, both dressed in white as they had been for their original wedding. He showed her a diary he kept of his months in Los Angeles and burned it as proof of his commitment to their relationship. And it worked. "A lot of people when they separate get angry with each other," said Bob Gruen. "John and Yoko were never angry with each other, so when they reconciled, they seemed better friends than before."

Almost immediately, Yoko, forty-two, was pregnant again. She offered to have an abortion. "I didn't want to trap him. I wanted him to be there because he wanted to be there. I said, 'What do you want to do about it? It's up to you.' John said, 'We're gonna have it'. . . . I wanted to make it up to him for all the suffering I had caused him because of the separation. He wanted the baby, so I was determined to have it."

Yoko and John each had a child of their own, and neither would have won a parent-of-the-year award. John's engagement with Julian would prove fleeting, and he was cruelly dismissive of the boy in some of his public comments, all too candidly characterizing him as an "accident" in contrast to his second, a "planned" child. "Ninety percent of the people on this planet, especially in the West, were born out of a bottle of whiskey on a Saturday night, and there was no intent to have children," said John, lumping Julian in with the other "Saturday night specials." Not surprisingly, Julian would grow up to wonder about the sincerity of his father's heart and his public persona of idealism. "Dad could talk about peace and love out loud to the world but he could never show it to the people who supposedly meant the most to him," he said. "How can you talk about peace and love and have a family in bits and pieces, no communication, adultery, divorce?" Yoko, meanwhile, had completely lost track of Kyoko, although not for lack of trying, and the pain of that separation only added to her existing reservoir of childhood angst all her own.

At least both parents were admirably determined to do better this time, especially John, who doted on his wife, wary of her previous miscarriages, rarely letting her do anything for herself. At her request, they waited until the fourth month to announce the pregnancy. "John was so proud about it, and he tried to show the other guys 'it's fun to have kids.' And that really helped the whole world. Isn't that amazing?"

"We got back together, decided this was our life, that having a baby was important to us and that anything else was subsidiary to that," said John to *Playboy*. "We worked hard for that child. We went through all hell trying to have a baby, through many miscarriages and other problems. He is what they call a love child in truth. Doctors told us we could never have a child. We almost gave up. . . . We were told something was wrong with my sperm, that I abused myself so much in my youth that there was no chance."

They chose a natural childbirth. Sean Ono Lennon, eight pounds, ten ounces, was born in Manhattan at the Weill Cornell Medical Center on October 9, 1975, John's thirty-fifth birthday. It was a difficult delivery, with Yoko requiring blood transfusions afterward. John waited outside her room, worried for the health of both mother and child. "Then I hear this crying," he reported. "I'm paralyzed, thinking 'Maybe it's another one next door.' But it was hours. And I was jumping around and swearing at the top of my voice and kicking the wall with joy, shouting 'Fucking great!'"

When Yoko woke up, she learned from John that their child was in good health. They cried together and eventually discussed names. They settled on Sean, meaning "gift from God." Weakened by childbirth, Yoko didn't see Sean for three days. When they finally left the hospital, Yoko recalled, "John carried Sean through the long hallway of the hospital and got into the car. He sat still looking at the bundle in his arms and said, 'Okay Sean, we're going home.' And that was that."

John largely kept himself from the public eye afterward, retreating to that other living movie called "The Yoko Show," where he would quietly appear as her celebrated guest, a living ghost of New York. He used the private time carefully, to decompress and renew himself both personally and creatively.

The year 1975 also marked the final dissolution of Apple Corps, the troubled utopian venture launched by the Beatles in a burst of optimism that now felt like a century rather than a decade ago. It had taken five years of negotiation and litigation to close the business down. The four former bandmates all signed what Lennon caustically referred to as "The Famous Beatle Agreement," which at long last freed them from one another. As John stayed home, a retired living legend, looking after the baby, claiming to bake bread, Yoko took over management of the family business. He was forthright about his inability to look after his own affairs. "Somebody has to take care of business—and there's no way I can do it. So she had to do it . . . And so I had to contribute something, so I had the early relationship with Sean, which was fantastic."

In another, later interview with *Playboy*, he described his domestic scene more graphically: "When I was cleaning the cat shit and feeding baby Sean, she was sitting in rooms full of smoke with men in three-piece suits they couldn't button. . . . We had to face the business. It was either another case of asking some daddy to come solve our business or having one of us do it. Those lawyers were getting a quarter of a million dollars a year to sit around a table and eat salmon at the Plaza. Most of them didn't seem interested in solving the problems. Every lawyer had a lawyer. Each Beatle had four or five people working. So we felt we had to look after that side of the business and get rid of it and deal with it before we could start dealing with our own life. And the only one of us who has the talent or the ability to deal with it on that level is Yoko."

Perhaps thanks to her Yasuda banking background, and her father's insistence on her making appointments to see him, the Ono family business couldn't have been in better hands. Her assignment was to clean the corporate litter box, although she described it more as another conceptual art exercise. "I was doing it as a chess game," she said. "Not on a Monopoly level—that's a bit more realistic. Chess is more conceptual. Doing things conceptually means something like 4-D. The beyond possible dimension."

Theoretical as that sounds, Yoko's actual approach was hardheaded. She studied the legal and financial aspects of their lives, and before long was giving instructions to her lawyer and accountant rather than receiving instructions from them, a change they found difficult to deal with. "A lawyer would send a letter to the directors, but instead of sending it to me, he would send it to John or send it to my lawyer. You'd be surprised how much insult I took from them initially. There was all this, 'But you don't know anything about law; I can't talk to you.' I said, 'All right, talk to me in the way I can understand it. I am a director, too.'"

"They can't stand it," added John to the *Playboy* interviewer. "But they have to stand it, because she is who represents us. They're all male, you know, just big and fat, vodka lunch, shouting males, like trained dogs, trained to attack all the time. Recently, she made it possible for us to earn a large sum of money that benefited all of them and they fought and fought not to let her do it, because it was her idea and she was a woman and she was not a professional. But she did it, and then one of the guys said to her, 'Well, Lennon does it again.' But Lennon didn't have anything to do with it."

"I think that in order to survive and change the world," Ono cannily told *Playboy*, "you have to take care of yourself first. You have to survive yourself, first. I used to think that money was obscene, that artists didn't have to think about money. But to change society there are two ways to do it: through violence or through the power of money within the system. The law is not a mystery to me anymore, politicians are not a mystery to me. I'm not scared of the establishment anymore."

These years showed again that however difficult her early upbringing, Yoko owned considerable internal forces that she was able to marshall and use to make a stand in the larger world. She is credited with quadrupling the fortune earned by John's music. At the same time, she refused to apologize for leaving primary care of her child with her husband, an unusual step at the time. "I am very clear about my emotions in that area," she said. "I don't feel guilty. I am doing it in my own way. I may not be the same as other mothers, but I'm doing it the way I can do it. In general, mothers have a very strong resentment toward their children, even though there's this whole adulation about motherhood and how mothers really think about their children and how they really love them. I mean, they do, but it is not humanly possible to retain emotion that mothers are supposed to have within this society. Women are just too stretched out in different directions to retain that emotion. Too much is required of them. . . . So I said to John, 'I am carrying the baby nine months and that is enough, so you take care of it afterward'. . . . The responsibility is shared."

She even frankly suggested that after having carried the baby inside her for nine months, it was John's turn to do the work, rock star or not. While she stubbornly refused to see herself as beholden to any human tradition, the writer Alan Clayson notes that her father's impact on her appears to have been powerful, even in his absence. "For all the opaque mystery, he continued to govern family behavioral patterns, especially those rooted in appreciation of the value of money and the notion that hard work and tenacity are principal keys to achievement."

Her role at this stage in the Ono family further clarifies her position vis-à-vis her husband, or who was leaning on whom. Had John not met Yoko, it is doubtful that he, in his amorphous post-Beatles state of mind, would have been able to find the creative structure he so desperately needed to ensure his survival as an artist. Had she not been back in New York, he may have had no buffer against his dark self-destructive and misogynistic ways, and he may have succumbed to a life of dissipation in Los Angeles. And had he not been able to rely upon her emerging executive management skills, his financial future and artistic legacy may have been lost to those salmon-stuffed lawyers at the Plaza.

One interviewer from *Playboy* who sensed his dependency on Yoko told John it sounded like a "teacher-pupil" relationship. He agreed. "It is a teacher-pupil relationship. That's what people don't understand . . . I'm the famous one, the one who's supposed to know everything, but she's my teacher. She's taught me everything I fucking know. She was there when I was nowhere, when I was the nowhere man."

For Yoko, it seemed the natural order of things. "[John] had a lot of experience before he met me, the kind of experience I never had, so I learned a lot from him, too. It's both ways. Maybe it's that I have strength, a feminine strength. Because women develop it . . . in a relationship, I think women really have the inner wisdom and they're carrying that while men have sort of the wisdom to cope with society, since they created it. Men never developed the inner wisdom; they didn't have time. So most men do rely on women's inner wisdom, whether they express that or not."

# CHAPTER TWELVE

# A New Lease on Life

**P**ART OF THE AGREEMENT between Yoko and John when they began their new experiment in parenthood was that both would put their creative lives aside for a time. "We decided—well, mainly John decided—that from here on, he was going to raise Sean and I was going to look after the business," said Yoko to *Playboy*. "He had read somewhere that Paul had made $25 million. He said, 'We'll never have that kind of money. We haven't got any Daddy Eastman behind us, the way Paul has. I said, 'Okay, I'll try to make $25 million, but it's going to take me at least two years.' The deal was that we both stopped any kind of creative work. Neither of us was going to do any writing or recording, and I wasn't going to do any art."

Lennon's recording contracts all expired in 1976, and he did not seek to renew them. He found it liberating to live without the pressure of having to produce yet another hit album, which had been a constant in his life since the early years of the Beatles. "My contract," he said, "was the physical manifestation of being in prison." He wasn't terribly interested in what his former musical colleagues were producing and he didn't bother attending their shows. He dropped his subscription to *Billboard* and quit buying records. "He didn't want to know anything about what was happening in the business," said Bob Gruen. "If he ever had the radio on, it would be WPAT, the easy-listening station. He wasn't signed to anyone or contracted to anyone or trying to keep up with anyone or to surpass himself any more. He just dropped out."

John's former life as a Beatle was unobtrusive in his apartment, especially where Sean was concerned. None of the old records were played at home, none of the old stories rehashed. "Beatles were never mentioned to him," reported Lennon proudly. "He did see 'Yellow Submarine' at a friend's, so I had to explain what a cartoon of me was doing in a movie." There were musical instruments and an abundance of recording equipment in the capacious apartment, but he made no serious effort to produce new work, and a lot of the equipment fell into disrepair.

His sense of responsibility for Sean was sincere. He took real pride in how hard he worked as a parent. He changed diapers. He was in charge of getting Sean to sleep, often singing him old folk songs and lullabyes. He would get up in the wee hours for feedings, occasionally with a glass of Cognac to help get him through the night. Yoko would come home from a day at the office and complain of how tired she felt. Even though he might retort sardonically that he, too, was tired from spending twenty-four hours a day with their child, he knew he was fortunate to be able to share so fully in the first five years of Sean's life, and he liked to say that of the three of them, he got the best deal.

Being John Lennon, he also developed fierce and uncompromising opinions about child rearing. "The reason why kids are crazy is because nobody can face the responsibility of bringing them up," he once observed. The ones who survive are the conformists, he believed, and perhaps in an unconscious attempt to explain himself and Yoko, he surmised that the ones who don't fit their suits are either put in mental homes or end up becoming artists. An extreme analogy, but possibly apt in their unique domestic case.

Being prone to creative hyperbole, he also managed to make his house-husbanding sound like a revolutionary act. The women's movement, he liked to say, was just getting started. The real changes were far ahead in the distance, and it was men like him who were pointing the direction. Perhaps he was right with regard to his own personal evolution, which was considerable. He often expressed relief at no longer having to be a macho rock-and-roll singer, maintaining, "I got over that a long time ago. I'm not even interested in projecting that. So I like it to be known that, yes, I looked after the baby and I made bread and I was a househusband and I am proud of it. It's the wave of the future and I'm glad to be in on the forefront of that, too."

For public purposes, Yoko only spoke obliquely of her business activities. News of her deals would occasionally make the papers. There were stories that the Ono-Lennons were buying up all the great estates of the Eastern Seaboard, and that they owned $60,000,000 worth of dairy cows. She did invest in real estate, including an additional five apartments in the Dakota which were mostly used for storage. Yoko, once careless about such things, now even surpassed her mother as a clothing maven. Even a world-class shopper like Elton John once marveled at her collections. "Yoko has a refrigerated room just for keeping fur coats. She's got rooms full of the clothes-racks like you see at Marks and Spencer. She makes me look ridiculous." After his tour of the Dakota, Elton rewrote Lennon's recent hit: "Imagine six apartments / It isn't hard to do / One is full of fur coats / The other's full of shoes."

Two grand rooms on the main floor were converted to Studio One, the headquarters of Lenono Music, where Yoko would go to work every day. It had a wall of eighty-eight white filing cabinets under its high ceilings, with a library ladder to reach the highest of them. She worked at a massive desk inlaid with gold, surrounded with pictures of herself and John on the walls.

She did buy a farm in Delaware County, upstate New York, to take advantage of tax breaks afforded American dairy farmers, and stocked it with highly productive Holstein-Friesian cattle (122 cows and ten bulls) at a total cost of close to $2.7 million. She was able to close the deal with only $375,000 in cash, providing a note for the balance. It was one of several farms in her portfolio.

Perhaps her most surprising purchase was a mansion on "Billionaire's Row" in Palm Beach. Built by the famed architect Addison Mizner in 1919, the massive residence sits on a 1.3-acre property with two pools, a tennis court, and direct beach access. It had previously been owned by a Vanderbilt. Yoko paid $725,000 for the property without visiting it, so as not to inflate the asking price. After some restoration work, she resold it for $3.15 million six years later. It was a beautiful old Art Deco place. One room had a high ceiling like a ballroom. The perfect place to park her husband, who used to love just sitting at the window and looking out at the ocean.

The couple was as eye-popping a presence in Florida as anywhere else. "Lennon was often chased by giddy teenagers while driving down the well-manicured streets of Palm Beach in his red Cadillac," wrote Palm Beach chronicler James Goss in his book Pop Culture Florida. When Julian visited Florida, John hired a yacht to host his sixteenth-birthday party. It was buzzed by young women in a speedboat shouting "We love you, John."

Feeling Palm Beach was too far for regular visits, Yoko searched from Rhode Island to Virginia for another estate. Fred Seaman, John's assistant, was dispatched to scout the properties on her behalf. She settled on a secluded waterfront mansion at Cold Spring Harbor in the quiet community of Laurel Hollow. It was an ivy-covered Tudor-style house sitting on a large property with a grand view of the harbor, with more than a dozen rooms on three floors, including a large master bedroom with a balcony that offered a spectacular view of the harbor. They had a small beach, as well as a private dock. There is even footage on YouTube of John and Yoko relaxing in lawn chairs on the bluff, with him cornily singing "Oh Yoko!" for the camera.

Yoko bought art through Sam Green, a New York dealer with connections to some of the city's most interesting people, including the Rothschilds and Greta Garbo. Yoko had known Green since her Fluxus days. He helped her build an impressive collection, with works by her friend Andy Warhol, as well as by Jean-Michel Basquiat, and Auguste Renoir's *Jeunes filles au bord de la mer*, which had belonged to the French American soprano Lily Pons.

Green also got Yoko invested in ancient Egyptian art and artifacts, which appealed to her in part because of her belief that she and John were reincarnations of ancient Egyptian royalty. He found her a gold sarcophagus which took pride of place in the Egyptian room at the Dakota, and a twelve-foot statue of the goddess Sekhmet that was eventually donated to a Philadelphia park in return for a large tax receipt.

In January 1977, Green's contacts informed him of a clandestine archaeological dig aimed at unearthing an ancient temple in Egypt. The dig, he said, was low on funds. Yoko agreed to wire money to the treasure hunters and arranged to visit the site. It was a tricky expedition, given that Egyptian authorities were stepping up efforts to protect the nation's heritage from international grave robbers. Yoko and John checked into the Nile Hilton in Cairo. He toured the city while Yoko attempted to finalize arrangements to reach the dig. It turned out the site and its treasures did not exist. Green's contact had been planning to pass off some inferior artifacts to the unsuspecting Yoko, never expecting her to actually visit the site herself.

Their return to the US was delayed because the phone system was out of order at the Cairo Hilton. Yoko could not contact the numerologist who advised her on the safest routes to fly. This was the unconventional side of her business practices. She rarely made a decision without consulting her numerologist. She also read tarot cards and kept a full staff of psychics busy. She once admitted to having five psychics altogether, "But never more than three at one time."

Notwithstanding the mystic gloss she insisted on putting on her investments, the guiding philosophy for her appears to have been quality, strong brands, and good locations. Lennon took pride in his wife's acumen, confiding that "Sean and I were away for a weekend and Yoko came over to sell this cow and I was joking about it. We hadn't seen her for days. She spent all her time on it. But then I read the paper that said she sold it for a quarter of a million dollars. Only Yoko could sell a cow for that much."

He also admitted that his wife had toughened him up when it came to his attitude toward money, since he used to feel guilty about being successful and having so much. He even imagined that this was the reason he squandered his own wealth over the years, either by giving it away or by allowing himself to be deceived by managers of various sorts. Yoko helped him accept that wealth wasn't inherently evil, assuming you used it properly.

For Yoko, business was a godsend, especially given that she'd consciously put aside her art for a period of time. She was better able to deal with a lot of bad memories of how she'd been treated in the early part of her relationship with John, when not only Beatles fans but the band's employees, too, wanted her gone from the scene. She would be in bed with John and Beatles assistants would waltz right into the room and speak to him as though she wasn't there. Back then she was invisible. Even hangers-on who considered themselves sympathetic to her tended to discount her individuality and talent, telling her that she needn't work anymore now that she was Mrs. Lennon.

For a woman who had always been her own breadwinner and had earned her freedom and control over her own career, sometimes at great personal expense, the dismissiveness had been unbearable. She intimated to *Playboy* that "This society doesn't understand that the woman can be castrated, too," she said. "I felt castrated. Before I was doing all right, thank you. My work might not have been selling much, I might have been poorer, but I had my pride. But the most humiliating thing is to be looked at as a parasite."

Now in firm control of a family fortune estimated in the late 1970s to be worth $150,000,000, thanks in no small part to her endeavors, she was able to leave those wounds in the past and regain her pride through her many financial accomplishments.

While the Lennons were deliberately keeping themselves out of the public eye, the newspapers continued to be fascinated with them. As the years went by, with no further albums or art exhibitions from them, rumors about their activities ran wild. People said Lennon had become a recluse in the manner of Howard Hughes, or that he was being held captive in the Dakota fortress by his sorceress of a wife. Stories about their lives, their relationship, their decision to "go underground," and never-ending speculation about possible Beatles reunions were standard entertainment-page fare throughout the seventies. Lennon was able to see the lighter side of all this celebrity madness, even calling himself Greta Hughes or Howard Garbo to get through it all. Despite their best efforts, they never stopped being in the press, with the odd result being that there seemed to be more written about them when they weren't talking to the press than when they were.

Beatles reunions were never a serious possibility, despite offers as high as $50 million for a single concert. Lennon's relationship with McCartney had come apart again early in John's new embrace of his revolutionary fatherhood mode. Some reports have Paul turning up at the Dakota with a guitar. The first few times, John let him in, but eventually he had laid down the law, requesting that he call before coming over. Given that it wasn't 1966 anymore (in fact, it was April 24, 1976, on April 24th), and turning up at the door wasn't quite the same anymore, he suggested his old friend should give him a ring first. As he shared with *The Express*, McCartney was somewhat upset by the demand, according to Lennon, who claimed to mean it in a friendly way, in that he was busy taking care of a child all day and didn't have time for impromptu playdates. They never saw each other again.

Nor was Lennon spending time with the other Beatles. He claimed not to listen to their music, or to care much what was happening in their lives, that he was too busy living his own life to be following what other people might be doing. Although he admitted that George Harrison's book, *I Me Mine*, had touched a nerve by not crediting Lennon as an influence, leaving him to imagine that George even still felt resentment toward him for splitting up the group. An odd perspective to have, given that Harrison had wanted to leave the group as early as 1966, practically before John had met Yoko. Paradoxically, Lennon was mentioned by Harrison more often in the book than either McCartney or the Beatles in general.

Despite the headlines and idle speculation, the Ono-Lennons were just getting on with their lives without the Beatles or anyone else. John really was looking after Sean, teaching him to swim, baking bread, and complaining about the annual rock concerts across the street in Central Park that kept his son from sleeping. Yoko really was buying furs, cows, and estates. John had an inkling that he should be making more of his life, said Elliot Mintz, but he was never unhappy enough or motivated enough to make a change.

In the summer of 1977, Yoko and John took Sean to Japan for the first time. John enrolled in an intensive six-week Berlitz course to learn the language before they departed, and did his best to present a respectable face to Yoko's family. He prepared handmade invitations to invite a hundred of her relatives to a reception to meet Sean, and even took a lot of trouble to look very dapper for Yoko. She was a bit puzzled by his enthusiasm, since she was minimally interested in people solely because they were relatives. To some degree, she felt that these were the people she had abandoned in order to make her own independent life. But she went along with John's sincerely felt wishes regardless, posing alongside him for a panoramic family photo. He was nattily dressed in a black suit with a pink carnation.

They toured the Ueno Zoo with Sean, and spent several weeks at Karuizawa, the mountain resort town where Yoko had spent time with her brother and her mother, and where her own father had played piano before entering the family banking business. Here they embarked again on a healthier lifestyle, eating fresh fish and taking mineral baths and massages in a serious effort at detoxification. To Yoko, the resort was very much like the Hamptons except for its mountainous location. There is a coffeehouse in a pine forest near Karuizawa and she and John fell in love with the place, finding themselves going there almost every day with Sean. To get there, you had to cycle for about thirty minutes from the town but they loved the spot. There was a big hammock in the backyard, and she, John, and young Sean used to spend the afternoons lying in it, giggling, singing, and watching the sky.

They would spend four consecutive summers in Japan, with John studying up on Kabuki theater, calligraphy, and the haiku. Despite having no time for honors or heraldry in his home country, he designed a personal chop, or official seal, which he would apply to his drawings. On their return to the US after the first Japan trip, Anthony Cox materialized once again. Kyoko was now fourteen and had spent her formative years in the Church of the Living Word. Ironically, the cult had given her the only experience of stability she'd known in her young life.

Her father, Tony Cox, was in difficult circumstances once again, and living in Oregon. On November 10, 1977, he called the Dakota to suggest some sort of rapprochement. Kyoko was anxious—excited at the prospect of seeing her mother and John again, but fearful of more chaos in her life. John answered the call and had a friendly chat with Cox. They discussed their mutually deceased fathers, but failed to make concrete plans for further contact, and Cox went silent once again.

John Lennon turned forty on October 9, 1980. The onslaught of middle age, along with Sean reaching school age, seems to have given him a push back toward productive creative activity. It also helped that Paul McCartney and Wings were enjoying enormous success, playing to larger crowds on longer tours than even the Beatles had managed. He was still writing number one hits and now also Oscar-nominated songs for James Bond movies. *Band on the Run* hadn't been a one-off: it was the first of seven platinum albums for McCartney and Wings, including the hugely successful *Venus and Mars*, and *Wings over America*. The old Beatles competitiveness was not completely extinguished. It never could be.

Yet another factor was Lennon's dissatisfaction with the whole Beatles oeuvre. His old producer George Martin visited him for dinner at the Dakota, and being ever the distinguished gentleman, overlooked John's insults toward him in the 1970 *Rolling Stone* article. Yoko remained tactfully out of the way for the whole evening, and the two old friends just reminisced about the good old times. When Martin challenged John about his disparaging comments about him and his bandmates in the press, Lennon wasn't terribly apologetic. Always prepared to put his foot in his mouth even further, as if his insecurity couldn't prevent it, Martin reported that he was told, "You know, George," he said, "if I could, I would record everything the Beatles did all over again."

"Blimey, John," returned Martin. "Everything?"

"Everything."

"What about 'Strawberry Fields.'"

"Especially 'Strawberry Fields.'"

As another possible source of John's drastic doubts about his own musical accomplishments, John and Yoko began having long conversations about why Paul McCartney's songs were covered more frequently than his. When he was feeling secure enough, which was not very often, Lennon would acknowledge that he'd had two great partnerships, one with Paul McCartney, the other with Yoko Ono. But being incapable of just letting it be, he usually felt compelled to add that he had "discovered" both of them and that wasn't bad going in the end.

John decided to sail with a crew to Bermuda, where Sean would meet him. Rejuvenated by an unexpectedly adventurous passage through a vicious storm, he was seized by a desire to make music again. While visiting some Bermuda pubs, he happened to hear a new American band, the B-52's, and was impressed that they featured female singers doing high-pitched vocalizations that reminded him of Yoko. He called her on the phone and shared the surprising fact that there were some new artists who were "doing her act" and that this time around, the public might be more ready for the inimitable style she had first featured so much earlier in her career.

It was suddenly a swiftly moving creative current for the notoriously lazy Lennon. Totally in awe of his young second son, he wrote a song about Sean, "Beautiful Boy," another one about Yoko, "Woman," and a third about himself and how the music world seemed to be moving on without him, "Watching the Wheels." Yoko hired Jack Douglas, who had engineered *Imagine* and gone on to work with Patti Smith, the New York Dolls, Aerosmith, and others, as the record producer. By the summer of 1980, they were recording at the Hit Factory on West Forty-Eighth Street in New York. There were no drugs or alcohol evident at the sessions, which were even timed to allow John to get home to put Sean to bed every night. Times had changed.

The idea for the album, *Double Fantasy*, was that John and Yoko would alternate, track by track, in a musical dialogue. Lennon led with the up-tempo rock song "(Just Like) Starting Over." Yoko followed with the erotic and punk-influenced "Kiss Kiss Kiss," in which she gasps her way to an apparent orgasm. Yoko felt as if John were saying in his song, Okay, we had the energy in the sixties, in the seventies we separated, but let's start over in the eighties. He's reaching out to her, reaching out after all that's happened, over the battlefield of past families, and it is more difficult this time around. In "Kiss Kiss Kiss," which was the B side to "Starting Over" on its release as a single, she felt it was the other side of the same issue. There is the sound of a woman coming to a climax on it, and she is crying out to be held, to be touched. Altogether, she felt that both sides were a prayer to change in the eighties.

Implicit in much of the songwriting was a sense that their marriage had gone through a rough patch over the summer but that both of them were committed to seeing it through, which seems to have been the case. Both seemed to gain a new lease on life by returning to creative work. Once they were satisfied with the material for the album, they had a publicist leak that they were back in business, which brought a long line of record companies eager to make a deal. John insisted that they were signing as a couple, and that any label failing to appreciate Yoko's full involvement in the project would be written off, and at least one was, for just that reason. In the end, they signed with David Geffen, who had worked with Jackson Browne, Linda Ronstadt, the Eagles, and many other mostly West Coast artists in the seventies before retiring briefly for health reasons. His newly formed Geffen Records was his own comeback project. That Geffen was careful to speak to Yoko first and also to rate her as an equal contributor to the project pretty much sealed the deal for Lennon.

The single "(Just Like) Starting Over" was released in late October and the album *Double Fantasy* followed on November 17, 1980. The single received abundant airtime but did not come close to the top of the charts. Sales of the LP were respectable, reaching number eleven in the US and fourteen in the UK, although the critical response was harsh. "Those expecting the return of the mythical Lennon—a man with an insightful, brilliant mind and a biting wit—will be sorely disillusioned," wrote the *Los Angeles Times*. "Isolated instances of strong music can't redeem an album whose emotional core is as vapid as this one's." Yoko, unexpectedly, fared better. "Her contributions outclass John's," said the same newspaper. "'Kiss Kiss Kiss' is the record's most ambiguous, challenging song as it obscures the line between love and violence, and 'Give Me Something' and 'I'm Moving On' at least question John's complacency."

These intensely personal themes had already come into sharp focus in an interview with Andy Peebles of the BBC on December 6, two days before his murder. The journalist asked the couple, "What about your private life and your own sense of security these days?" John responded wistfully, "Yoko told me, you'll be able to walk down the street here (in New York). I can go right out this door now and go to a restaurant. You want to know how great that is?"

John and Yoko would do another interview for RKO Radio on the morning of December 8. He no doubt startled listeners with his observation that "we've been together longer than the Beatles, do you know that? People always think in terms that John and Yoko just got together and then the Beatles split. We've been together longer than the Beatles!"

Later that same day, the couple gave David Sheff of *Playboy* a 20,000-word interview, in what would be their final media encounter, to publicize the new album. As usual, John did most of the talking, rehashing a lot of old Beatles controversies and explaining his time away from the recording studio. Perhaps the most interesting part of the conversation was Yoko's response to the conspiracy theorists who believed her to have put John under a spell and kept him to herself: "Why should I bother to control anybody?"

While John was contemplating the meaning of his fortieth birthday and his relationship with his lovely son, Yoko was still surprising interviewers with her quirky take on popular culture, extolling the virtues of pop music, a medium in which she had always been something of an outlier. "Pop music is the people's form," she told David Sheff, "Intellectuals trying to communicate with the people usually fail. Forget all the intellectual garbage, all the ritual of that, and get down to the real feeling—simple good human feeling—and express it in a sort of simple language that reaches people. No bullshit. If I want to communicate with people I should use their language. Pop songs *are* that language."

She also expressed her ongoing puzzlement that the public and the media were so fascinated by her personal beliefs and private life, and what she had been up to for the last five years. "I'm amazed that people can be so concerned about someone else's life," she told *Playboy*. "I mean, what about their own lives? Every life is interesting, every life is an encyclopedia. There's not much difference between our lives and someone else's."

That ironic observation has to go down in the annals of great understatements for sure.

# PART THREE

# AFTER THE END: LEARNING TO SWIM ALONE

*"I can swim like everyone else, only I have a better memory than them. I have not forgotten my former inability to swim. But since I have not forgotten it, my ability to swim is of no avail and in the end I cannot swim."*

— Franz Kafka, *Notebooks*, 1920

# CHAPTER THIRTEEN

# Passing the Time

To PARAPHRASE JOHN LENNON'S most ambitious song, "A Day in the Life": we all read the news that day, oh boy, about an unlucky man who made the grade. He was happy that day. "John and I were gloriously happy," Yoko later recalled. "In our minds, we were a team—old soldiers." In retrospect, she must have felt that it was exactly what Lou Reed later called "a perfect day" in his tenderly melancholy song of that title: "I'm glad I spent it with you, such a perfect day you just keep me hanging on."

John arose at 7:30 on December 8, put on his black kimono, and stood looking out at the Manhattan skyline from his living room window. Sun was streaming into the room when Yoko found him. It was one of the brightest, warmest winter days in New York in some time. They dressed and walked to Café La Fortuna on West Seventy-First Street where John ordered a breakfast of eggs Benedict. Afterward he got a fresh haircut and returned to the apartment to give his attention to the waiting *Rolling Stone* photographer Annie Leibovitz.

Leibovitz photographed a naked John clinging like a child to the fully clothed Yoko on their bed, underlining (or perhaps playing with) his notorious dependence on her. She had wanted to capture him on his own. He insisted that Yoko be in the frame. The moment the image was taken Lennon told her she had "perfectly" captured his relationship with his wife.

Around 1:00 p.m., the Onos did their RKO Radio interview and headed for the Hit Factory studios. On their way out of the Dakota, a young man wearing a scarf and a dark overcoat asked John to sign his copy of *Double Fantasy*.

Yoko and John spent almost five hours at the studio, working on "Walking on Thin Ice," a single by Yoko that John was convinced would be her first number one hit. David Geffen popped by to tell the couple that *Double Fantasy* had already gone gold, meaning that 250,000 copies had shipped. They packed up just after 10:00 p.m. and traveled by limo up Eighth Avenue to Columbus Circle and north up Central Park West to the Dakota. The plan was to say good night to Sean and head to the Stage Deli restaurant. Yoko was first out of the vehicle. John followed, carrying a tape machine.

The same young man who had asked Lennon for an autograph earlier in the day was waiting for him. Mark David Chapman was a mentally disturbed twenty-five-year-old who believed his musical hero, a onetime prophet of peace and love, had sold out. As John passed, Chapman dropped into a crouch and fired five hollow-point bullets from a .38 Special revolver. One bullet missed and crashed through a window. The other four hit John in the shoulder and back from a distance of less than ten feet. He staggered up the steps to the Dakota's reception area and said, "I'm shot! I'm shot!" before falling to the floor.

Within seconds, Yoko was at his side screaming, "John's been shot! Help me! Help me!"

A doorman took the gun from Chapman's hand and a front-desk worker covered Lennon with his uniform jacket before alerting the authorities. A call went out over the police radio: "Man shot, One West Seventy-Second."

Chapman stood on the street reading J. D. Salinger's *Catcher in the Rye*, which he considered a manifesto of anti-phoniness, until police arrived to arrest him. He was put in handcuffs without incident and later charged with second degree murder. He would be sentenced to twenty-two years to life in prison. His sad bids for parole have been perpetually declined.

The first officers on the scene recognized that Lennon's injuries were serious. He was pleading profusely through the mouth. Rather than waiting for an ambulance, they loaded him into a squad car and sped to Roosevelt Hospital. Yoko followed in another police vehicle. They passed John off to staff at the emergency ward but it was already too late.

John Winston Ono Lennon, age forty, was dead on arrival at 11:07 p.m. More than a thousand people had gathered on the street outside the Dakota by 1:00 a.m., many of them crying, many of them reporters. They would stay for days. Some for months and years.

The front page of the *New York Times* the next day featured a picture of a distraught Ono being led out of the hospital by a policeman and David Geffen. A policeman said she had been "very hysterical" after the shooting, sobbing, "Tell me it isn't true."

An official statement was released on her behalf the following day: "There is no funeral for John. Later in the week we will set the time for a silent vigil to pray for his soul. We invite you to participate from wherever you are at the time . . . John loved and prayed for the human race. Please do the same for him. Love, Yoko and Sean." The inclusiveness of the statement was consistent with her approach to art and life.

Yoko has said very little about what went through her mind that tragic evening. We don't know if she asked herself why it had happened, or if she was next, or why she was spared, or whatever else might have flashed through her mind on the sidewalk, in the squad car, in the hospital. She had been hated, the one more likely to receive death threats, over the years. Surely the whole fourteen years of their life together—fourteen sometimes exhilarating and sometimes horrible years, filled with all that music and all those happenings and a million private moments—must have flashed before her eyes. Even a decade later, she was to say, "I don't know if I'm ready to talk about it. I'm sure most people can imagine what I went through."

All we really know for certain is that her first concern, after it was clear there was no hope for her husband, was to get home to Sean so he would learn of his death from her rather than from television.

In the days that followed, the Lennon song "Imagine" would be played to death. "I was still shaking in bed," commented Yoko. "All night these people were chanting or playing John's records. What I learned was that I didn't have much control over my destiny or fate—anything."

The darkly schizophrenic and accidentally elegiac album *Double Fantasy* would suddenly top the charts and become one of the worst records ever to win album of the year at the Grammy Awards. "(Just Like) Starting Over" would hit number one, as would the follow-up single, "Woman." Annie Leibovitz's photo of the naked John embracing Yoko was released on the cover of *Rolling Stone* in January 1981, part of a whole issue dedicated to Lennon's life and death. In 2005, it would be chosen as the best magazine cover of the previous four decades. A brown paper bag would be delivered to the Dakota from the coroner's office containing John's clothes and the belongings he had on him at the time of his death. It struck Yoko as strange that a larger-than-life figure such as her husband could have his physical legacy delivered to her in a plain brown bag.

Two years later she was still reeling from the murder. "To tell you the truth," she said, "I still haven't gotten over the initial shock." Her life was irretrievably changed, in ways that she would never stop processing. Mostly, she felt lonely. "I feel the loneliness of many, many people now, so I'm trying to find a method of how we can *not* be lonely." She said she couldn't imagine herself in a relationship with another person, "being concerned about this person and this person's career or this person's neuroses, listening to the person's childhood, what the mother is like and the father and the brother. I mean, I can't connect like that with a person . . . Also, I'm still in this apartment where John and I shared a happy life, and everything is as it was—John's picture is over there, et cetera. It's not that I'm being Miss Havisham, you know, in Dickens: 'Let's keep everything like the wedding night.' It's not that. I don't intend to live as a widow per se, but I don't seek out that sort of communication at this point."

She credits Sean with helping her through the worst moments. "Work is consoling and gives you strength," she observed, "but without your family, who needs you? Sean gave me the drive to survive. Some days, I felt life wasn't worth it, but it was important that I stay around for Sean. Or he would have lost two parents."

From 1981 to 2021, Yoko Ono would continue to reside in the ghost-filled Dakota apartments, playing two roles throughout the long decades. The first was as custodian of her late husband's estate and legacy, a never-ending responsibility she took seriously. The other role was the widowed singer-songwriter and solo artist engaged in an expansive return to the art world in which she was to be reclaimed as a groundbreaking feminist artist and social activist, exactly what she had been all along.

The first role—"keeper of the wishing well," she called it—was thrust upon her in the immediate wake of Lennon's death. Several Lennon fans committed suicide in despair over his passing in the days that followed, prompting her to tell the newspapers that each one of us had to find the courage to carry on. On December 15 she released another statement directed at the hundreds of thousands of people who had gathered across from the Dakota in Central Park for ten minutes of silence and prayer the day before: "Bless you for your tears and prayers. I saw John smiling in the sky. I saw sorrow changing into clarity. I saw all of us becoming one mind. Thank you. Love, Yoko." She received thousands of letters from people upset at John's death, many of them asking her for help in coping with their feelings. She read them all.

There were endless memorials. No other musical personality has been kept alive so assiduously by fans and the public. "The death of John is something you can clearly understand is not finished yet," Yoko would say almost a quarter century after the event occurred.

His Beatles colleagues, George, Paul, and Ringo, released a tribute song, "All Those Years Ago," in 1981. Elton John wrote "Empty Garden (Hey Hey Johnny)," and both Yoko and Sean would join him onstage when he performed it at Madison Square Garden in the summer of 1982. Paul Simon, Queen, David Bowie, and Bob Dylan were among the many others to write or perform musical elegies.

There were physical monuments, most notably Strawberry Fields, a dedicated tear-drop shaped area of Central Park across the street from the Dakota, dedicated in 1985 and funded and maintained by Yoko. It has served as a destination and gathering place for Lennon fans ever since.

The year 1990 was the ten-year anniversary of Lennon's death; it would also have been his fiftieth birthday. Yoko knew something had to be done. "I thought that somehow I wanted to direct the celebration into a positive direction," she said. "Already last year, people started to say, 'What about this, what about that?' The suggestions were made mainly from a business point of view. I didn't want the year to become a pandemonium of trying to sell Lennon out on the market. I wanted something that was more positive and in the spirit of 'Imagine.'"

The outcome was a United Nations ceremony commemorating Lennon's life: "Imagine All the People." Yoko made a brief and familiar statement, one drawn from her early book *Grapefruit*: "The dream we dream alone is only a dream. But the dream we dream together is reality." She played a recording of John pleading for peace, and a thousand radio stations around the world simultaneously broadcast "Imagine" to an estimated billion people.

On it went. On she went. In 2000, Yoko founded the John Lennon Museum in Saitama, Japan, to preserve knowledge of Lennon's life and music. Among the displays are some of Yoko's personal memorabilia as well as a "reflection room" full of chairs facing a slideshow of moving words and images designed to encourage people to pause and think about not thinking. Not thinking had always been one of her most profound thoughts.

In 2002, Yoko bought John's childhood home in Liverpool and gave it to the National Trust, a gesture I've always found to be a haunting overlap with one of his songs from the *White Album*, "Happiness Is a Warm Gun": "A soap impression of his wife which he ate and donated to the National Trust." For Yoko it was a heartfelt gift: "I loved the fact that his bedroom was preserved exactly as it was. He spoke about it so much. When I'm there, I think about what he was dreaming. Because the dreams he had there influenced the whole world, eventually. That's why I like young people to see it. They might think they don't have anything—a piano, say, And they can see what little he had, and yet how many beautiful dreams started there."

In 2006, New York City welcomed an annex to the Rock and Roll Hall of Fame in SoHo. It closed in 2010 after the financial crisis weakened the city's tourism trade. Its final exhibition had been dedicated to John Lennon's New York years, to which Yoko contributed an array of his personal effects, including the brown paper bag from the coroner's office containing the clothes he was wearing the night he was shot.

In 2018, Yoko created a piece of art called *Sky* for an art-and-design program directed by the New York City Transit authority. It was installed at the Seventy-Second Street subway station near the Dakota as yet another memorial to John.

Those are only the highlights of the onslaught of commemoration that has kept alive the memory of a unique artist, musician, and cultural personality.

For Yoko, the legacy of her dead husband was more complicated than the public might have imagined, and sometimes darker. There were so many dimensions, including all the people they had known together, some of whom were eager to exploit John's fame and her vulnerability. A former employee, Fred Seaman, walked off with tapes of John's unreleased recordings. Seaman and May Pang cashed in with quickie books about their relationships with John, and a scurrilous 1998 biography of Lennon by Albert Goldman, now largely discredited, made him and most of the people around him look nasty and depraved. Over time, Yoko developed a method for dealing with the negativity, later sharing with the *Tampa Bay Times*: "To be a widow is hell. Hell. Total, total nightmare of despair. The widows of the world, they understand this."

When John passed away so suddenly . . . I discovered that there were people who specialized in taking advantage of widows. Nobody thinks they will be a widow, and when you are, you are so shell-shocked you don't feel like speaking out about something like that. So these are things that are not spoken of so much in our world. I was getting hit left and right. It was getting so heavy, I was worried that it would effect my health. So to release myself from the weight of it, I kept blessing the names that came to my mind, every night before I went to sleep . . . Sometimes I would get a shock, and say to myself "I'm not going to bless that one, am I?!" But I kept going.

I realized something very interesting. The names that came up more often than not were the names of people who were particularly not nice to me. The names of the worst enemies, so to speak. So I ended up blessing those people. Strange things started to happen. The enemies were still attacking me. But some of them were getting more interested in something else. Some of them started to have some difficulty in their own lives that made them focus their energies on those things more than on me. One group of people started to fight amongst themselves. One of them, in fact, came to me complaining about his gang of friends how unfair they were to him about his take and confessed to me what they were up to! I may have been just lucky, and the change of the situation may not have had to do with my nightly blessings. But, at least, it released me from the resentment and fear I held within me. I started to feel lighter. It helped me to move on and be active in health.

Some of the bad karma she claims dogged her through the 1980s appears to have been her own fault to some degree. She was successfully sued by *Double Fantasy* producer Jack Douglas, the Elephant's Memory band, and others for unpaid royalties. She also refused to grant Cynthia Lennon rights to have John's music performed at a Liverpool concert in celebration of John's fiftieth birthday. Yoko held her own concert there instead, claiming that Cynthia had been set up by unethical promoters trying to stage a Beatles reunion *sans* John.

That she had already begun a new relationship with Sam Havadtoy, an antiques expert eighteen years younger, didn't sit well with some observers. A former BBC disc jockey called Havadtoy's presence in her life "scandalous," never mind that the Lennons, and especially John, had both had their own ideas about what constituted marital fidelity. Havadtoy had been a Lennon assistant, just like May Pang. He and Yoko were indeed living together, "boyfriend and girlfriend," he said, through much of the eighties and nineties. She has said almost nothing about what appears to have been a relationship of convenience, in either public statements or in her art.

Other people surprised Yoko in a positive manner, not least of all Paul McCartney. The supposed animosity between the two artists has always been something of an urban myth. They loved the same person, and shared a creative intimacy with that person, even though he also occasionally rubbed them both the wrong way and was a difficult being to know.

Around the time Lennon was to be inducted into the Rock and Roll Hall of Fame in 1994, Yoko bestowed upon Paul, whom she had seen from time to time in New York, a special gift, one from her as well as John in absentia: the raw Lennon demos of two unrecorded songs, "Free as a Bird," and "Real Love." Through some sonic necromancy, McCartney took Ringo and George into the studio and produced a Beatles single fifteen years after the group had disbanded. "I knew what I was doing when I gave them "Free as a Bird" and "Real Love," said Yoko, "because I thought it was a great thing to happen. I think this world is so depressed and a lot of people are feeling directionless and everything, that for them to have an *up* feeling is great, even it's just for three minutes."

Yet another aspect of the Lennon legacy involved the business affairs Yoko had been managing five years before his death. John left behind unreleased songs, albums in need of remastering, song catalogues and publishing rights, film and audio recordings, and artwork. "Now that he belongs to the world," says Yoko, "I feel responsible about sharing things that were meant to be shared . . . things that he expected to communicate because he was an artist. Things I can't sort out because it's painful for me and because I'm a very busy person too. It's a slow process and a difficult one, because I don't want to present anything to the world that he wouldn't have liked. That's how I look at it. It's not so much resenting sharing him, but now he belongs to the world and I have that responsibility."

Much of John's work with the Beatles has been in litigation of one form or another since the band broke up but that hasn't prevented new product from reaching the market. The Beatles studio albums were rereleased on CD in 1987. A two-volume compilation entitled *Past Masters* came out a year later. Two albums of live performances at the BBC appeared in 1994 and 2013. All told, the band has by now released twenty-one studio albums, five live albums, and fifty-four compilation albums, seventeen boxed sets, and a couple of mash-ups, most notably *Love*, released to acclaim in 1996. Five separate documentary film projects have been launched since Lennon died, not least of them Peter Jackson's magisterial epic *The Beatles: Get Back*.

Yoko released five separate records of Lennon material in the 1980s, including a soundtrack for the movie *Imagine*, a live album, and a boxed set. That inevitably led her critics to accuse her of cashing in on John's memory. The Associated Press published a feature noting that the dead Beatle had managed to put out as many albums during the decade as Michael Jackson and Bruce Springsteen combined. It didn't help that Yoko's new look, with short hair, stylish clothes, and oversized dark glasses, was expressly businesslike. She was unapologetic, observing: "I didn't sell out John," she said. "I'm sure John would be happy I'm still keeping him out there. There's a commercial aspect, yes, but I mean, why not? I was a partner, and I still feel that I'm a partner." The world seemed to have forgotten just how much Lennon liked to sell his work, including sketches of his naked wife at a premium price of £550. And, as Havadtoy rightly commented, Yoko was in a no-win situation: "After John's death, newspapers wrote that [she] was this selfish person hoarding John's memory, controlling it, not willing to share it with his fans. So after two years, she puts out 200 hours of film footage and a record and they say she's exploiting John's memory."

Some of the new ventures worked, and some didn't. Jackson's documentary was as magnificent a project as anyone could have imagined, but *Lennon*, the Broadway musical, approved by Yoko and written by Don Scardino using John's songs as its primary material, bombed. Yoko had high hopes for the twelve-person show, which had a variety of actors playing John: "What we present on stage should again give people insight, encouragement, inspiration and fun, so they can go on with their lives with some assurance and hope." The show was canceled after a forty-one-day run. The *New York Times* summed up the critical response: "A fierce primal scream of the kind Ms. Ono is famous for as a performance and recording artist is surely the healthiest response to the agony of 'Lennon,' the jerry-built musical shrine that opened last night at the Broadhurst Theater."

While she sold Lennon's share of the Beatles catalogue to Sony, Yoko receives an array of licensing fees and royalties from his solo work, and continues to control the family's investments. Her net worth is estimated at $700 million.

The money has been a bone of contention with other Lennon family members. There were no provisions for Julian Lennon (or first wife, Cynthia) in John's will. Everything was left to Yoko. Seventeen years old at the time of John's death, Julian had only the £100,000 trust fund his father had arranged at the time of his divorce, and his memory of his father telling him he was the accident of a whiskey bottle. He sued Yoko and the Lennon estate for more. They fought through the courts for fifteen years before eventually reaching a settlement that awarded Julian an undisclosed sum rumored to be around £20 million.

Julian claimed to be unhappy with the settlement, which he considered unfair, but said he wanted to be rid of the litigation out of concern for his half brother. "I think the key point to all this, for me at least, has been Sean," he said. "If I hurt Sean's mother, then I hurt Sean. It's a roundabout way of thinking about things. But because I love Sean so much, I just don't want to hurt him. I can get over it. Have gotten over it."

As for Yoko, Julian expresses grudging admiration, calling her "a hardball, a very strong woman. . . . I admire her. She's a tough cookie. But I don't necessarily agree with her."

On a happier note, Yoko's long-lost daughter, Kyoko, called her mother out of the blue in 1998. She had spent most of the interim years with Anthony Cox, who had left the Church of the Living Word, divorced his wife Melinda, and moved in with the Chicago commune, Jesus People USA. Kyoko had received an education under the name Ruth Holman. After Lennon's death, Cox and Kyoko sent a sympathy telegram to Yoko but did not indicate their location. In response, Yoko published an open letter: "All these years, there has not been one day I have not missed you. You are always in my heart. However, I will not make any attempt to find you now as I wish to respect your privacy. I wish you all the best in the world. If you ever wish to get in touch with me, know I love you deeply and would be very happy to hear from you. But you should not feel guilty if you choose not to reach me. You have my respect, love, and support forever."

It was concerns for her privacy, according to Cox, that made Kyoko reluctant to approach her huge celebrity of a mother. In the meantime, impostors, some of them blue-eyed with blond hair, tried to weasel into Yoko's good graces. In 1994, Kyoko telephoned Yoko, leading to a tearful reunion and her first meeting with half-brother Sean. "Kyoko is happy to be reunited with her mother and family," said a friend. "She's happy with her life. But she doesn't want that quiet, peaceful life to be disturbed by media attention." A teacher with a daughter of her own, Kyoko has been photographed with her mother but does her best to keep a low profile. Yoko and her publicists have said almost nothing about their relationship, undoubtedly at Kyoko's request. Anthony Cox subsequently dropped out of sight, and was last reported living in a Volkswagen in Colorado and trying to sell Lennon memorabilia.

In the final dimension of her custodial role, Yoko is the go-to resource for anyone wanting to know more about John Lennon. No one knew him better, and certainly no one else can come up with such idiosyncratic and highly specific descriptions such as these:

> He had three small but distinct moles straight down the center of his broad forehead, ending where the third eye was. Buddha was supposed to have had one mole in the center of his forehead, and that was considered in the Oriental physiognomy as a sign of a very wise man. I always thought John's oval and well-chiseled classic face looked very much like a Kabuki mask or a face you'd expect to see in a Shakespearean play. . . .
>
> He carried his body with a certain lightness that gave grace to his movements. He was in his twenties when I met him. I was eight years older. But I never thought of him as somebody younger than me. When you were near him, the strong mental

vibe he sent out was too heavy for a young person. Some people are born old. That was John. His slumming, clowning and acting the entertainer was just a kind of play-acting he enjoyed. But it was obvious to anybody around him that he was actually a very heavy dude; not a prince but a king.

Her work as keeper of the Lennon flame had a strange effect on Yoko's own public profile. At the time of his death, she was still largely reviled as someone who had broken up the world's favorite band and stolen its leader for her own selfish reasons. Almost overnight, she became the grief-stricken widow, an oracle for the Lennon obsessed, and a vessel for all the good things he meant to the world. People began to call her Mrs. Lennon, with none of the nasty connotations the term had carried during John's lifetime.

She wasn't fooled. "For ten years I was the devil, now suddenly I'm an angel," as she said in 1981. "Did the world have to lose John for people to change their opinion of me? It's unreal. If it brought John back, I'd rather be hated." Over time, however, she reached an accommodation with Lennon's public. By 2007, it seemed perfectly normal to see her on *Larry King Live*, sitting beside Paul McCartney, Ringo Starr, and Olivia Harrison, representing John's place in the band. She joined the same trio onstage at a Microsoft event in 2009 to launch the *Beatles: Rock Band* video game. That same year, Montreal's Museum of Fine Arts presented the exhibition *Imagine: The Peace Ballad of John & Yoko* on the fortieth anniversary of her bed-in at Montreal's Queen Elizabeth Hotel. Over one hundred drawings, photographs, and films were mustered for the event. A photographic book was released. There were tours of the hotel, with hordes of people asking "Is this the room? Is this the bed?" Simultaneously, a new play called *John/Yoko Bed Piece* was staged in Toronto. Yoko attended the exhibition's opening and, far from being resented, was treated as cultural royalty.

It helped that she had not only continued but expanded the activism she and John undertook in his lifetime. When a UK couple, Andrew and Christine Gale, announced they were performing a bed-in to protest the impending US-UK invasion of Iraq, Yoko picked up the phone: "It's good to speak to you. We're supporting you. We're all sisters together." The Gales told her that they'd been inspired by the songs "Give Peace a Chance" and "Imagine." In 2011, Yoko organized and hosted a benefit concert for victims of the Japanese earthquake and tsunami, inviting a dozen artists from the rock, jazz, and avant-garde worlds to join her onstage. "I'm still in a daze, in a way," she told Rolling Stone. "Of course, I'm Japanese, too. It's something that happened in my home country. It's an incredible shock." That she felt it necessary to remind people of her Tokyo roots is indicative of how identified she'd become with her adopted home of New York City.

She was named the first global ambassador for autism in 2010, and five years later was awarded a lifetime achievement award from the *Observer* Ethical Awards for a wide range of activities, starting with her bed-ins and up through her more recent work as an advocate of same-sex marriage, an opponent of industrial fracking, and a critic of America's lame gun control laws.

As usual, she sees her activism as an outgrowth of her art. "Art to me is a way of showing people how you can think," she said. "Some people think of art as like beautiful wallpaper that you can sell, but I have always thought it is to do with activism."

She founded the Yoko Ono Lennon Courage Award for the Arts, presented annually to artists, writers, musicians, or curators who seek truth in their work and demonstrate courage, leadership, and resourcefulness in their work, risking their careers by pursuing a larger vision of the local or natural interest "despite pressure to succumb to commercial and political constraints." Promotional material for the award italicizes the last part of that sentence for emphasis. The $25,000 prize is given to several recipients a year, and has been awarded to the likes of WikiLeaks founder Julian Assange and performance artist Laurie Anderson, "one of America's major, and majorly confounding, modern artists," according to the *New York Times*.

"To be an artist, you need courage," says Yoko of the award, "and most people don't think that. It's an age where people are only interested in entertainment. People are just entertained every day, like crazy, and that's all they're doing. And they say: 'This is boring, let's see something else.' We are all kings and queens now, asking others to entertain us. It's a very sad situation, because there are many things that we have to do if we want to survive." That courage has long been evident in her case, as a deeply brave person with enough gravitas to declare: "You change the world by being yourself."

Few think of her anymore as merely an outrageous figure from the art world's lunatic fringe, in fact, it's hard to even imagine today those kinds of misguided sentiments. Perhaps it's because of how deftly she has handled her role as custodian of the Lennon legacy, but also because she has never abandoned her primary personal role as a singer-songwriter, solo artist, and social activist. Her resilience and staying power are now fairly commonly lauded and her tenacity almost universally applauded. After all, one of her first public responses to her husband's murder was to go ahead and release a song that suddenly sounded far different than when it was recorded in the hours just before his fatal encounter outside the Dakota.

# CHAPTER FOURTEEN

# Burning Bridges

YOKO'S MEMORIES OF HER second-last day in the studio with John would remain crystal clear thirty years later. "The last Sunday. I'm glad in a way that we didn't know that it was our last Sunday together, so we could have had a semblance of normalcy. But it turned out that it was not a normal Sunday at all. Something was starting to happen, like the dead silence before a tsunami. The air was getting tenser and tenser, denser and denser. Then I distinctly saw airwaves in the room. It was wiggly likes, like on the heart monitor next to the hospital bed, just before it becomes a flat straight line. 'John, are you all right?' I asked through the density. He just nodded and kept listening to 'Walking on Thin Ice,' playing it loud."

"I think you just cut your first number one, Yoko," said John in the last hours of his life. The song, with its twisted dance-club rhythm, was melancholy and hauntingly prophetic. "Walking on thin ice. / I'm paying the price, for throwing the dice in the air," followed by still more lyrics on the fragility of human life, and the inevitability of tragedy. John had the tape in his hand when he was shot. It went skittering across the ground outside the Dakota.

Yoko chose to release the record less than a month after John's death, so soon that the public winced. The Geffen label probably had a say in the timing, but for Yoko it was an opportunity. "Walking on Thin Ice" was an anti-anthem, the direct opposite of "Imagine" or "Give Peace a Chance," one that used reality as a teacher. "There's some songs that start to affect our life," she said. "I found that it's true with many of my works. After I wrote 'Walking on Thin Ice,' my life was literally like walking on thin ice." She had spent her whole life transforming personal trauma into art. There was no reason to stop now. Besides, as she often said, "art is like breathing for me. If I don't do it, I start to choke."

Five months later, she would release a studio album, *Season of Glass.* It contained some songs she'd written as early as 1974, but most of it was new material addressing John's murder. The devastating saxophone lullaby, "Goodbye Sadness," with its lyric "Hello, happiness, wherever you are, I hope you hear my song." The angry "I Don't Know Why" in which she cries "You bastards! / Hate us, hate me! We had everything." And the startling "No, No, No," which opens with four gunshots and Yoko wailing "Noooooo!," a vocalization the musician/journalist Alan Clayson calls "one long scream, and it sounds like it will never end."

"No, No, No," says Yoko, "was written and sung by a woman who was in such a pain that her heart was cracking while she kept her mind clear so she could survive for herself and for her son. If course that was me, right after John passed away. When John was still alive, he kept whispering to Sean that he will always be there for Sean and protect him. So when John left, Sean kept saying, 'a promise is made to be broken.' Making it lighter than what it was. He was in pain. Sean loved this song. Each time when I sang, 'I don't remember what you promised,' and elongated the end of it, he used to let his body go down at the same time to the floor. I remember

213

how hard it was for me to go through that period, especially knowing how Sean was managing to hide his tears."

It's a distressing and lovely record, *Season of Glass*. Again, there were people saying it was too soon after John's death to be making music, although no one questioned the former Beatles on their rush to the studio. Yoko was happy to explain: "Music was my salvation. When I started to sing, I noticed that my throat was all choked up and my voice was cracking. I seriously thought maybe I should quit making the album because, as some people had advised me, 'It was not the time.' But the question was, 'When *would* be the time?' I thought of all the people in the world whose voices were choking and cracking for many reasons. I could sing for them. I could call it a choke or a crackle. Well, wasn't that what the critics had been saying about me for all these years anyway? That gave me a laugh, and it became easier."

Another startling dimension of *Season of Glass* was its cover, featuring Lennon's blood-covered glasses on a table beside a half-empty glass of water with the Manhattan skyline looming in the background. The performance artist Lisa Carver first encountered the image as a teenager in a used record store, observing in *Reaching Out With No Hands*: "I think the significance of that half-drunk glass of water was a demonstration of impermanence," she says. "Undrunk forever, frozen unfinished."

Yoko felt the cover was meant to be frank with people about what had happened. "John was killed. And it was very important for me to show that to the world, and for people to remember. Because I think that all of us are responsible for his death, of course, including myself, and both John and I were always trying to make a peaceful world. And it's very ironical that John, who loved peace so much, died in a violent way." She considered it "a very, very mild expression" of the reality of the killing. She had seen her husband's blood pooling on the ground. That people felt it was too graphic or exploitative astonished her. "I felt the oneness with [John] and we were saying, 'Please look at me. This is what you do to me.' I mean, that's what John wanted to say, I think."

*Season of Glass* broke into the *Billboard* top fifty, Ono's best showing to that date, and was listed as one of the best two hundred albums of the decade by *Pitchfork*.

She was still brooding over John's death in 1982 when she returned to the studio to make *It's Alright*, her sixth solo album. While managing a more upbeat tone, the record was in some ways even more difficult to make than its predecessor, because of her awareness that life was indeed moving on. "I had to walk and talk normally," she said, "while I knew that somewhere inside me there was a clock that had stopped in 1980." She was also dealing with stalkers and bomb threats, and worried about Sean's security. The phrase "it's alright" wasn't a statement of fact so much as a prayer, or a therapeutic exercise. "After John, music was the thing that kept me going. The support of the public helped. I'm thankful for that. I was aware of the fact that making music for me is very therapeutic and relaxing. It's home, it's family. It's like knitting might be for some women. When I was making the music, I literally felt that the music lifted up my spirits."

Yoko would follow *It's Alright* with the album *Starpeace*, which billed itself as a response to the Reagan administration's "Star Wars" strategic defense plan. Unfortunately for her, it interested neither the press nor the public and a tour in support of the record was canceled almost as soon as it began, in response to low turnouts. The only release associated with her in the mid-eighties was a tribute album, *Every Man Has a Woman*, timed for her fiftieth birthday. It had reportedly been suggested by John before he died, and included recordings of a dozen Yoko songs performed mostly by their friends, including Harry Nilsson, Roberta Flack, and Klaus Voormann.

One of her earliest reentries to the art world also came in 1981, with the sculptural project *Wish Tree*, a perpetual decentralized art series involving the planting of a tree native to its location, under Yoko's direction. People are invited to tie a written wish to the tree, until the tree is covered in wishes. Over time, twenty-one trees have been planted, including eucalyptus and lemon trees. "As a child in Japan," explains Yoko, "I used to go to a temple and write out a wish on a piece of thin paper and tie it around the branch of a tree. Trees in temple courtyards were always filled with people's wish knots, which looked like white flowers blossoming from afar." The series is identical in spirit to one of the instruction poems from *Grapefruit*.

All of the wishes, more than a million to date, have been gathered up and buried at the foot of the Imagine Peace Tower, yet another memorial to John Lennon. Located on Viðey Island near Reykjavik, Iceland, the tower consists of a wishing well, thirty feet in diameter, with the words "Imagine Peace" carved into it in twenty-four languages, and fifteen searchlights with mirror-like prisms that reflect a column of light straight up into the sky. The tower is lit every year from Lennon's birthday, October 9, until December 8, the date on which he died, and on other special occasions.

With the mid-1980s taken up by Lennon memorials, business management, and caring for Sean, who was eventually enrolled in a Swiss boarding school, Yoko was largely absent from the art world until 1987. Cincinnati's Carl Solway Gallery hosted a John Cage tribute for which Yoko minted eight of her all-white chess sets. They are in enameled bronze, and priced at $7,500 each. Two years later, a curator of film at the Whitney had the idea of exhibiting all of Yoko's films. When she made other elements of her collection available, too, the museum decided to hold a major retrospective featuring 150 of her works from her avant-garde days. In museum terms, said the *New York Times*, it was a "blockbuster." It later went on a seven-city tour, attracting large crowds at each stop. "Now her work appears quite timely—refreshingly uncomplicated, minimal, with a whiff of the New Age about it, right down to the primal screams that emanate from a cell constructed at the centre of the exhibition," wrote the *Guardian*.

It was Havadtoy who suggested that Yoko cast some of her early works in bronze, including the chess sets and the infamous apple. "I got very upset," she said, "because I thought that this person just didn't understand anything about my work. My work was about a representation of ideas, and ideas are just like water or air. The work had an ethereal quality."

But eventually she came around. "I realized that for something to move me so much that I would cry, there's something there. There seemed like a shimmering air in the Sixties when I made these pieces., and now the air is bronzified. Now it's the Eighties, and bronze is very Eighties in a way, solidity, commodity, all of that. For someone who went through the Sixties revolution, there has of course been an incredible change. . . . I call the pieces petrified bronze. That freedom, all the hope and wishes are in some ways petrified."

The bronze work did detract from the appealingly ephemeral nature of her originals, and together with her decision to join forces with the galleries once shunned by Fluxus, it made clear that Yoko had moved on somewhat from her earlier aesthetic values, but most of the critics didn't mind. "Yoko has a lyrical, poetic dimension that sets her apart from the other conceptual artists," said David Bourdon, former art critic at the *Village Voice*. "Her approach to art was only made acceptable when white men like Joseph Kosuth and Lawrence Weiner came in and did virtually the same things as Yoko, but made them respectable and collectible."

To the extent she received criticism, it was because the whimsical elements of Fluxus were not aging well with every audience. "Yoko Ono's art consists of play," said the Norwegian poet Skjalg Bye of her 2005 Oslo show curated by Hans Obrist for the Astrup Museet, "a form of play that once might have been viable. But in our time, we need more than to see a chessboard with only white pieces, broken tea cups for the audience to glue back together, and to jump of a stool, or shake hands through an unpainted canvas. The most sensational thing is that the Norwegian intellectual elite shows up in flock to behold and participate in the Yoko Ono 'kindergarten for grown-ups.'"

If the Whitney show put her back on the cultural map as an important artist, Onobox, a six-disc collected works released in 1992 by the Rykodisc division of Warner Music, did the same for her music. It begins with the albums *Fly* and *Yoko Ono/Plastic Ono Band*, followed by a remixed and reordered *Approximately Infinite Universe, Feeling the Space*, a selection of her tracks from *Double Fantasy* and Lennon's posthumous *Milk and Honey*, and the previously unreleased 1974 LP *A Story*. A companion compilation of her singles called *Walking on Thin Ice* was released simultaneously. The box set, said *Entertainment Weekly*, speaking for the consensus, finally "gave Yoko Ono, the avant-garde heroine, her due."

The positive critical response was overwhelming. The *New Yorker* covered the launch at the Vrej Baghoomian Gallery in Soho and was shocked to see the likes of Cyndi Lauper, Joey Ramone, and Kim Gordon of Sonic Youth come out to pay their respects. Music and entertainment publications accustomed to portraying Yoko as a witch or using her as a punch line were suddenly noticing that she had performed with such avant-garde colossi as John Cage and Ornette Coleman, that her sounds were as contemporary as, if not more advanced than, a lot of the fashionable music then being played in New York clubs.

At the age of fifty-nine, in her fourth decade of performing music, she was discovered, finally, on her own terms, as a major voice and talent. "The uniformly favorable reviews of *Onobox*," wrote Rob Tannenbaum in

*Newsday*, "have the whiff of apology, as though some critics feel ashamed of the way Yoko was maligned. It would be irresponsible not to note that there is dross on each CD, failed experiments, droning ballads, songs that drift aimlessly. But the dross is outweighed by the delights. Ironically, Yoko had the kind of career—protean, curious, funny, risky—that Beatles' fans expected but never got from George, Ringo, and Paul. And far more than the seamy biographies or accusations of hirelings, *Onobox* fearlessly depicts the complex romance between Yoko and John."

And that was only the beginning:

Onobox . . . shows that behind her idiosyncratic, aggressive and sometimes abrasive early vocal style lurked an inventive, original composer.

The way she invents what others took for granted, renewing the ordinary by finding it odd, turns this collision of rock's primitive energy and performance art's self-dramatization into a preview of today's musical hybrids.

Her catapulting "Move On Fast" is a punk-jazz answer to the Beatles' "Ticket to Ride"; the meeting of asperity and pity makes "I Want My Love to Rest Tonight" a women's-lib update of The Threepenny Opera.

[Onobox] reveals that her later songs, in a more conventional pop style while quirkily left of center, have a lot to say about a great many topics, ranging from the uneasy sides of relationships to feminism, sexism, economy, anger, pain and loss.

Among the sparks that fly are searing rockers like "Why" and "Don't Worry Kyoko," in which Ms. Ono uses her voice as if it were a wailing, overdriven electric guitar, competing virtuosically with those of Lennon and Eric Clapton.

Ono grinds syllables into pointy weapons, braying in a signature vocabulary that anticipates the rubbed-balloon screech at the core of Public Enemy records.

The homely, gray power of these songs shames the "fox-core" raving of current female punkers like Babes in Toyland and Hole.

From the erotic gasps of "Kiss Kiss Kiss" to the recriminations of "I'm Moving On" to the soul-combo succor of "Every Many Has a Woman Who Loves Him," few songwriters have delineated the daily joys and sorrows of marriage so clearly.

Most importantly, *Onobox* introduced Yoko's otherwise difficult-to-find work to a lot of younger listeners who had grown up long after the Beatles had disbanded. Her forgettable 1995 album *Rising*, a collaboration with Sean, sold only 11,000 copies in the US but spawned a follow-up of remixes with a wide range of performers from Adam Yauch of the Beastie Boys to Thurston Moore of Sonic Youth and the Japanese noise band Incapacitants.

When the California rock band Beulah found itself in a period of turmoil in 2002, with lead singer Miles Kurosky breaking up with his longtime girlfriend and three of six band members divorcing in short order, it came out of the studio with a new item titled *Yoko*. Said Kurosky: "Yoko had to be the title since the record is about love, my growth as an artist, and the changes I've been going through as a human being. I wanted to make a more mature, confident and daring artistic statement. The word 'Yoko' says it all: change, progress and risk."

By the time the aughts generation brought hordes of DJs looking for material to remix, Yoko's music was a favorite source. The Austrian Paul Rauhofer, who performed under the names Club 69 and Size Queen, remixed Yoko along with Cher, Madonna, and Britney Spears. New

York–based Danny Tenaglia, also known as Soulboy and a half-dozen other aliases, turned Yoko's "Walking on Thin Ice" into a dance track that fulfilled Lennon's prophecy by hitting number one on the Billboard dance charts. It was the first of a long string of top hits.

By 2011, *Rolling Stone* was writing that "Yoko Ono has overcome the likes of Rihanna, Britney Spears, Lady Gaga, and Katy Perry to score her sixth consecutive Number One on the Billboard Hot Dance Club chart with 'Move on Fast.' The song is her eighth Number One dance hit overall." The magazine noted that the rest of the music industry had finally caught up with Yoko, appreciating what were once obscure tunes and remaking them for contemporary audiences. "Those are all incredibly creative people on the chart with me," she said. "I respect Lady Gaga very much. I feel a touch guilty that I'm up there. But it's all right, that happens."

Yoko confessed to having initially opposed the idea of remixes. The idea of monkeying with tracks that she'd painstakingly recorded, and especially ones that John had played on, seemed sacrilege. "I had the pride of a rocker," she said. "People can get very elitist very quickly, and that's how I was." Yet when she first heard what producers were able to do with her songs: "I just started crying. It was so beautiful that somebody understood my work so well."

She had become the queen of the dance clubs while scarcely setting foot inside them. "I did go to a few clubs just so people can be like, 'Yes, Yoko was there,'" she said at age seventy-eight, underselling the fact that she had requested a mike in one club so that she could augment the orgasmic moans of a track being played. "But it does get a bit nerve-wracking to go to those places. I would love to be dancing every night until dawn, but somehow it's not conducive for my life right now."

*Rolling Stone*, which had never stopped chronicling her every move, compared guesting on a Yoko album to getting cast in a Woody Allen film: "an artistic validation and New York City-branded rite of passage. It's also clearly a hoot." For her 2007 remix album, "Yes, I'm a Witch," she made her vocal tracks from seventeen of her songs available to what the magazine called "a generation of alternative-rock and dance-music pupils, including Peaches, Cat Power, the Flaming Lips and torch singer Antony, too young to care if she broke up the Beatles (which she did not) but the right age to appreciate the radical modernism of Ono's early-Seventies LPs. Her long-underrated talent for simple, direct melodies makes it easy for these disciples to rescore Ono's song-writing in their own lingo. Peaches amplifies the sexual undercurrent of 'Kiss Kiss Kiss' with electro-bump-and-grind. The Polyphonic Spree, usually on the wrong side of twee, bring the right comfort and light to 'You and I,' and Le Tigre punk up the vintage feminism of 'Sisters O Sisters. . . .' Jason Pierce of Spiritualized takes the avant-disco of 'Walking on Thin Ice' further out, with a drone-rock backdrop that echoes Suicide's 'Cheree' and noise-guitar eruptions that Lennon surely would have loved."

Of all the new collaborations, none stunned like her work with her dead husband's former songwriting partner. After John's induction into the Rock and Roll Hall of Fame in 1994, Yoko visited Paul at home and wound up standing in her housecoat in his kitchen like any other McCartney houseguest, along with her twenty-five-year-old son, Sean, who by then had launched a serious music career of his own. Paul took them on a tour of his home recording studio, where albums like *Press to Play* had been produced, as well as his own experimental albums under the alias Fireman.

Sean began noodling with a few of Paul's vintage instruments, some of which had been used on the Beatles' greatest tracks, including the electric spinet that had helped make "Because" such a luscious song. Paul suddenly suggested that all three of them record something together.

Yoko suggested they might try a new song she'd written for Ron Destro's upcoming stage play about the Hiroshima tragedy, something obviously of huge significance for her. Destro, said Yoko, had "reminded me that 1995 was the fiftieth anniversary of the tragedy. In his script there's a scene where a little girl tries to fold 1000 paper cranes. In Japan, there's a tradition of folding 1000 paper cranes to make a wish. The little girl dies before she is able to fold all 1000 cranes. I was particularly touched by this scene."

Before long, Paul and Yoko were vocalizing, Sean and Linda McCartney and her son James were playing instruments and the three McCartney daughters, Mary, Heather, and Stella were providing a chorus. "Since it was a song for Hiroshima and world peace," said Yoko, it made sense that "we should have his whole family involved." And so it was that "Hiroshima Sky Is Always Blue," or a version of it, came to be. It was totally spontaneous, and improvised on the spot. Yoko felt it was very much in the tradition of the Plastic Ono Band: "What happens in the moment is what's important."

Paul let Yoko take the tape of "Hiroshima Sky" back with her to New York to add some additional dubs of Sean's guitar. Rather than release it as a single, as McCartney had suggested, she used it on a future album. Ian Peel would describe the song as a "live free form jam. . . . A track which unites the extremes of both the avant-garde and the emotions. At times the result of Ono and McCartney's collaboration is disturbing and haunting. At others it's comforting and playful. Proof positive that the last thing avant-garde music should be is cold, inhuman and soulless."

The remixes, reissues, reconsiderations, and retrospectives turned the later years of Yoko's life (she is now eighty-nine) into one long victory lap, and a well-deserved one at that. The art world has been especially generous to her, with major shows in New York, Frankfurt, London, and Bilbao. The Venice Biennale handed her its Golden Lion Award for lifetime achievement in 2009. Austria awarded her the 2021 Oskar Kokoschka Prize, its highest honor for contemporary art.

As always with Yoko, there have been misses along with the hits, some of them bewilderingly odd. She tried to launch a fashion line inspired by sketches she had given John as a wedding gift. At the time of drawing, she had been "amazed at how my man was looking so great. I felt it was a pity if we could not make clothes emphasizing his very sexy bod." The collection, according to *Rolling Stone*, contained tailored sportswear, footwear, headwear, and accessories. It turned out there wasn't much of a market for "suit pants embossed with a cut-out of a hand sewn over the crotch and a jersey pullover with eyelets cut out around the nipples."

And just as controversy had stalked her early years, it retained its interest in her as she aged. In 2006, her longtime chauffeur, Koral Karsan, accused Yoko of sexual harassment and demanded $2 million or he would release certain audiotapes and photographs of her. According to police, he claimed to have been involved in an affair with Yoko and also threatened to kill her and Sean Lennon. Karsan was arrested. He later pleaded guilty to attempted grand larceny and was ordered deported to his native Turkey. Years later, a German auction house would file for bankruptcy, leading to the discovery of eighty-six items, including Lennon notebooks and drawings, that turned out to have been taken out of the Dakota by Karsan, with, he would falsely claim, Yoko's permission.

Yoko being Yoko, she also sought out controversy on her own. By the time Donald Trump was elected in 2016, she had 4.6 million followers on Twitter. To that time, she had used the platform primarily to distribute her instructional poems and keep fans updated on releases and performances. Three days after Trump's victory, she tweeted: "Dear Friends, I would like to share this message with you as my response to @realDonaldTrump. Love, Yoko." She attached a short clip of one of her familiar tortured wails. Embedded was a nineteen-second clip featuring the octogenarian expending a trademark anguished cry. "I think John would feel the same as all of us," she said. "Terrible."

In recent years, Yoko has tended to allow her work to speak for itself, giving fewer interviews, and most of them shorter than those granted in midlife. On turning eighty, however, she sat for *Interview* magazine and explained to a disbelieving journalist, Elvis Mitchell, why such fine work as her recording of "AOS" with Ornette Coleman in 1968 hadn't been appreciated at the time. She patiently explained how everything she'd done at that time had been colored by public perceptions of what was happening with the Beatles. "It feels like I was accused of something that I didn't do, which was breaking up the Beatles," she said. "That was like being somebody who is in prison without having done anything wrong. It's like you're accused of murder and you're in prison and you can't get out. . . . I wasn't valued by people, or if they did value me, it was in a particular way."

In some respects, Mitchell's questions and statements in *Interview* are more interesting than Yoko's answers. He professes astonishment that people ever saw her as anything less than an artist, and that those who thought of her only as the woman who broke up the Beatles "weren't really looking at or listening to what you were doing—they were just paying attention to what other people were saying. But it seems like you were built, on some level, to not care about what other people say." Yoko, brushing aside all the pain those years had caused her, responds blithely: "I know. Isn't that funny?"

Mitchell is similarly surprised that Yoko still feels that most people think of her first in relation to the Beatles.

"That was a little while ago," he says.

"Five minutes ago," she responds.

"But even Paul McCartney is saying now in Rolling Stone that Yoko is a badass!"

Yoko goes on to speak of Fluxus and George Maciunus, performing *Cut Piece* for the first time, writing *Grapefruit*, shooting "Bottoms," and forming the first Plastic Ono Band, as though it all happened five minutes ago, and it is received by Mitchell as a great and bold adventure that could only have turned out well and that all of us should be sad to have missed out on.

She credits the difficult early years with Lennon with teaching her self-love, and self-appreciation, lessons she attributes to the fact that she has been "the one who survived regardless." She came to see rejection as a blessing of sorts, "a very strange blessing. Because if what I was doing back then would have been totally accepted—you know, 'Now, Yoko, do that one again! We love it!'—then I would have been dead as an artist, stuck in one place. But I couldn't get stuck in one place because people kept whipping me, so I always thought, 'Go on, do another thing.'" Left unsaid was the obvious fact that her late husband, who had been massively accepted, even idolized, had been stuck after leaving the Beatles and needed her to lead him out of his rut.

She admits that it has been hard for her to admit that she's finally been accepted by the music and art worlds. Accustomed to fighting and struggling, she's uncomfortable with anything else. "Suddenly they're saying, 'No, you don't have to fight. We understand you!' It's like you've been knocking on the door for forty years and then someone suddenly says, 'You don't have to knock on the door—the door is already open.' Oh . . . Okay! So how are you going to deal with that? And I have to be very cautious. It's better that you're criticized than complimented as a person."

Similarly, she feels an ongoing need to nurture her rebellious streak and to reject the formal, traditional culture into which she was born.

From time to time, she still says to herself, "I don't want to start thinking like my mom."

The last public appearance of Yoko Ono Lennon was at a 2019 women's march in Columbus Circle. She attended in a wheelchair with a blanket over her knees, still wearing her trademark dark shades. An unspecified illness has made movement difficult for her. At eighty-nine, she remains in her nine-room suite at the Dakota with round-the-clock care. She has dinner with Sean two or three times a week, and he organizes her birthday party every year.

"She is a particularly special being," said her old friend and publicist Elliot Mintz. "In her eighty-nine years, she's lived 400." Yoko herself put it most succinctly in a recent posting on her Twitter account: "I want my epitaph to be: Here is a woman who loved life, and still does."

# EPILOGUE

# What Did It Mean?

*There's no goodies in it. There's no baddies in it. There's no villains, there's no heroes. It's just a human story.*

—Peter Jackson

There are many revelations in filmmaker Peter Jackson's majestic documentary, *Get Back*. It opens huge windows into the lives, personalities, and creative processes of the four Beatles in their last year together. But the one revelation everyone seemed to be waiting for, the smoking gun that would confirm Yoko Ono's demolition of the world's most beloved rock band, never materialized. After plowing through sixty hours of original film footage, and twice as much audio tape, Jackson himself made the unexpected pronouncement that "Yoko was a benign presence in the studio."

Andy Welch put a finer point on things in the *Guardian*: "The world owes Yoko Ono an apology," he wrote. "Blaming it all on her constant presence was always an absurd, lazy accusation grounded in misogyny and racism (seeing Paul, Ringo and George's partners and various guests wander in and out of the studio really hammers home those double standards) but hopefully we can once and for all put to bed any nonsense about how she brought about the band's decline. Yes, there were tensions—complicated, deep-seated and long running—but as McCartney says in Part Two, Yoko's presence was only an obstacle if the rest of the band allowed it to be. 'It isn't really that bad. They just want to be together.' Watching *Get Back*, Peter Jackson takes a sad song and makes it better."

Jackson's blockbuster finally put to rest that old canard that Yoko killed the Beatles. It was fifty-two years in coming, but it allowed the public to consider afresh the enigmatic artist in black who so hauntingly shades and shadows the documentary's entire storyline.

No one seemed more relieved than Yoko. During the hoopla surrounding the documentary, *New Music Express* reported that she shared with her 4.6 million Twitter followers an article saying that the new Peter Jackson film proved she wasn't the cause of the band's demise, making clear how raw her feelings remain over half a century later.

She celebrated this turning point by releasing a limited-edition artwork that reprised a singular object she had first exhibited in 1966 at the Indica Gallery in London, the very show where she first bumped into Lennon. Entitled *Mend Piece for John*, and available through the Whitechapel Gallery, the piece is basically a broken ceramic teacup and saucer that each new owner can reassemble using scissors, glue, twine, tape, and ribbons, each in a personal way. It is a perfect expression of a four-hundred-year-old Japanese tradition known as *kintsugi*. Its technique involves repairing broken vessels often using gold leaf as glue, reflecting the idea that by highlighting and embracing a piece's flaws and imperfections one can create a stronger and more beautiful work of art. Making art from trauma and scars is also vintage Yoko. *Mend Piece for John* further underlines her interest in construction rather than destruction, the stubbornness of her optimism, and the persistence of her hope that maybe, after all this time, some shared mending can take place.

We may yet have another filmic look at Yoko. Jean-Marc Vallée, the acclaimed French Canadian director of *Dallas Buyers Club, Big Little Lies,* and *Sharp Objects,* was making a movie about the whirlwind romance and shared domestic and professional lives of Yoko and John when he died from a heart attack on December 26, 2021, at the untimely age of fifty-eight. *Variety* magazine reported that Vallée had written a script with Anthony McCarten, best known for *The Theory of Everything* and *Bohemian Rhapsody.* Yoko is listed as a producer on the film, in cooperation with Universal Pictures.

Vallée had been so keen on the project that he reportedly dropped out of the running to direct the latest James Bond film to concentrate on the Ono-Lennon biopic. Co-producer Nathan Ross told *Deadline* magazine: "We are all huge Beatle fans and this is a dream come true. There were inner and outer struggles John had . . . the thing we loved about the script was its stark honesty. You see so many biopic scripts where you can see that the cooperation of the family had something to do with the editorial, and that wasn't the case here." That sounds consistent with what we've seen from Yoko both in her work and in her public comments about her life with Lennon. It remains unclear who the new director will be, if the film proceeds at all.

If it does, it will have an opportunity to correct an imbalance in her portrayal in *Get Back,* a project that could never do justice to Yoko because it is framed by the Beatles experience, and in that context, she is always a hanger-on. She appears day after day with John, in his studio. Standing back and asking what was really happening in the lives of Yoko and John in their years together, we know, as the artist Lisa Carver urgently said, that Yoko was not there with John: he was there with her. John was hanging on to Yoko as if his life depended on it, adopting her aesthetics, her ideas, her lifestyle, even her color schemes, without attribution.

If anyone was being used, especially early in their relationship, it was Yoko, although with typical generosity she seemed not to mind. She was happy to offer Lennon the opportunity to explore far more rawness and experimentation in his own music, and also in his art. That he needed the change seems obvious when one listens to both his shredded, wailing guitar, along with Ringo's frenzied drumming on Yoko's 1970 *Plastic Ono Band* album, not to mention his primal wailing and almost bestial voice on his companion album that year. Both are keen moments of stylistic liberation. Their two years together prior to the Beatles' breakup and the two subsequent years, prior to the bizarre trial separation, were remarkably fruitful periods of artistic expansion, musical growth, and lifestyle experimentation.

"Frenzied" is probably a better word to describe the conceptual carousel they were on, and through it all John, hungry for self-liberation, was nourished by Yoko's taste for free-form artistic self-expression. It was through her that he became steeped in the ideals of peace and feminism, and learned how to advance them through art and revolutionary acts. She was undoubtedly the senior cultural partner in the Ono-Lennon venture. *She* took *him* to her adopted home, New York City, introduced him to her radical friends and the local avant-garde scene and, as a professional survivor, taught him how to stand on his own. Unhinged as he often was through his late twenties and thirties, it is difficult to imagine Lennon anything but broke and in ruins without her confident guidance. The considerable estate about which he had naively boasted to Maureen Cleave also would likely have dissipated without Yoko's almost genetic business acumen.

Performance artist Lisa Carver argues that we need to flip our entire notions of what happened between them to really understand their relationship: it wasn't John and Yoko; it was Yoko and John. She is explicit about this, titling one of her written reconsiderations of the couple, "John Ripped *Her* Off!" "[Yoko] influenced and changed and expanded him much more than he did her," she says. "She was doing things like bed-ins for a long time before she met John."

Having her role misunderstood was not a new experience for Yoko, adds Carver. She had been doing happenings for years before Fluxus was formed, only to see its mostly male participants receive the lion's share of credit for her ideas in the years after.

A corollary observation from Carver is that no one ever considers that *John* destroyed *Yoko's* career by infiltrating and dominating her work, driving her conceptual framework, instructional objects, and poetic installations wildly off course into the more conventional realms of pop and rock music.

Viewing them through this alternative lens is a useful exercise, but if we're fair to both Yoko and John, we acknowledge that in her company, he voluntarily crossed over from his suffocating career as a performing flea to an experimental art world that gave him the higher degree of artistic risk he sought, and she crossed over from the arid and frustrating realm of avant-garde art to the seething marketplace of pop music with its enormous stage and vast reach. They were each other's muse and met in a middle of their own creation, bringing all sorts of colliding worlds to a new equilibrium with its own aesthetics, spiritual politics, and reservoir of personal pain. Carver nails it when she identifies their collaborations as "an experiment of what happens when man and woman, east and west, truly mix, consume and give freely and become one new, fascinating hybrid."

But enough about her and him, and him and her. John Lennon was a crucial person in Yoko Ono's life, but the point of this book is that she had a fascinating and important life of her own apart from him, one worthy of consideration on its own merits. Here, too, Lisa Carver is a helpful guide:

> Yoko's always been a way *out* for me, from the moment I encountered her work, in 1985 as a sixteen-year-old. My father was in and out of prison, my mother was on a lot of pills. I was in a small town exploring the library, looking for escape routes, looking for other worlds that must have existed no one had told me about yet. I took the bus to a town that had a used record store and I found Yoko Ono's *Season of Glass* for 25 cents. . . . She has meant so many different things to me as I've grown and changed, but really, every reincarnation she takes in my heart is always the same thing: a doorway made out of what I thought was a wall. It's just the shape of the trap she helps me get out of that changes through the years.

"Yoko stands outside of time," continues Carver. She refused to accept the loneliness and isolation and rejection in her life as debilitating. Others might have taken it all as a curse. Not Yoko. Far from it. "Yoko Ono has so uncursed herself, as an artist, as a Japanese woman, as a wife and mother," says Carver. "She's gotten so much curse from practically the whole world, and she's shaken it off. She's done for herself the same thing she tries to do for every person on earth: she recognizes the violence, even just of prejudice, aimed at her, she tries to see it for what it really is, and then she tries to absorb the power or energy of the hate and deflect the ugly bent of it, to transform it with love and freedom. She is uncursed and unleashed. She absorbs but is not absorbed."

A perfect example of Yoko absorbing curse is the initial reception of the critical world to her work as an artist. Just when she was coming into her own and critics were turning their attention to conceptual and feminist artists of the sixties, she was ostracized by the avant-garde. Just as Beatles fans turned on her for apparently stealing their living totem, the avant-garde brushed her aside for marrying and presumably selling out to a commercially successful performer and for becoming a global prankster/celebrity alongside him. Just like the Beatles crowd, the critical gods and goddesses assumed that Yoko was following John, and not vice versa, and no longer trusted her sensibility.

Yoko passed unnoticed in Linda Nochlin's important 1971 essay "Why Have There Been No Great Women Artists." The influential 1994 book *The Power of Feminist Art: The American Movement of the 1970s, History and Impact* managed to exclude Yoko as well. She was missing in action when the Guild Hall, East Hampton, launched its exhibition *Personal and Political: The Women's Art Movement, 1969–1975*. And while the Queens Museum of Art would include works by Yoko in its huge survey exhibition *Global Conceptualism: Points of Origin 1950s–1980s*, that was primarily because she was capable of "representing Japan" in an internationalist show.

One of the few exceptions to this trend was Lucy Lippard, author of the groundbreaking 1973 essay "The Dematerialization of Art: 1966–1972." In that and subsequent works, Lippard charted the course of the new art's elimination of the "visual, physical element" in favor of "ultra-conceptual or dematerialized art," and probed the ideas, ambitions, and works of Yoko's generation of conceptual artists. She came up with the ideal metaphor with which to describe the manner in which Ono and others were seeking to liberate both themselves and what they saw as the art system: that of the escape attempt.

"On a practical level," writes Lippard, "conceptual artists offered a clear-eyed look at what and where art itself was supposed to be; at the utopian extreme, some tried to visualize a new world and the art that would reflect it." She admits that conceptual art was "all over the place in style and content," but materially it was specific, and for a chaotic period of time it "was the only race in town."

One can see in Lippard's work how conceptual art was an ideal point of entry for someone like Yoko: "The inexpensive, ephemeral, unintimidating character of the conceptual mediums themselves (video, performance, photography, narrative, text, actions) encouraged women to participate, to move through this crack in the art world's walls," writes Lippard. These women brought new subjects and approaches to their practice, including role-playing, guise and disguise, body and beauty issues, and new focuses on autobiography, interrelationships, daily life, and, of course, feminist politics. "They played a role similar to that of women on the Left. We were slowly emerging from the kitchens and bedrooms, off the easels, out of the woodwork . . . By 1970, thanks to the liberal-to-left politics of many male artists, a certain unprecedented amount of support for the feminist program was forthcoming." This environment, writes Lippard, allowed Yoko to continue "her independent proto-conceptual work."

It wasn't until all the retrospectives and reconsiderations began in the new century that Yoko was absolved of the crime of embracing popular culture and, in Carver's words, was "uncursed and unleashed." The masterful survey of her complete body of work called *YES: Yoko Ono* perhaps came closest to a comprehensive appreciation of her remarkable creative presence. It captured the protean quality of her activities in conceptual art, print, film, and music, her deep engagement with visceral feeling and high concept. True, her work is often exotic, her remarks quizzical, her character elusive and even strange to many people, but she has always been a unique force in her times, and usually so far ahead of her times that her meaning is still unfolding. Even after all these years, individual pieces have a striking immediacy, a freedom from pretension and false contrivance that comes across as dramatically new.

The shows at the Whitney and Museum of Modern Art and the traveling *YES: Yoko Ono* were all well-attended and well-reviewed, and accompanied by commentary and essays by experts arguing for her place in the contemporary art scene. "I had been invisible for quite a long time, for about a quarter of a century," said Yoko, adding that she was pleased to be emerging from the shadows to "have an exchange, to enjoy, and to have fun."

On the occasion of her receiving the Venice Biennale's Golden Lion award, the exhibition director Daniel Birnbaum credited her with opening "new possibilities of poetic, conceptual and social expression for artists all over the world," and with giving new form "to our comprehension of art and its relationship with the world we live in." Birnbaum estimated that her work had "revolutionized the language of art and will remain a source of inspiration for generations to come."

This book has been intended to show that there is still much more to learn about her career. As Birnbaum notes, younger artists will find their own way to her.[1] Because her legacy contains so much more than individual works, they will benefit from it whether they recognize it or not. For instance, it has become increasingly clear that she deserves recognition for the development of the parallel gallery system. She literally invented the self-curated, artist-run gallery concept with her loft series on Chambers Street in 1961. No one even knew what a loft was

1   As this book was going to press, a new Yoko tribute album curated and produced by Ben Gibbard was released to coincide with her eighty-ninth birthday. The likes of David Byrne and Yo La Tengo perform versions of her compositions. As well, it was announced that in the spring of 2022, Yoko's art work would be featured in a group thematic exhibition of the Pulitzer Art Foundation in St. Louis.

back then, let alone considered it a space where an artist lived and worked instead of trying to get a dealer to represent you. Artists can represent *themselves*, she declared, and it worked for her and many others who have subsequently bypassed agents and middlemen to take their work directly to their audiences. Artist-run centers such as A Space, Mercer Union, YYZ Gallery, Transmission, Arc Gallery, Park Place, and a horde of others with international nonprofit status owe their existence to Yoko's free-form, do-it-yourself approach.

New generations will come to their own determinations of the merits of Yoko's enigmatic, poetic, sad, funny and inspiring pieces, instructions, music, and events, which, in true conceptual fashion, she never distinguished or separated from the life that lived them. It will be fascinating to see what they make of her oeuvre with its complete absence of sour irony, with her utopian candor and early commitment to subverting the entire art market with novel art-making processes and presentations.

It will also be interesting to see what they make of her as a person and a persona. She has been both a brave individualist who lived her life as art, and a sometimes savvy, sometimes naive creator of a Warholian public image that has taken on a life of its own. If recent years are any indication, she will be appreciated in both dimensions as an enigmatic, gifted, generous, quirky, surprising, thought-provoking, paradoxical, and thoroughly mesmerizing presence, and a mirror not only of her own times but of times to come.

# APPENDIX

# A Yoko Ono Archive

## MUSIC

*Unfinished Music #1: Two Virgins*
Released November 11 1968. Apple Records (US)/November 29 1968 (UK) Recorded Nay 19 1968 at Kenwood, Surrey. Duration 29:27. Produced by Yoko Ono and John Lennon.

Personnel: John Lennon and Yoko Ono, vocal, spoken dialogue, screaming, piano, organ, mellotron, percussion guitars, tape loops, sound effects / Pete Shotton: Tape loops.

*Unfinished Music #2: Life with the Lions*
Released May 26 1969 (US)/ May 9, 1969 (UK). Apple Records. Recorded November 4-25 1968, Charlotte's Hospital London. Duration: 50:56. Produced by Yoko Ono and John Lennon.

Personnel: Yoko Ono, vocals, radio, John Lennon, vocals, guitar, feedback. John Tchicai saxophone, John Stevens percussion

*Wedding Album*

Released October 20 1969 (US) / November 7 1969 (UK) Apple Records. Recorded March 25-31 1969 Hilton Hotel Amsterdam and Abbey Road Studios London. Duration: 47:38. Produced by Yoko Ono and John Lennon.

Personnel: Yoko Ono vocals, rare sounds, heartbeat sounds / John Lennon guitars, keyboards, vocals, heartbeat sounds / Klaus Voorman electric guitar, bass / Nicky Hopkins piano chimes / Hugh McCracken piano, chimes.

*Live Peace in Toronto*

Released December 12 1969 Apple Records. Recorded September 13, 1969 Varsity Stadium, Toronto. Duration: 33:49 Produced by Yoko Ono and John Lennon.

Personnel: Yoko Ono; wind, presence, backing, art / John Lennon lead vocals, rhythm guitar / Eric Clapton lead guitar, backing vocals / Klaus Voorman bass / Alan White drums

*Plastic Ono Band / Yoko*

Released December 11 1970. Apple Records. Recorded October 10 – November 6 1970. Royal Albert Hall, Abbey Road Studios. Duration: 40:29. Produced by Yoko Ono and John Lennon.

Personnel: Yoko Ono vocals / John Lennon guitars / Klaus Voorman bass / Ringo Starr drums / Ornette Coleman trumpet AOS / Charlie Haden bass AOS / Ed Blackwell drums AOS / David Izenzon double bass AOS / Phil McDonald, Andy Stevens and John Leckie engineering Mal Evans.

*Fly*

Released September 21 1971 (IS) December 3 (UK). Apple Records. Recorded at Abbey Road Studios London and Record Plant New York Duration: 94:52 (double album). Produced by Yoko Ono and John Lennon.

Personnel: Yoko Ono vocals, claves / John Lennon guitar, piano, organ / Klaus Voorman bass / Eric Clapton guitar / Jim Keltner drums / Ringo Starr drums / George Marino engineer.

*Sometime in New York City*

Double album. Released June 12, 1972 Apple Records. Produced by Yoko Ono, John Lennon and Phil Spector. Duration: 90:52 Personnel: Eric Clapton, Klaus Voorman, Nicky Hopkins, Keith Moon, Frank Zappa, George Harrison, and the Elephant's Memory Band

*Approximately Infinite Universe*

Released January 8 1973 (US), February 16 1973 (UK) 1973, Apple Records. Recorded Mid Oct-Nov. 1972 at Record Plant NY and Butterfly Studios. Duration: 93:09 (double album) Produced by Yoko Ono and John Lennon. Engineer Jack Douglas.

Personnel: Yoko Ono vocals, piano / John Lennon guitar backing vocals / Stan Bronstein saxophone / Richard Frank drums percussion / Daria Price castanets / Gary Van Scyoc bass, trumpet / Adam Ippolito piano Hammond organ / Wayne Gabriel guitar.

*Feeling the Space*

Released November 2 1973 (US), November 16 1973 (UK) 1973. Apple Records. Duration 55:15. Produced by Yoko Ono.

Yoko Ono vocals and backing vocals / David Spinozza guitar / Ken Ascher piano and organ / Gord Edwards bass / Jim Keltner drums

Michael Brecker saxophone Arthur Jenkins percussion David Freedman vibraphone Pete Kleinow steel guitar / John Lennon occasional guitar / Don Brooks harmonica / Jeremy Steig flues / Something Different Chorus / George Marina, Master Engineer.

*Welcome: The Many Sides of Yoko Ono*
1974 (Limited Edition) Apple Records/ Toshiba EMI. A unique compilation of songs by Ono, a promotional pressing by Apple Records available only in Japan, which was divided into tonal categories: "Gentle and Emotional Yoko" and "Rocking and Driving Yoko."

*Double Fantasy*
Released November 17, 1980, Geffen Records. Recorded at the Hit Factory New York, Produced by Jack Douglas, Yoko Ono and John Lennon. Duration 45:01.

Personnel: Yoko Ono, lead and background vocals, arrangements/ John Lennon lead and background, rhythm guitars, keyboards / Earl Slick, lead guitar / Tony Levin, bass guitar / George Small, piano and synthesizer / Andy Newmark, drums / John Parran, Seldon Powell, George Opalisky, Roger Rosenberg, David Tofani, Ronald Tooley, horns.

*Season of Glass*
Released June 3 1981 (IK) June 12 1981 (US). Geffen Records. Recorded at The Hit Factory, New York. Duration: 51:05. Produced by Yoko Ono and Phil Spector.

Personnel: Yoko Ono vocals, cover photography, design / Hugh McCracken guitar / George Small keyboards / Tony Levin bass / Andy Newmark drums / Arthur Jenkins percussion / David Friedman vibraphone / George Opalisky saxophones / Michael Brecker tenor

/ Ronnie Cuber baritone / Howard Johnson tuba / Conductor Tony Davilio.

### It's Alright (I See Rainbows)

Released November 2 1982 (US) December 16, 1982 (UK). Polygram Records. Recorded at The Hit Factory New York. Duration: 36:43 Produced by Yoko Ono.

Personnel: Yoko Ono vocals / Paul Griffin keyboards and synthesizer / Pete Cannarozzi synthesizer / Gordon Grody backing vocals / Elliott Randall guitar / Michael Holmes, Paul Shaffer keyboards / Neil Jason bass / Yogi Horton drums / Reubens Bassini percussion / Badal Roy tabla / Howard Johnson baritone sax.

### Milk and Honey

Released January 9, 1984 recorded October 1979, December 1980, 1982-83, Polydor/Geffen Records, Produced by Yoko Ono. Duration: 36:49.

Personnel: Yoko Ono, vocals and piano / John Lennon, guitar, keyboards, vocals/ Earl Slick guitar / Tony Levin bass / Andy Newmark drums / Paul Griffin piano / Carolos Alomar, backing vocals.

### Starpeace

Released November 18 1985. Polygram Records. Recorded in Right Track Studios, New York. Duration: 40:21. Produced by Yoko Ono and Bill Laswell.

Personnel: Yoko Ono vocals, cover concept / Bernie Worrelll keyboards / Eddie Martinez guitar and electric sitar / L. Shankar violin / Tony Williams drums / Sly Dunbar drums and percussion / Tony Levin, whistle / Bernard Fowler backing vocals / Non Hendryx backing vocals / Sean Lennon, vocals on "Starpeace."

*Live in New York City*

Released February 10, 1986/Recorded August 30 1972. Parlophone EMI, Capitol Records. Produced by Yoko Ono. Duration 42:30.

Personnel: Yoko Ono vocals and keyboards / John Lennon vocals and rhythm guitar / Jim Keltner drums / Elephant's Memory Band.

"New York City" (Lennon) 2:56 / 2) "It's So Hard" (Lennon) 3:18 / 3) "Woman is the Nigger of the World" (Yoko Ono, Lennon) 5:30 / 4) "Well Well Well!" (Lennon) 3:51 / 5) "Instant Karma!" (Lennon Ono) 3:40 / 6) "Mother" (Lennon) 5:00 / 7) "Come Together" (Lennon McCartney) 4:21 / 8) "Imagine" (Lennon Ono) 3:17 / 9) "Cold Turkey" (Lennon) 5:29 / 10) "Hound Dog" (Leiber Stoller) 3:09 / 11) "Give Peace a Chance" (Lennon Ono) 1:00.

*A Story*

Released 1997 / Recorded 1974, Record Plant New York. Duration 38:56. Produced by Yoko Ono and David Spinozza , Rykodisc. All songs composed by Yoko Ono.

Personnel: Yoko Ono vocals and back / Ken Ascher keyboards /Leon Pendarvis keyboards / Gord Edwards bass / Arthur Jenkins percussion / Rick Marotta, drums / Hug McCracken guitars / David Spinozza guitars.

*Blueprint for a Sunrise*

Released November 9 2001. Capitol Records. Recorded at Quad Rock Studios New York. Duration 46:59 Produced by Yoko Ono and Robert Stevens. All songs composed by Ono.

Personnel: Yoko Ono vocals / Sean Ono Lennon guitars keyboards / Timo Ellis guitars / Chris Maxwell guitars / Erik Sanko bass/ Zeena Parkins electric harp / Hearn Gadbois percussion / Phil Hernandez drums / Sam Koppleman drums.

*Yokokimthurston*
Released September 25 2012. Chimera Music label. Recorded 2011 at Manhattan's Sear Sound Studios. Duration: 60:35. Produced by Ono, Gordon, Moore.

*Take Me to the Land of Hell*
Released September 17 2013. Chimera Music Label. Duration: 42:47.

Personnel: Yoko Ono vocals / Sean Ono Lennon guitars, bass, percussion, piano, shakers, synth, sound design / Andrew Wyatt rhodes / Questlove and Lenny Kravitz drums / Erik Friedlander cello / Joyce Hammann violin / Yuka Honda keyboards, sound design. All songs composed by Ono.

*Warzone*
Released October 24 2018. Sony Music International. Duration 44:10 Produced by Thomas Bartlett.

## FILMS AS DIRECTOR

- *Cut Piece* (1965, 9 min)
- *Eye blink* (1966, 5 min)
- *Bottoms* (1966, 5½ min)
- *Match* (1966, 5 min)
- *Film No. 4* ("Bottoms") (1966/1967, 80 min)
- *Bottoms*, advertisement/commercial (1966/1967, approx. 2 min)
- *Wrapping Piece* (1967, approx. 20 min)
- *Two Virgins* (1968, approx. 20 min), a portrait film consisting of super-impositions of John's and Yoko's faces

- *Film No. Five ("Smile")* (1968, 51 min)
- *Self Portrait* (1969, 42 min)
- *Rape (Chase)* (1969, 77 min), filmed by Nick Rowland, a young woman is relentlessly pursued by a camera crew
- *Bed Peace* (1969, 71 min)
- *Honeymoon* (1969, 61 min)
- *Apotheosis (with Lennon)* (1970, 18½ mins)
- *Freedom* (1970, 1 min), a slow-motion film showing a woman attempting to take off her bra
- *Making of Fly* (1970, approx. 30 min)
- *Up Your Legs Forever* (1970, 70 min), a film consisting of continuous panning shots up a series of 367 human legs
- *Erection (With Lennon)* (1971, 20 min), a film of a hotel's construction over many months, based on still photographs by Iain McMillan
- *Sisters, O Sisters* (1971, 4 min)
- *Luck of the Irish* (1971, approx. 4 min)
- *Imagine* (1972, 70 min)
- *Blueprint for the Sunrise* (2000, 28 min)
- *Onochord* (2004, continuous loop)

## BOOKS AND MONOGRAPHS

- *Grapefruit* (1964)
- *Summer of 1980* (1983)
- (Tada-no Watashi – *Just Me!*) (1986)
- *The John Lennon Family Album* (1990)
- *Instruction Paintings* (1995)
- *Grapefruit Juice* (1998)

- *YES YOKO ONO* (2000)
- *Odyssey of a Cockroach* (2005)
- *Imagine Yoko* (2005)
- *Memories of John Lennon* (editor) (2005)
- *Aftershocks: Stories From the Japan Earthquake* (contributor) (2011)
- *Vocal China Forever Love Song*
- Acorn (2013)

## MUSIC VIDEOS

- "Mrs. Lennon" (1971)
- "Mind Train" (1972)
- "Don't Count the Waves" (1972)
- "Midsummer New York" (1972)
- "Walking on Thin Ice" (1981)
- "No, No, No" (1981)
- "Goodbye Sadness" (1981)
- "My Man" (1982)
- "Hell in Paradise" (1985)
- "New York Woman" (1996)
- "Bad Dancer" (2013)

# Select Sources & References

Ashton, Dore. *The Delicate Thread*, Kodansha International, 1997.

Berman, Stuart. "Yokokimthurston," *Pitchfork*, 2012.

Birmingham, Stephen. "Ono," *New York Times*, September 8, 1996.

Birnbaum, Daniel. Statement, Venice Bienalle, 2009.

Boxer, Sarah. "Non-Art for Non-Art's Sake." *New York Times*, August 6, 2000.

Carver, Lisa. *Reaching Out With No Hands*, Backbeat Books, 2012.

Clayson, Alan. *Woman: The Incredible Life of Yoko Ono*, Chrome Dreams, 2004.

Cleave, Maureen. "How Does a Beatle Live?" *Evening Standard*, December 1966.

Commager, Henry Steele. *The American Mind*, Yale University Press, 1949.

Compton, Todd. *Who Wrote the Beatles Songs?* Pahreah Press, 2017.

Corbett, John. *Pick Up the Pieces: Excursions in Seventies Music*, University of Chicago Press, 2019.

Cott, Jonathan. "16 Track Voice," *Rolling Stone*, March 18, 1971.

Courrier, Kevin. *Artificial Paradise: The Dark Side of the Beatle' Utopian Dream*, Praeger Publishing, 2009.

Danto, Arthur. "Life in Fluxus," *The Nation*, December 2000.

Doggett, Peter. *You Never Give Me Your Money: The Battle for the Soul of the Beatles*, Bodley Head Press, London 2009.

Dorment, Richard. *Penguin Book of Art*, Penguin Books, 1999.

Enright, Robert. *Peregrinations: Conversations with Contemporary Artists*, Talonbooks, 1997.

"Onobox," *Entertainment Weekly*, 1992.

Friedman, Ken. "Fluxus & Co," Emily Harvey Gallery, 1989.

Garland, Rodney. *The Heart in Exile*, Valancourt Books, 1953.

Goldman, Albert. *The Lives of John Lennon*, William Morrow, 1988.

Graustark, Barbara. "Yoko: An Intimate Conversation," *Rolling Stone*, October 1, 1981.

Hapgood, Susan, *Art in America*. Fall, 1990.

Harris, Mary. *Arts at Black Mountain*, MIT Press, 1987.

Hopkins, Jerry. *Yoko Ono*, Macmillan Publishing, 1986.

Hotta, Yoshi *Hojoki Shiki* (transl. Jane Corddry), Lotus Publishing. 1984.

Johnstone, Nick. *Yoko Ono Talking: In Her Own Words*, Omnibus Press, 2005.

Junod, Tom. "What I've Learned: Yoko Ono," *Esquire*, January 2011.

Kaido, Kazu. *Reconstruction*, MOMA, 1987.

Lippard, Lucy. *Escape Attempts*, University of California Press, 1995.

Lisle, Laurie. *Louise Nevelson: A Passionate Life*, IUniverse, 1967.

MacDonald, Ian. *Revolution in the Head: The Beatles Records and The Sixties*, Fourth Estate, 1994.

Maciunas, George. *Fluxus Manifesto*, Maciunas, MOMA, 1963.

Melly, George. *Revolt into Style: The Pop Arts in Britain*, Faber & Faber, 1970.

Mostel, Raphael. "Music; Freedom is one Thing, but Liberty Is Going Too Far," *New York Times*, April 7, 2002.

Munroe, Alexandra. Interview for Japan Society, August 1997.

Munroe, Alexandra, *Spirit of Yes*, Abrams Publishing, 2000.

Nechvatal, Joseph. "John and Yoko/Plastic Ono Band," *Whitehot*, 2021.

Oe, Kenzaburo, *Crazy Iris*, Grove Press, 1985.

Okamoto, Taro. "The Non-Sense, The Laugh," Atelier, 1950.

Okamoto, Taro. "Reconstructions," Oxford/MOMA, 1987.

Ono, Yoko. "The Feminization of Society," *New York Times*, February 23, 1972

Ono, Yoko. Catalogue, Indica Gallery, London 1966.

Ono, Yoko. *John and Yoko/ Plastic Ono Band*, Thames and Hudson, 2020.

Ono, Yoko. "To the Wesleyan people," *Anthology* 14, 1966.

Palmer, Robert. Ono Box Liner Notes, Rykodisc, 1992.

Peel, Ian. *The Unknown Paul McCartney: McCartney and the Avant Garde.* Reynolds and Hearn, 2002.

Rexer, Lyle, *The Art Newspaper*, 1989.

Rexroth, Kenneth. *Art of the Beat Generation*, Crowell Press 1971.

Savage, Jon. *England's Dreaming*, Macmillan, 1991.

Sugaya, Miyuki. Statement, Tokyo 360 Degrees Gallery, 2019.

Swenson, Gene. "Reviews and Previews," *Artnews* 60, 1961.

Taylor, Paul. "Yoko Ono's New Bronze Age At the Whitney," *New York Times*, February 5, 1989.

Tomii, Reiko. "Global Conceptualism," Queens Museum of Art, 1999.

Van Ghent, Dorothy. "Comment," *Wagner Literary*, 1959.

Weschler, Lawrence. *Asian Traditions, Modern Expressions*, Abrams, 1997.

Wiener, Jon. *Come Together: John Lennon in his Time*, Random House, 1984.

Womack, Kenneth. *Solid State: The Story of Abbey Road and the End of the Beatles*, Cornell University Press, 2019.

Yamamura, Midori, "The Word of a Fabricator," translated by Ono, Yoko, 1962.

# Index

Abe, Kobo

AG Gallery

Apple

Ashton, Dore

Baer, Jo

Baldessari, John

Bare Naked Ladies

Bauhaus

Belting, Hans

Berman, Stuart

Birmingham, Stephen

Birnbaum, Daniel

Black Mountain College

Bloom, Harold

Borack, John

Bourdon, David

Browning, Robert

Browning, Elizabeth

Buffy the Vampire Slayer

Cage, John

Carnival of Light

Carter, John

Carver, Lisa

Clapton, Eric

Cleave, Maureen

Commager, Henry Steele

Conrad, Tony

Coppola, Francis Ford

Corbett, Jon

Cott, Jonathan

Cotter, Holland

Cox, Anthony

Courrier, Kevin

Cunningham, Merce

Dada

Danto, Arthur C.

De Duve, Thierry

Destro, Ron

Dorment, Richard

Douglas, Mike

Drake, Nick

Duchamp, Marcel

Dunbar, John

Dylan, Bob

Edelson, Mary Beth

Enright, Robert

Epstein, Brian

Esquire Magazine

Everson Museum of Art

Fallowell, Duncan

Fitzgerald, F Scott

Fitzgerald, Zelda

Fluxus

Gakushuin

Garland, Rodney

Goldman, Albert

Gomez, Edward

Grapefruit

Graustark, Barbara

Greenburg, Clement

Hamilton, Richard

Hapgood, Susan

Harrison, Jim

Hendricks, John

Higgins, Dick

Hopkins, Jerry

Hoffman, Abbie

Hotta, Yoshie

Harris, Mary Emma

Hesse, Eva

Hughes, Robert

Ichinyanagi, Toshi

Imagine

Indica Gallery

Ives, Charles

Jano, Arthur

Japan Society

Japan Times

Jikken Kobo

Jones, Joe

Jung, Carl

Kaprow, Allan

Kazu, Kaido

Kazuko, Okahura

Kintsugi

Kureshi, Hanif

Munroe, Alexandra

Kennedy, Jacqueline

Kerr, Clark

Kosuth, Joseph

Kozo, Tanaka

Kupferman, Meyer

Leary, Timothy

Lennon, John

Lester, Richard

Lewitt, Sol

Lisle, Laurie

Lippard, Lucy

Lost Weekend

Lozana, Lee

MacDonald, Ian

Maciunas, George

Maddin, Guy

Mailer, Norman

Mansell, Katherine

Marcus, Greil

Martin, George

Matsumoto, Shunsuke

McCartney, Paul

Melly, George

Milligan, Spike

Mishima, Yukio

Moon, Keith

Moorman, Charlotte

Mostell, Raphael

Motherwell, Robert

Myers, Mike

Myers, Toni

Nancarrow, Conlon

Nevelson, Louise

New School

Nilsson, Harry

Nochlin, Linda

Noh Drama

O'Brien, Conan

Oe, Kenzaburo

Okamoto, Taro

Ono, Keisuke

Ono, Yeisuke

Ono, Isoko

Ototano

Ozamu, Dazai

Paik, Nam June

Palmer, Robert

Pang, May

Partch, Harry

Peel, Ian

Pet Shop Boys

Picasso, Pablo

Pitchfork

Plastic Ono Band

Presley, Elvis

Rabkin, Richard

Rape (Chase)

Rexer, Lyle

Rexroth, Kenneth

Rubin, Jerry

Rollin, Betty

Ruggles, Charles

Sarah Lawrence College

Sayle, Murray

Seaman, Norman

Season of Glass

Shinto

Skywriting by Word of Mouth

Smithson, Robert

Sogetsu Art Centre

Spector, Phil

Spinozza, David

Stein, Gertrude

Stiles, Katherine

Sugaya, Miyuki

Suzuki, DT

Takemitsu, Toru

Taylor, Paul

Tendai Lotus

Teshigahara, Hiroshi

Tomii, Reiko

Tougas, Kirk

Tudor, David

Updike, John

Van Ghent, Dorothy

Vetrocq, Marcia

Voormann, Klaus

Walters, Barbara

Warhol, Andy

Watson, Gerry

Wei, Lily

Weiner, Lawrence

Wechsler, Jeffrey

Wenner, Jann

Wiener, Jon

Williams, Raymond

Womack, Kenneth